One Family Under God

EARLY AMERICAN STUDIES

Series editors
Daniel K. Richter, Kathleen M. Brown, Max Cavitch,
and David Waldstreicher

Exploring neglected aspects of our colonial, revolutionary, and early national history and culture, Early American Studies reinterprets familiar themes and events in fresh ways. Interdisciplinary in character, and with a special emphasis on the period from about 1600 to 1850, the series is published in partnership with the McNeil Center for Early American Studies.

A complete list of books in the series
is available from the publisher.

One Family Under God

*Love, Belonging, and Authority
in Early Transatlantic Methodism*

Anna M. Lawrence

PENN

UNIVERSITY OF PENNSYLVANIA PRESS

PHILADELPHIA

Copyright © 2011 University of Pennsylvania Press

All rights reserved. Except for brief quotations used for purposes of review or scholarly citation, none of this book may be reproduced in any form by any means without written permission from the publisher.

Published by
University of Pennsylvania Press
Philadelphia, Pennsylvania 19104-4112
www.upenn.edu/pennpress

Printed in the United States of America
on acid-free paper

10 9 8 7 6 5 4 3 2 1

A Cataloging-in-Publication record is available from the Library of Congress
ISBN 978-0-8122-4330-7

For Dan, in the best of bonds

Contents

Introduction: The Transatlantic Methodist Family … 1

1. Transatlantic Methodism: Roots and Revivals … 17
2. Loosening the Bonds of Family and Society … 44
3. The Best of Bonds: Joining the Methodist Family … 72
4. Religious Ecstasy and Methodist Sexuality … 96
5. Celibacy in the Methodist Family: The Case Against Marriage … 133
6. "The Whole World Is Composed of Families" … 158
7. One Family, Two Nations … 187

Conclusion … 218

List of Abbreviations … 225

Notes … 227

Index … 273

Acknowledgments … 281

Introduction

The Transatlantic Methodist Family

In 1771, Freeborn Garrettson had a life-changing conversation with Methodist preacher Francis Asbury. Their talk was so affecting that Garrettson wondered, "How does this stranger know me so well!"[1] Many Methodists in the eighteenth century described their entry into the group in a similar fashion. "He spake to me," converts recounted, feeling that the preacher knew their own story, marking the intimacy of the moment of awakening.[2] As a result of Asbury's instrumental role in his conversion, Garrettson claimed Asbury as his "spiritual father."[3] Like most Methodists at this time, Garrettson was not born into the Methodist church; his parents had been members of an Anglican church in Maryland. After Garrettson's conversion, he wrote, "something told me, these are the people. I was so happy in the time of preaching, that I could conceal it no longer; so I determined to chuse God's people for my people."[4] These people would become Garrettson's Methodist family.

In this book, I examine the Methodist family as paradigmatic of the influence of religious ideas on the eighteenth-century family. During these formative years, Methodists used the central metaphor and organizational principle of "family" to organize themselves across a great geographical expanse. Methodism was a movement that spanned the transatlantic world, spreading throughout England, Wales, Ireland, and America during the eighteenth and early nineteenth centuries. By the late eighteenth century, Methodism was the fastest growing denomination in America. In the early nineteenth century, Methodists and Baptists competed to claim the greatest number of souls in Protestant America.[5] In England, Methodists dominated the revivalist scene of the eighteenth century and became a serious challenge to the Church of England.[6] This group rose originally as a subset of the Anglican church, but they sought to associate with each other in a closer, more spiritually watchful way than could be done within a formal denomination. Instead of starting by building churches or congregations, they began by forming societies and bonds between each other as evangelicals. In this book, I explore how men and women related to one another within this rapidly growing transatlantic network of familial relations and how they claimed authority over the personal decisions within their own lives and within the family as a whole.

This book addresses contemporary disputes over the history of family and marriage by examining this crucial period in which the contexts and meanings of family were open to debate.[7] Most research has confirmed the dominance of the nineteenth-century romantic marriage model in both England and America, by opposing it to the earlier mode of spousal choice, in which economic concerns and parental control were the primary considerations.[8] In examining this shift, historians have often pointed to secular literature, legal trends, the rise of the romantic novel, and prescriptive literature, but the roles of religious families and the significance of religious literature are almost entirely left out of the conversation. For the most part, we have assumed that religion had a conservative effect on the rise of individualistic, love-based marriages.[9] I argue that we should revisit and reassess religious families to understand their effect on the formation of the modern family. I measure their impact on family history along three interrelated trajectories: (1) religious families were quite elastic in their ideas of membership, since unrelated evangelicals became "brothers," "sisters," "mothers," and "fathers"; (2) this flexibility of familial association strengthened the emotional bonds of family by emphasizing the intimacy of this chosen family; and (3) evangelicals accelerated the turn toward romantic marriage through their exaltation of the "soul mate" as a central consideration for marriage.

While it is easy to associate religious notions of family with conservative, backward-looking principles, religious groups have also prompted radical reconsiderations of family formation, gender roles, and marriage. This is particularly true of dissenting religious groups, which critics have frequently characterized as sexually deviant.[10] Early Quakers excited suspicion for the ways that they allowed women to preach in public, and critics accused Quakers of sexual flagrancy behind closed doors. Similarly, antipopery movements in seventeenth- and eighteenth-century England, France, and America fostered the idea that Catholics were sexually aberrant; images circulated of publicly prudish priests and nuns who were secretly lascivious. The Moravians, who were Methodists' contemporaries, shared similarly pietistic, ecstatic language with Methodists. Moravian communities also challenged the normative patriarchal family through their separation of the sexes in worship and life. Polygamous Mormons in the nineteenth century faced violent public opposition to their marital practices. A common component of these religious dissenters' challenge to the larger society was their countervailing notions of gender and sexuality.

The preponderance of anti-Methodist literature written in the eighteenth century demonstrates how disturbing and provocative this group was to outsiders. During the eighteenth century, critics contributed to a deluge of material written against Methodists, and publishers turned out more than six hundred anti-Methodist pamphlets.[11] Common themes in this literature were the interdependent ideas of evangelicalism's power and women's susceptibility to that power. The writings characterized itinerant preachers as poor, uneducated, irrational, self-interested, rapacious, seductive, and dangerous.[12]

The opposition to this group illustrates the ways in which early Methodists were a revolutionary community. While we are now more likely to associate modern Methodism with middle-class morality, conservative denominationalism, and temperance, Methodism is historically rooted in dissent. In the eighteenth century, Methodists dissented from the Church of England to form their own religious and social culture. In opposition to the dominant social and political beliefs of broader secular society, early Methodists championed antislavery, women's religious participation, and leadership from a variety of social classes.

Methodist Family

"Family" as a term does not have a static meaning throughout history. The sociological conditions of family have always been contextual, and the cultural and emotional meanings of family changed rapidly during this period in history. There were also variations among families, due to location, race, class, and ethnicity, which make it difficult to speak of "the family." The geographic scope of Methodists ranged across a variety of settings from London to the newly industrialized areas of North England, and from the American South and Middle Atlantic to the Northeast. Methodists came from elite families and very poor families. Methodists drew from primarily English ideas of family, but the American Methodist family encompassed African Americans as well, especially in the South and Middle Atlantic.

The eighteenth century marks an important, but also a somewhat ill-defined, period in family history. In 1976, Nancy Cott marveled that "the eighteenth century is the most mysterious of times in the history of American families."[13] In 2003, Ruth Bloch reiterated the call for further definition of eighteenth-century family culture. "The transition from seventeenth to eighteenth century ideas about sex and marriage was far from smooth . . . and remarkably little has been done by historians to give an account of the change."[14] Evangelicalism was the predominant emergent moral and religious movement of this era, and it brought a new sensibility to the domestic and social ideas of family in this "mysterious" eighteenth century.

In this study, I analyze the Methodist discourse of family with a concern for both the language and roles of the Methodist family. In using the concept of "family" as a broad association of unrelated people, I depart from family histories based in demographic surveys, a field that has been well established since the late 1960s.[15] In going outside the definition of "family" as a unit of the household, I seek to understand how evangelicals used the terms of family as a broader measure of association.

At the outset, this book asks the reader to think of family in two ways: family as metaphor for a profound sense of association for people with few blood ties; and family in the more traditional sense of legally defined families. Just as the alternate metaphorical meaning of family is distinct from the traditional blood family, the religious family is also distinct from the more concrete sense of community. In this current virtual age, a nonphysical community seems very familiar and probable. In the eighteenth century, community was largely a local identification, with a bounded set of peoples and territory. The eighteenth-century evangelical family certainly had a sense of its own membership, but its people were scattered throughout the Atlantic world. Its members were drawn from multiple denominations, races, and nationalities. This was the essence of the evangelical mission, to expand the work of God in every direction. Thus, evangelicals necessarily saw the scope of their mission spreading beyond the boundaries of community.

The Methodist family pulled people out of their identification with local communities into an expansive sense of identity within the larger world of godly people. Furthermore, the Methodist sense of family went beyond the shared elements implied by a community to emotional, personal ties that one finds in affectionate blood families. Family also implied the sense of eternal bonds for Methodists, who saw their commitments to each other and God as eternal ones that would exist beyond the world of the living. As an interesting point of contrast, eighteenth-century Moravians had both a community and a religious family. For Moravians, founding local communities was just as important to their mission as expanding the sites of those communities and reaching various different kinds of people throughout the Atlantic world.[16]

Methodists evoked the ideas of family by widespread use of terms such as "fellowship," "our people," "our society," and "the connection" when referring to the broader group of Methodists. While eighteenth-century people generally used the term "connection" to refer to extended kinship, the Methodist "connection" meant the whole group, or Methodist associations in different geographical areas.[17] When Methodists employed broader associative terms like "our people," it was a way of talking about their sense of being a distinct family, their shared sense of religious experience, and their linked fates in the world beyond. The concept of "family" underlies all of these terms and encompasses their shared sense of intimacy, obligation, and cohesion.

In researching the accounts and letters written by early Methodists, I came across a consistent use of family terms to describe various kinds of evangelical relationships. The use of the family as metaphor is simultaneously everywhere and nowhere in studies of Methodism. Almost every work references the titles of "brother" and "sister," but very few examine the context and meaning of those titles.[18] At the same time, there has been little attention paid to the exact nature of early Methodist approaches to individual family formation and sexual activity. In 1984, religious historian David Hempton wrote, "The influence of Methodism on family life is also under-researched. On one level, families could be useful in recruitment, as converted parents or children shared their faith within the household. . . . On another level, however, the austerity of Methodist religion could be recognized by their dress, hairstyles and physical detachment from the world of revelry, sports and dancing."[19] Hempton's call to study Methodism's influence on family life underlines the need to study family from both the perspective of conjugal families and the broader body of believers. Hempton wonders how Methodist families expanded the sect's membership, but also how converts joining the "the austerity of Methodist religion" might have ignited segregations of or divisions within individual families.

This book expands on Hempton's questions by looking at how individual families viewed their children's conversion and how these adult children took up new roles in the "Methodist family."

Familial language and organization defined the first sixty years of Methodism in particular, and it pervaded early evangelicalism in general. From the 1730s into the 1790s, the language and institutions of the religious family helped to incorporate newly converted individuals like Freeborn Garrettson into a larger organization and culture. On the individual level, Methodists like Garrettson, who took "God's people for my people," were born again into a religious family, often after painful separations from their own parents' religious traditions. As individuals, they were welcomed into the Methodist fold with the alternative bonds of a voluntary family. Unrelated Methodists called each other "brother," "sister," "father," and "mother," and they offered one another spiritual, emotional, and economic support as family members. Often these familial bonds helped to loosen or dissolve ties to their birth families. At the same time that individuals temporarily or permanently broke their bonds with their blood families through conversion, Methodist leaders and laity provided a way to assuage this loss through the institutions and culture of the religious family.

In the eighteenth century, men and women used "family" flexibly, and it took on varying meanings in different religious associations during this period. I argue that eighteenth-century Methodists understood family in a way that seemed compatible with current models, yet they also redefined them. They based their family on the model of the nuclear family, but they were also operating outside of nuclear families. If they challenged nuclear families in some ways, they also expanded and elaborated on nuclear families, providing crucial support from outside of nuclear families. When Quakers and Baptists called themselves brother and sister, their language and actions implied the erasure of hierarchical distinctions between people, acknowledging each other, to some extent, as real equals.[20] When Methodists used the terms "brothers" and "sisters," they also evoked egalitarian spiritual bonds. Fathers and mothers held more authority, having earned those titles by being mentors and leaders to other converts. As Susan Juster shows in her work on American Baptists, evangelical use of family terms changed distinctly over the course of the eighteenth century. It generally evolved from a fraternity of equals to an association of duty, rule, and authority.[21] The metaphor of family was a sword that cut both ways in the Methodist family as well. Sometimes the family ideal emphasized the equal nature of believers and at other times, highlighted the need for conformity to the rule and discipline of the fathers and mothers.

Anti-Methodists saw the bonds of family as a cult-like encroachment on legal families and as a unifying force that caused divisions outside the Methodist family. The religious divisions within their own families often alarmed parents of converted Methodists. Parents witnessed psychological and social transformations in their children after they joined the Methodist family, and parents often blamed the religious group for radically altering their children's behavior. Examining anti-Methodist literature is crucial to understanding how Methodism became synonymous with insanity, infidelity, illness, and insurrection. Consistently, anti-Methodists accused this group of causing converts to reject their families' ways and prevailing cultural mores, to wear serious clothes, to think serious thoughts, and to avoid irreligious company including their friends and family. So unified did this religious family seem that it caused its opponents to charge that, like a close family, they seemed to care only for their members and to shun everyone else.[22] Juster writes, "Evangelicals did consider themselves a 'family' united by the bonds of grace, but they were nonetheless a peculiar family—one in which the parental authority was reserved for God alone and earthly domestic ties were irrelevant."[23] A family of like-minded converts who created a unified culture and closed ranks was not a comforting idea to those who fell outside those bonds.

The Methodist family did not replace individual nuclear families altogether. However, I argue that the religious family did affect the meaning of family bonds, both natural and chosen. Although nuclear families have been central to European societies for more than five hundred years, their emotional, social, and economic meanings have changed.[24] A significant trend in the development of modern families has been the growing concentration on emotional relationships and the focus on children as the center of family life. In the eighteenth century, families were cultivating this mode of affective relationships, developing some of the hallmarks of what would become the domestic Victorian model. Another aspect of the family that has changed remarkably over the modern period is the extent to which families were dependent upon a network of associates outside of the nuclear family. In the eighteenth century, extended family members and close family friends were invaluable to children and young adults. The Methodist family was similar to an extended kinship network, forming a voluntary network around individual converts.[25] Although Methodists used the titles of the nuclear family, they did not entirely replace nuclear family bonds; rather, they supplemented the converts' nuclear family and became a kind of familial network. Methodists further imbued their religious family members with a more modern emotional significance, coming closer to the sorts of sentimental bonds exhibited among Victorian family members. Significantly, evangelicals assigned these meanings to chosen family members, not reserving them for their blood family ties.

Gender and the Methodist Family

In the First Great Awakening, women's spirited participation in revivalism concerned some Protestant onlookers, even though women were only a slight majority of all converts. Anti-Methodists claimed that preachers like George Whitefield drew women away from their fathers and husbands and then encouraged these unruly women to take over roles normally reserved for men. As *Gentleman's Magazine* complained in 1741, "Many silly women" attended Methodist meetings "every morning, leaving their children in Bed until their return, which sometimes is not til 9 O'Clock." This movement caused women to neglect their duties as mothers, "contrary to the Laws of Nature."[26] The vocal participation of early American Methodist women drew the criticism that in Methodist meetings "women often prayed, and even stood up and made speeches just like men."[27]

This study of gender within evangelicalism uncovers not simply the participation of women but also the way that both women and men took up new roles within the evangelical family, influencing broader secular understandings of marriage, sexuality, and familial roles. By examining the particular language and practice of evangelical sexuality and family formation, I highlight how the evangelical movement in the eighteenth century was central to the rise of familial and romantic discourse in England and America.

To understand the roles that evangelicals enacted within their chosen religious families, we must first understand the gender implications of evangelical discourse and practice. Philip Greven was one of the first historians to specifically categorize evangelicalism and its gendered discourse, both masculine and feminine. In *The Protestant Temperament,* Greven paints a portrait of the evangelical temperament: "While the aggressive and bold public behavior of evangelicals who saw themselves as soldiers in Christ's army provided many people with a sense of self-assertion and of manliness, the ideal evangelical, nevertheless, was self-less and feminine."[28]

Greven argues that in order to be saved, men and women accessed and emphasized their feminine sides; they had to become submissive, passive, and guilt-ridden in order to be fit for conversion. Susan Juster's work on Baptists, Cynthia Lynn Lyerly's study of early Methodists in the South, and Christine Heyrman's expansive study of southern evangelicals also demonstrate how eighteenth-century men and women tapped feminine language and affect, which was particularly challenging to codes of masculinity in the American South.[29]

Establishing the feminine discourse and behavior of evangelicals alongside the broad swell of women involved in this movement could lead us to the conclusion that eighteenth-century evangelical movements empowered women. Methodist women did have more powerful positions within this group than in the Church of England, due to the increased emphasis on lay participation. Even though female preaching was not broadly encouraged, Methodist founder John Wesley approved some English female preachers. There was an expansive network of female leaders within English and American Methodism.[30] Many women took on a more widely acceptable feminine role as exhorters, who spoke publicly to lead prayer or expand on a particular biblical passage, oftentimes in connection with a preacher's sermon.[31] Women also assumed lay leadership of classes and bands, two of the basic units of Methodist organization. Classes were groups that met regularly to provide discipline and improve each other spiritually. Female band leaders organized selective groups of women, who met in small, intimate sessions to provide mutual spiritual support. Similar to other evangelical denominations, Methodism seemed initially open to female lay leadership and even preaching, but by the nineteenth century most Wesleyan Methodist women were limited to being band leaders and exhorters. As the nineteenth century progressed, an increasingly hierarchical conservatism was compounded by the embourgeoisement of Wesleyan Methodism in England and America.[32]

Yet, early Methodism did not always mirror the larger Anglo-American society. In the evangelical family, separation and isolation from the corrupting influences of the world were the optimum conditions for leading religious lives. This tendency to separate from the world, Greven argues, intensified both the cohesion of the nuclear family and the authority of parents over children, as well as husbands over wives.[33] I complicate some of Greven's assertions by demonstrating the ways in which many Methodists loosened ties to their birth families. This work illustrates how Methodists formed an alternative family, which lessened the cohesion and isolation of the traditional hierarchal, patriarchal family. Though early Methodists formulated a strong sense of hierarchy and men were at the top levels of institutional power, the extent of female participation in this group tended to mitigate patriarchal tendencies both within individual families and in the religious group as a whole.

Transatlantic Methodism

The test for eighteenth-century Methodists was to be truly "one family under God" and to expand this family in a coherent way over a large geographic area. The Methodist family was transatlantic in the sense that there was a steady interaction between English and American religious culture in this period. For example, the popular preacher George Whitefield was a member of the Holy Club, the Oxford meeting that helped formulate Methodism in the 1730s.[34] He was also one of the main engineers of the Great Awakening in America, which spread to broad areas of the eastern seaboard in the 1740s and 1750s, even while he continued his ministry in England. The exchange of ideas between America and England continued in the eighteenth century, as American revivals greatly influenced English Wesleyan Methodism. John Wesley's emphasis on the conversion narrative, his encouragement of evangelical visions, his establishment of the band meeting, and the basis for his pietistic theology all reveal the deep and lasting influence of Wesley's visit to America and his interest in American religious ideas.[35]

The chronology of Methodism's rise on both sides of the Atlantic makes it a difficult story to tell within the existing categories of revivalism in American and English history. While the Methodist movement had a role in sparking the Great Awakening in America, Methodism did not establish itself as a distinct religious group in America until the 1760s. Thus, it was only at the end of the Great Awakening that American Methodists began to organize (and to catch the attention and resources of English leadership). Paradoxically, while every other religious group was struggling to get their congregants to attend church through the American Revolutionary War, Methodists were gaining in numbers and growing their organization.

Scholars of English Methodism have been for the most part unconcerned with its connections to American Methodists, and vice versa.[36] Histories of American evangelicalism have been very good at explaining the regional forces that have complicated or abetted in the rise of revivalism but have sometimes slighted the wider transatlantic connections and contexts.³⁷ In the established historiography, the calls for revival were issued locally and triggered by regional issues: in the case of New England, the dissipation of the Puritan community; in the Middle Atlantic, with the diversity of eighteenth-century immigration; and in the South, opposition to the gentry class and the low levels of ardent religiosity within many southern communities. Methodist histories of the South have been particularly convincing in showing how evangelicalism appealed to southern men and women by overturning embedded class and race hierarchies.³⁸ Yet, by expanding the framework into the much broader situation of early Methodism in England and America, we obtain a different picture of early evangelicals; we see a constant exchange of religious ideas and practices that influenced the way that Methodism was enacted on both sides of the Atlantic. As Methodist personnel and print culture circulated throughout the Atlantic world, evangelicals in England and America shared common views about how to live a religious life, a common language to speak about their deepest spiritual desires, and common ideas about their place in society. English and American Methodists also shared the same organizational structures; bands, classes, circuits, and conferences took root on both sides of the Atlantic.

In the recent decades, religious historians have delved into these transatlantic waters; transatlantic studies of revivalism, Quakerism, and Moravianism expand our understanding of seventeenth- and eighteenth-century religious culture.³⁹ Scholars of transatlantic evangelicalism in particular have focused on the extent to which eighteenth-century print networks helped to create a transatlantic culture of revivalism. Frank Lambert's study of George Whitefield, for instance, emphasizes the commercial aspects of revivalism and the many ways in which his success relied upon newspapers and evangelical magazines to spread the news of his preaching.⁴⁰ Similarly, Susan O'Brien's research on transatlantic networks shows how the fervid letters exchanged between preachers and the laity became fodder for a transatlantic print culture.⁴¹ Crucial to transatlantic studies, however, is the recognition that the Atlantic was a circulatory system of culture, rather than a unidirectional transmission of people and practices.

This book looks at these transatlantic cultural links in order to examine the cohesion of the Methodist family. Transatlantic religious links were present throughout the eighteenth century, but they also persisted beyond the American Revolution and into the early nineteenth century. As the Methodist movement circulated evangelical experience, ideas, and persons throughout the Atlantic world, it became a family bound together across national, regional, racial, and political lines.

The Politics of Early Methodism

Political developments of the eighteenth century obscure rather than clarify the boundaries of this emergent transatlantic movement. In many ways, English Methodists envisioned American Methodists as simply a branch of the same family, one that included Irish, Scottish, and Welsh Methodists under the same umbrella. In other ways, American Methodism quickly emerged as a distinctive branch and during the Revolutionary era became a peculiar offshoot with its own problems, in terms of integration into the English Methodist religious structure. As the Revolutionary era progressed, English and American Methodists struggled to redefine the purpose, organization, and scope of the collective Methodist mission. This book, spanning the first eighty-five years of Methodism, circa 1730–1815, examines the ways in which religious communities reformed themselves during the Revolutionary and post-Revolutionary era.

During the Revolutionary and early national period in America, Methodists experienced a crisis of identity. As the American Revolution progressed, divisive politics and the ultimate formation of the Methodist church as a distinct denomination challenged Methodists on both sides of the Atlantic during the 1770s and 1780s. Whether American and English Methodists could remain a coherent, unified transatlantic family was subject to intense debate.

Even as they struggled to formulate possibly opposing political and social identities, Methodists on both sides of the Atlantic tried to maintain symbolic, political, and pragmatic ties that they conceived and enacted as familial bonds. By examining the Revolutionary era, and by focusing on the transatlantic network, this work highlights the lines of evangelical power and filial duty. John Wesley expected American Methodists to respond in accordance with his own wishes by staying out of the political fray. He hoped that his American coreligionists would send their preachers back to England for the duration of the conflict. Yet, English and American Methodists found themselves divided politically over the issue of American sovereignty. They were torn over whether Wesley had the power, as the "dear old Daddy" of Methodism, to recall American ministers and, further, to expect a unified political response to the issues of the Revolution.[42]

E. P. Thompson argued that the Methodist movement preempted the revolutionary impulses of the eighteenth-century and early nineteenth-century working class, since Methodist empathetic and emotional language co-opted the revolutionary sentiments of the English working class. Thompson's branding of Methodism as antirevolutionary prompts questions about how to understand the relationship between religious faith and political movements.[43] In many places, Methodists sought to separate political and religious beliefs, denying that the spiritual should ever associate with the secular. John Wesley drew this distinction when he wrote to his American and English ministers that they should stay out of political disputes in the case of the American Revolution. He wrote that because this was not a religious dispute, Methodists should not take sides or arms in it.[44]

In contrast, Bernard Semmel counters Thompson's thesis by arguing that English Methodists were indeed revolutionary. According to Semmel, the Arminian Methodist theology of universal grace incited social liberalism, formulating an English quasi revolution.[45] On the other side of the Atlantic, historian Dee Andrews demonstrates that American Methodism benefited from and absorbed the rise of republican languages and ideas. In her view, Methodism provided the best fit with this nascent political ideology. Her work emphasizes the elements of Methodism that drew from this Revolutionary period, specifically the republican elements of democratic decision making and religious equality.[46] The underlying question for historians on both sides of the Atlantic was: how revolutionary were the Methodists? One particular way to measure the political impact of Methodism is to examine the movement's ability to promote the leadership of dispossessed sectors of society, particularly white women, African American men and women, and the lower classes. But historians must still grapple with the relationship between spiritual and secular forms of authority. Therefore, Andrews can credibly point to measurable claims of authority by these groups within Methodist societies, while Thompson is also correct in his view that the Methodist hierarchy failed to assuage the serious class divides in English society more generally.

Methodist Conformity and Divine Providence

The Methodist family, like all families, reflected the limitations of family unity, on multiple levels, from demands for uniform responses within political disputes to prescriptions for social and sexual control. These social and political struggles reveal that Methodism was never monolithic in definition or in practice. This evangelical movement combined both primitive and modern forms of Christianity; it joined individualistic and hierarchical impulses. The disestablishment of churches following the Revolution was a key moment in American religious history, paving the way for a proliferation of sects and churches, including Methodism.[47] However, scholars debate the relationship of institutional proliferation to populism. On the one hand, Nathan Hatch argues that the early national period witnessed the realization of American democratic ideals precisely through this proliferation of denominations.[48] On the other hand, Jon Butler contends that while Methodism and other evangelical movements were individualistic in many ways, the eighteenth century was paradoxically a period of increasing denominational authoritarianism.[49] Susan Juster also argues that the early national period marked an era of increasing power for evangelical denominations, but that this came at the price of marginalizing Baptist women.[50]

Part of the disagreement about how to characterize the political impact of evangelicalism is that this movement simultaneously emphasized rigid authority, collective identity, and individual religious expression. Methodists' ability to redefine the family allowed them to move between these polarities of absolute individualism and committed adherence to collective codes of conduct. Methodists formulated many different levels of authority in the various relationships among family members, and Methodist authority asserted itself in a multitude of ways. There were the standard nodes of religious authority, including the quarterly and annual meetings and conferences that issued rules of discipline. Authority was further reinforced through the letters that preachers and exhorters wrote to the laity, through the sermons that preachers delivered, and through the publications that proliferated in this period.

Yet, Methodists still retained their individualism, varying their responses to official directives and other authorities within the group. While this disjuncture is present in any religious tradition, early Methodists had a particular way of making life decisions that empowered the layperson to act in accordance with individual impulses rather than conformity to external rules and leadership. Particularly regarding questions of social practices and ecclesiastical organization, Methodist men and women called on providence to demonstrate the correct path. Sometimes providence aligned with Wesley's or other preachers' directives; at other times, it produced a subversion of hierarchical power in favor of individual autonomy. In the case of celibacy, for instance, Methodists interpreted this injunction from Wesley as a call to consider marriages more seriously in some cases, to delay marriage indefinitely in others, and in still others to deny completely the practicality of celibacy. An entire spectrum of response came out of even the innermost circles of prominent Methodist ministers and laypersons, and Wesley himself debated the merits of celibacy and marriage.[51]

Laity and ministers alike described the source for their spiritual authority as providential and based in a communication between God and the individual. Providential signs could appear in randomly occurring dreams, but at other times they arose directly in response to petitions and prayers, combined with the individual's sense of God's will. Methodists formed close relationships with God, so much so that many believed that they could ascertain divine will in diverse arenas. Women and men relied on providential signs to point the way in deciding whether they should marry, where they should minister, how they should worship, and in making every kind of religious, social, or political decision.

Overview

This book opens by describing the span and sociability of early Methodism. As Methodists began meeting during American and English revivals from the 1730s to the 1760s, they established themselves as a transatlantic group. The central chapters of the book engage the social and emotional design of early Methodist life through an examination of the early narratives and personal writings of English and American Methodists. In Chapter 2, I discuss the themes found in conversion narratives, the single most important genre of early evangelical literature. In Chapter 3, I trace the familial culture of evangelicals in both the structures and the discourse of Methodism. This book explicates the basic organization and ethos of the Methodist family, the classes, bands, circuits, and larger print culture that connected this group. I also examine the specific roles of brother, sister, mother, and father within the family of Methodism. In Chapter 4, I explore the ways that early Methodists talked about sexuality by analyzing not just the self-definition of early Methodists, but also anti-Methodist views of evangelical language and behavior. In Chapters 5 and 6, I turn to an examination of how early Methodists approached the questions of marriage and celibacy. These chapters consider how Methodists debated the utility of marriage and their views on forming individual families. In Chapter 7, I examine the political dimensions of this group and the ways in which they struggled to balance their social and organizational imperatives toward the end of the eighteenth century. As the group matured and became more successful throughout the Atlantic world, American Methodists began to define themselves as a separate denomination in order to be able to act more like a traditional church with the power of sacraments and ordination. In many ways, this ethos of establishing themselves as a denomination warred with the original intent of being a social group that provided fellowship and familial support. As such, John Wesley and all Methodist preachers found themselves at a crossroads in the 1780s.

This study focuses on the Methodist family, but I also see this as an opportunity to rethink the concept of family more generally. This book is about the centrality of love and authority in the formation of the modern family and the role of religious groups in that development. In the eighteenth century, Methodist men and women negotiated their sense of self and individual authority within the terms of family. Early evangelicals infused a strong sense of religiosity into their social bonds with each other, and, conversely, they infused religious practices with social and intimate meanings. I hope this work sparks further exploration into the emotional and social history of the family, both blood families and metaphorical families like the Methodists. By more closely examining these historical senses of family, we also understand how we situate ourselves in the world, among the bonds of family we presume and the bonds of family we choose.

Chapter 1

Transatlantic Methodism: Roots and Revivals

The Atlantic world was a crucible of religious exchange in the eighteenth century. The Methodist family flourished in this transatlantic arena as early evangelicals established a missionary project to spread the word, both domestically and universally. The early evangelical movement had three main characteristics: transcendence, sociability, and mobility. Evangelicals repeatedly sought to transcend their physical bodies in order to have a better union with God, and they sought to connect with one another in order to find support for their individual religious journeys. They found sustenance among many different kinds of people, whose only essential commonality was their overriding desire for salvation. The religious family expanded connections between evangelical members who were not related by blood and not necessarily connected by nationality, ethnicity, or race.

Eighteenth-century evangelicals achieved this transcendence and sociability through the expansive print culture and mobility of people circulating throughout the Atlantic world. This mobility was central to how Methodism expanded as a family—from the circuits that kept preachers in constant rotation to the outdoor revivals where evangelicals traveled to meet with each other. Just as evangelicals were itinerant, their language was also mobilized by the increased circulation and production of print material. Methodists spanned the vast distance of the Atlantic through epistolary and print means more commonly than by actually crossing the ocean themselves. The circulation of evangelical discourse formed the basis of their spiritual unity, overcoming the great distance between evangelical groups.

Formative episodes in early Methodist history occurred in England, Wales, Ireland, America, and even on the Atlantic Ocean itself. This organization grew as a transatlantic movement with ideas, discourse, and people crisscrossing the Atlantic throughout the eighteenth and nineteenth centuries. Methodism was not an English transplant on American soil; it matured within a culture of exchange. Because of founder John Wesley's charisma and organizational strengths, Methodist histories tend to focus on Oxford or his home of Epworth, England, as the sites of Methodism's genesis. In some historical narratives, the transatlantic scope of Methodism only arises during the post-Revolutionary period when American Methodist leaders challenged John Wesley's leadership. But there were important earlier chapters of significant transatlantic cultural exchange. One such period was when John and Charles Wesley undertook an Anglican mission in Georgia in 1735 and put a number of early Methodist social and organizational ideas to the test. Subsequently, in the late 1730s and 1740s, American and English revivalists fed off each other, swapping conversion accounts and methods for evangelizing the transatlantic arena. Transatlantic dialogues occurred between American and English evangelicals and also between European pietists, like the Moravians, and nascent Methodists. Moravianism and the broader transatlantic evangelical culture helped to spark Methodists' simultaneous concentration on the mission of converting souls and formulating a domestic religiosity, the foundation for the Methodist family.

Origins of Methodism

Any discussion of the origins of a social or religious movement is tricky. A movement does not spring forth fully formed at one point in time; instead, multiple strains coalesce to produce a movement. Still, like any storyteller or listener, we appreciate even a provisional starting point. One date to begin talking about Methodism's birth might be 1729, when John Wesley, Charles Wesley, and others began meeting in "the Holy Club" at Oxford University.[1] Some historians frame the beginnings of Methodism with a biography of Wesley, starting with his birth in 1703, emphasizing his parents' interesting mix of high church and dissenting strains.[2] Some early histories of English evangelicalism choose a very specific beginning, John Wesley's conversion on May 24, 1738, at "about a quarter to nine," to be precise.[3]

Methodism came out of the broader evangelical movement, but it was not the only spoke in that wheel. While he was the primary founder of Methodism, it would be a mistake to locate the genesis of Methodism and its ideas solely in John Wesley. For one, George Whitefield, a fellow member of the Oxford Holy Club, had experienced his own conversion earlier, in

1735, and was a leading itinerant by 1738. Well before John Wesley's rise, Whitefield was touring throughout the Atlantic world, in the American colonies, England, and Wales. In addition, British evangelicalism began not with Wesley-centered revivals but with Welsh dissenters, who emerged prior to the inception of Methodism. The major formative period for evangelicalism in the British Atlantic world commenced as early as 1714, when there was a small Welsh revival led by Griffith Jones. There were larger numbers of successful revivals after Anglican clergymen Daniel Rowlands and Howell Davies began itinerating in 1735. In 1736, the renowned Welsh preacher Howell Harris started his itinerant preaching career, and he became particularly instrumental in fomenting robust revivals, forming small spiritual societies, and encouraging lay preaching; all these elements eventually became cornerstones of Methodist practice.[4]

If one links Methodist history to the Welsh revivals and the meetings of the Holy Club, it becomes clear that Methodism began as a collaborative movement, drawing upon a sometimes uncoordinated and contradictory set of leaders and influences. Charles Wesley started the Holy Club in 1729, before his elder brother John became its true leader.[5] The club's structure was less like a cohesive organization and more like a network of associations. The Holy Club was actually a diverse, shifting group of societies that met within different colleges at Oxford during the early 1730s.[6] The title "Methodist" was originally an aspersion, cast by fellow students who satirized the methodical, monotonous religious life that its members promoted.[7] John Wesley was particularly taken with rules for keeping one's life in the narrow way, as his mother, Susanna, had imposed a sense of spiritual order at an early age. He read widely and was particularly taken with Dr. George Cheyne's teachings on health and nutrition, as well as seventeenth-century devotional writer Jeremy Taylor's rules for holy living.[8] These rules included limiting entertaining diversions and mixing with the opposite sex in order to keep the mind focused on spiritual goals. The Holy Club meetings elaborated on the methodical practices of regular prayer and self-examination that John Wesley had begun to institute in his personal practice. These proto-Methodist meetings included a mix of discussions of classical literature and theology, alongside the dissection of a holy life.

If we take the Holy Club as the opening chapter of Methodism, a few aspects central to the Methodist character become apparent. The Holy Club established some of the key elements in Methodist religiosity, the spiritual fellowship and sociability found outside of formal institutions. The Holy

Club correlated religious goals with social ones; members held each other accountable for maintaining daily religious practices, but also for refraining from social practices that could be harmful to their souls. The club advocated getting out of bed when it was still dark and praying very early, so as to avoid masturbation.[9] The club also warned against running after the "pretty creatures" of London. Charles Wesley frequently attended London theaters and had some romantic relationships with actresses there.[10] When criticized by his older brother John, Charles responded, "What, would you have me be a saint all at once?"[11] Also, these proto-Methodists invoked a strong sense of association, formulating a network that went outside of blood family ties. One of the crucial aspects of family ties is religious association, and families expected that their children would grow up in the religious traditions of their family. In formulating their own religious society, the Wesley brothers provided a forum for religiosity that was distinct from their fellow students' religious practices of churchgoing. The Holy Club's underpinning belief was that institutional adherence was not enough. On the individual level, pulling away from traditional religious institutions had an effect on the individual's family; taken collectively, the innovation of new spiritual organizations was a form of dissent.

Religious dissent was not welcome in eighteenth-century English society. Yet Oxford, like many English institutions, was growing more tolerant of dissent in the early eighteenth century. The fact that Oxford University tolerated Holy Club meetings in the early 1730s demonstrates that the eighteenth-century Church of England was, to a degree, more lenient toward dissenters than it had been in the previous century. In fact, this toleration contrasted sharply with the violently fractured religious atmosphere of the seventeenth century, which witnessed the English Civil War. Dee Andrews writes that in the eighteenth century, "Nonconformists were no longer perceived by the Anglican majority as dangerous schismatics separated from the one true church, but as Christians called by a particular name in legal distinction from the established church. English religion, that is, was denominationalized."[12] Linda Colley similarly argues that while religious dissension generated hostility and violence during the English Civil War period, the eighteenth century was a time of cool disregard toward religious dissent. This shift in religious tolerance was significant. In the previous century, religious dissent had been viewed as a political and social scourge, but for most of the eighteenth century, dissension was reduced to a mere legal stigma. Adherence to the Church of England was still a requirement for public office, but the Toleration Act of 1689 had taken the sting out of dissenting. Colley maintains that, in practice, Protestant dissenters faced no discrimination, and religious discord centered on emotional and political opposition to Catholicism, rather than internal Protestant divisions. Britons, as Colley argues, became unified as Protestants against internal and external enemies; exactly which brand of Protestantism one espoused mattered less than ever before.[13]

American attitudes toward religious dissent were shifting by the eighteenth century as well. The Puritan hegemony of the North and the strictly Anglican culture of the South gave way to a deeply pluralist religious culture that had taken root in the colonial period.[14] During the late 1730s, the Great Awakening, which began with small revivals in New England, opened the way for the establishment of multiple churches. Additionally, fresh immigrants brought new religious institutions with them, especially in the form of Lutheran and Presbyterian churches in the mid-Atlantic colonies of Pennsylvania, New Jersey, and New York. This was a period of rapid institution building, and churches of many different denominations began to spring up on the American landscape.[15]

While official church and governmental policies were demonstrating some tolerance of Protestant dissent by the early eighteenth century, wider social acceptance of dissent was slower to emerge. In America and England, Methodists faced violence on the streets and repudiation in the press. Even though laws against dissenters were not enforced in the penal codes, dissenters were still barred from universities and civic offices. There were fewer legal penalties, but social penalties remained in the eighteenth century. Many Methodist preachers experienced the violence of mobs on their preaching circuits. Wives incurred their husbands' wrath when they joined with evangelical groups, and children felt their parents' displeasure after attending meetings. Pamphlets warned that Methodists were political and social scourges equal to the dissenters of the seventeenth century, even Catholics in disguise.[16] The eighteenth-century Methodist experience in England complicates Colley's assertion that hatred of dissenters dissolved in the face of anti-Jacobite fears, or that society drew a stark division between Catholicism and dissenting Protestantism. The early Methodist story points to the fact that eighteenth-century English religious culture was still an inhospitable place for dissenting religious groups to grow.

Throughout the eighteenth century, leaders within the Church of England feared nonconformist sects that threatened to woo believers away.

Dissent worked both inside and outside the Church of England. Though the church claimed that 90 percent of English people were members, their formal allegiance masked the fact that many English were no longer centrally involved with the Anglican Church. There were many people who called themselves Anglicans, while attending dissenting group meetings. The Church of England had lost numbers to the dissenting splinters of radical Protestantism, such as the Quakers and Baptists in England. As the eighteenth century progressed, the Anglican Church had a sense of withering, while nonconformist sects bloomed. Similarly, prior to 1740 in America, the Church of England was growing through its establishment of new churches and expansion of membership, particularly in Virginia. Yet during this same period, there was a sense of formal membership without much fervor.[17]

Faced with this sense of growing disaffection, Anglicans embarked on a missionary course. In the beginning of the eighteenth century, Anglican leaders became more active in recruiting and retaining their members. Though the Church of England had formerly repudiated itinerant preaching, it embraced the itinerancy of ordained ministers for the purpose of mission work in the eighteenth century. The Society for the Propagation of the Gospel in Foreign Parts (SPG) and the Society for the Propagation of Christian Knowledge (SPCK) formed as missionary branches of the Church of England. These groups were working in both England and America, seeing the home mission as important as the mission to convert the apathetic English populations in America.[18] Thomas Bray, the Anglican commissary for Maryland, founded the SPCK for colonial work in 1698. The SPG was specifically founded for missionary work abroad in 1701. In the same vein, thirty to forty reforming societies sprang up in London by the 1730s. They converted the unchurched and unbelieving in England and promoted the idea that the Anglican Church was fulfilling a primitive Christian mission by forming these societies.[19]

The Anglican missionary impulse was part of a larger wave of what David Hempton calls "a more benign religious version of the infamous triangular trade of slavery and cotton that fueled the economies of empire." As Hempton's work on transatlantic Methodism confirms, evangelical pietists, and particularly Moravians, fed an unprecedented wave of mobility. The movement included not just people, but also a print culture that spread its influence from areas in central Europe through western Europe and the broader Atlantic world. Hempton writes, "As the expansion of

Europe into the New World gathered pace in the eighteenth century, the spoils would go to those who were prepared to be mobile, and who had a powerful religious message to trade."[20] John and Charles Wesley volunteered to be part of the SPG mission to America, to retain the English souls of the colony and convert the Native American ones. The SPG was especially keen to remedy the underrepresentation of Anglican ministers in the less populated areas of America, particularly the American South where Anglo-American colonists needed ministerial attention.[21]

Methodist Beginnings in America

As John and Charles Wesley headed for Georgia during the winter of 1735, they found themselves in a motley, multinational shipboard community. John Wesley immediately began learning German in order to converse with the largest group of immigrants on board, a band of twenty-six Moravians, and he attended their evening services. Wesley wrote in his journals that he and his associates quickly reestablished their regularly scheduled ways once on board. They instituted daily public prayers and preaching to some of the eighty English-speaking passengers, alongside a few Moravians. The Anglicans and Moravians established regular Sunday services, and John Wesley noted that he administered communion to "[a] little flock" of half a dozen people, which included some unconverted shipmates. The Wesleys even set a schedule for catechizing and exhorting their fellow passengers. This evangelical pattern fit easily into the shipboard context where the diverse, captive audience would have provided a ripe opportunity for the Anglicans to try out their evangelizing methods.[22]

The trip to America was an important formative chapter in Methodism because this transatlantic journey prompted John Wesley to realize that he had not experienced a full conversion. The vulnerability of this realization, coupled with his exposure to Moravianism, made him ripe for incorporating Moravian ideas into the bedrock of Methodist practice. In the violent Atlantic storms, he confronted the shameful realization that he feared death, which revealed the unprepared state of his soul. During one particularly harrowing storm, he noticed his Moravian shipmates were wholly at peace. "In the midst of the psalm wherewith their service began the sea broke over, split the mainsail in pieces, covered the ship, and poured in between the decks, as if the great deep had already swallowed us up. A terrible screaming began among the English. The Germans calmly sung on.

I asked one of them afterwards, 'Was you not afraid?' He answered, 'I thank God, no.' I asked, 'But were not your women and children afraid?' He replied mildly, 'No: our women and children are not afraid to die.' "[23] The Moravians' stalwart faith and pietistic spirituality appealed to Wesley, and they became an important inspiration for Methodist spirituality and organization. Moravians possessed something else that Wesley envied—a sense of belonging, a real sense of religious family.[24]

In February 1736, after almost three months of rough sea travel, the ship made it to Georgia. Once on dry land, John Wesley was able to further observe the Moravian community in action when he set up his first temporary residence with the Moravians. In his journal, Wesley described the group's daily devotion to God and his surprise at their steadfastness and peacefulness. He continued to have regular contact with the Moravians, and considered them to be his spiritual family, even after setting up an independent house as a minister. Soon after landing, John Wesley met August Spangenberg, a well-educated and devout Moravian, who was the founder of American Moravianism. After talking with Spangenberg, he realized that his trials at sea had not been enough to prompt a real conversion, but merely an awakening to his sinfulness. When Spangenberg asked if Wesley had a personal feeling of salvation, Wesley realized he was unsure how thoroughly he believed he had this assurance.[25] He sought this sensibility of God's forgiveness of sins, which many Moravians possessed. Following his experience with American Moravians, Wesley also began a lifelong study of the works of German pietistic theology.[26]

As impressed as Wesley was with the Moravian community, the religiosity among Georgia's English population disappointed him. During his mission in Savannah, John Wesley discovered some of the difficulties of establishing regular religious worship in the colonies. The colonial leadership made it clear that his first duty was to the English settlers and that preaching to Native Americans took him too far away from his English flock. He admitted that organizing religious worship for white people in Georgia alone was a steep task, stating, "Even this work [Savannah's parish] is indeed too great for me."[27]

In Wesley's summary of the failures and successes of the Georgia mission, he counted spreading the gospel to "African and American Heathen" as one of his successes.[28] In reality, his mission to Native Americans was by every measure unsuccessful, but the goals of mission work had an important effect on Wesley's activities in Georgia. With the aim of converting

Figure 1. *Wesley Conversing with a Young Negress*, artist unknown, ca. 1890. Courtesy of the Drew University Methodist Collection.

Native Americans in mind, he developed his method of evangelizing, a process he would calibrate for many years. In addition, the goals of his mission established that the Methodist ideal was to have an inclusive fellowship of different peoples in the same religious family. Not evangelizing Native Americans was a missed opportunity, according to Wesley, who wrote that Indians were the ideal converts, like "little children, humble, willing to learn, and eager to do the will of God."[29] Wesley confirmed a common misperception of Native Americans, that they were open, passive, and ready to be religiously inscribed.[30] Closer to the end of his time in Georgia, he wrote in September of 1737 that his mission among Native Americas was pretty hopeless. There was "no possibility of instructing the Indians; neither had I as yet found or heard of any Indians on the continent of America who had the least desire of being instructed."[31] He had a little more success with meeting and having spiritual conversations with some African Americans. He had planned to travel to different plantations in order to reach slaves, after he identified the planters who would allow him to preach.[32] Yet, there is no evidence in his journal of any sustained contact with African Americans. Moravians likewise sought to establish a mission that included the conversion of non-Christians and crossed racial boundaries. Though Moravians also ultimately failed in their Georgia mission, they succeeded in expanding their community and fellowship to African Americans in the West Indies and in North Carolina during the eighteenth century.[33]

If John Wesley did not succeed in fulfilling his desire to convert Indians and African Americans in America, he did succeed in other ways; his American mission established the foundation of Methodist practices, such as individual assurance of faith, lay preaching and participation, hymn singing, and extemporaneous prayer.[34] The primary goal of Methodist spirituality became a personal experience of the promise of salvation, the assurance that he witnessed among the Moravians in America. Wesley also began to establish some of the touchstones of Methodist practice, especially the matrix of domestic meetings that would later become the basis for class and band meetings. Classes and bands were groups of Methodists who gathered in members' homes for the purpose of buttressing their spiritual commitment. Wesley's early Methodist organizations laid out a kind of compromise between church adherence and dissent. He advocated being a member of the Church of England, while attending extra-institutional meetings.[35]

While Wesley fairly strictly followed the Anglican Common Book of Prayer in Savannah, he was conducting meetings in individual homes as well by April of 1736. Wesley wrote about the purpose of these first religious meetings in Savannah: "(1) to advise the more serious among them to form themselves into a sort of little society, and to meet once or twice a week in order to reprove, instruct and exhort one another. (2) To select out of these a smaller number for a more intimate union with each other, which might be forwarded, partly by our conversing singly with each, and partly by inviting them all together to our house."[36]

This duality of early Methodists was fairly common throughout the first decades of the group's existence. Many held official membership in a standing church, but Methodism offered them the community of a spiritually dedicated fellowship. Like John Wesley himself, many were officially members of the Church of England and depended upon the Anglican Church for the rites of communion, along with the conferrals of baptism and marriage. The vast majority of eighteenth-century Methodist preachers were not ordained, but if they were ordained in the first decades of the group's existence, they were ordained in the Church of England. Thus, the Church of England offered a level of respectability and the necessary rites of sacraments, but Methodism offered something outside of those formal requirements.

What Methodism offered was an intimate union with other like-minded Christians. The idea of reinforcing religious practice through a social form, such as band and class meetings, defined Methodism and early evangelicalism, more generally. By designating bands as a central feature, Wesley wrote in *A Short History of the People Called Methodists* that this was a formative chapter in instituting bands and class meetings.[37] The "band" was a small group of Methodists, segregated by sex, and members were encouraged to provide mutual support and criticism. The band was a forum for complete openness and intimacy; in the band meeting, "we should come as close as possible, that we should cut to the quick and search your heart to the bottom."[38] These meetings were significant in establishing later Methodist practice, formulating the voluntary, lay-driven nature of Methodism, and particularly stressing the importance of forming a spiritually supportive, elective family.

Organized Women

Women were at the center of this nascent Methodist practice in colonial Georgia, becoming active as laity and as leaders. John Wesley appointed at least three female lay leaders in Georgia: Margaret Burnside, Mrs. Robert Gilbert, and Mary Vanderplank.[39] Yet, the impetus for Wesley's formation of the band structure and supporting female authority was planted well before his mission in America.

As a child, Wesley witnessed household religious meetings, and in these meetings he also observed his mother, Susanna Wesley, exercising domestic religious power. When her husband, Samuel Wesley Sr., was absent from the house on extended business, Susanna Wesley pulled her children together for religious meetings, consisting of prayers and reading sermons. When members of their parish began to attend as well and she preached to them, Samuel objected, saying it was improper for a woman to lead a congregation.[40] Susanna defended her right to lead them, arguing that, "as I am a woman, so I am also mistress of a large family. And though the superior charge of the souls contained in it lies upon you, as head of the family, and as their minister yet in your absence I cannot but look upon every soul you leave under my care as a talent committed to me, under a trust, by the great Lord of all the families of heaven and earth."[41] Susanna Wesley drew the ideas of home meetings from the missionary pamphlet *Propagation of the Gospel in the East*.[42] She saw herself as head evangelical of her family and thus instituted weekly meetings with her children to interview them about their spiritual well-being.[43] There is no doubt that John and Charles Wesley absorbed this strong, elemental example of women's religious authority being rooted in the family, particularly as they began to formulate social groups at the basis of Methodist practice. It is particularly striking that Susanna Wesley's basis for authority combined the religious inspiration of mission work with the mother's duties in the household. Through her example, this concept of evangelizing through the household was planted in Wesley's mind well before his time in Georgia. In addition, Welsh revivalists had been meeting in select groups by the mid-1730s, and Wesley would have been aware of this practice.[44]

The American experience sparked the creation of Methodist bands in that Wesley consciously synthesized these precedents and the religious structures of the Georgia Moravian community. In organizing the Anglican community of Georgia, John Wesley drew specifically from Moravian models, which had single-sex groups. The Methodist band was almost certainly inspired by the Moravian organization of "choirs." The Moravian family order was based in these choirs, which divided members according to sex, marital status, and age. In this sex segregation, Moravian women had considerable power overseeing other women.[45] Moravian women held various leadership offices: nurse, deaconess, eldress, and chief eldress. Wesley followed this innovation of appointing female leaders, which abraded local colonial sensibilities. The colonists complained that Wesley appointed "Deaconesses, with sundry other Innovations, which he called Apostolick Constitutions."[46]

Wesley's proto-Methodist family model was based on the Moravians, but there were also significant differences between the family order that Methodists adapted and the Moravian model. In contrast to Methodists, Moravians lived in self-contained societies and shaped their communities around their religious order.[47] The Moravian choir system became the basis for community organization in their settlements throughout the Atlantic Moravian world, starting in the late 1730s.[48] In 1741, American Moravians formed their largest community in Bethlehem, Pennsylvania, where choirs, not individual families, were the basic unit of social, religious, and economic organization.[49] The community lived in sex-segregated units, divided into groups designated as "Single Brethren," "Single Sisters," and "Married People."[50] The reasons for this segregation were practical and spiritual. All of the members slept, ate, worshipped, and worked within these units. By keeping individual members oriented toward the community and curtailing any inclination to pair off into couples or separate from the community into distinct nuclear families, Moravians kept individuals focused on their religious goals. As with other designed religious communities, the devolution of individual families contributed to the evolution of a higher religious family.

The Moravian model radically limited the influence of particular families, assigning child rearing to the larger community. Even before children were born, they were assimilated into the larger religious structures. Moravian leader Nikolaus Ludwig von Zinzendorf wrote, "When the marriage has been consecrated to the Lord and the mother lives in continuous interaction with the Saviour, one may expect that already in the mother's womb the children form a choir, that is, a grouping of the community consecrated to the Lord's work."[51] The community assumed responsibility for children at their weaning, when communal supervisors took charge of raising the children's choir. Parental authority was curtailed in this system, deferring to the broader group authority. Moravian marital and sexual practices diverged from those in mainstream Protestant groups. Matrimony was not solely an individual or family concern, but a decision in which the community had the primary stake and interest.[52] Historian Aaron Fogleman's work confirms that even the act of conjugal sex was part of Moravian religious teachings, making marital sex a holy and radically guilt-free activity. Moravians saw marriage and sexual acts as healthy contributions to their religious community.[53]

Methodists never separated themselves from society and never instituted any sort of community order as the Moravians did, but they shared some of the same ideals and practices regarding the religious family, social religious goals, and divine authority. Like the Moravian choir, the Methodist band was a place for intense spiritual sharing and growth. Both Methodists and Moravians presumed that the greatest growth would occur among like-minded individuals, who were at the same stage in their life and could support each other. After Wesley returned to Europe following his Georgia mission, he continued to draw from Moravian ideas, talked extensively with Moravian leaders, and even stayed in their community in Herrnhut. Even though Methodists and Moravians would eventually part ways, the two religious groups shared a common genetic component following this contact in America.

The Moravians also affected John Wesley on a personal level. As the Moravians in Georgia promoted the religious benefits of sex and family formation, Wesley also began to think about his own marital possibilities. At the start of Wesley's mission in Georgia, he was thirty-two, overripe for forming a romantic attachment. Propriety called for him to be married in order to claim respectability as a religious leader and as an upper-middle-class man. In 1736, John Wesley started a relationship with a younger woman in the Savannah congregation, Sophy Hopkey. Wesley and Hopkey visited various congregations around Georgia together, evangelizing together and planning a future together. However, as Wesley's own account confirms, he was ambivalent about his intentions toward Hopkey and about marriage in general.[54] He wrote that she was his soul mate and that they shared a physical and spiritual bond, but he also wrote that he was not sure he would ever marry.[55] When Hopkey accepted a proposal of marriage from another man, Wesley was hurt and confused.[56]

This failed relationship would have been a simple romantic misstep (and not Wesley's last one), but what unfolded after the dissolution of their relationship became much more complex, implicating the Anglican mission in Georgia and Wesley's career. Wesley proceeded to exclude Hopkey from communion on the grounds that her marriage had been improperly publicized.⁵⁷ Once he attempted this revenge, her family got involved and had Wesley arrested on charges of defaming Hopkey and failing to give her communion. He was also tried for "ecclesiastical innovations" and for being a "Jesuit, a spiritual Tyrant, a Mover of Sedition."⁵⁸ The essential maneuver that got Wesley in trouble was his legalism regarding Hopkey's apparently improper marriage. While the core of his mission in Georgia was to "regularize" the colonists' religious practices and sacraments, including marriage, baptisms, and communion, his stance on Hopkey's improper marriage seemed personally motivated.⁵⁹ In December of 1737, as authorities were moving to prosecute him on further related charges, he escaped to Charleston and then sailed to England.⁶⁰

Wesley's hasty retreat from Georgia and the mission's altogether ignoble conclusion embarrassed not only Wesley but also subsequent historians of Methodism. Wesley first published his journal in order to quell the controversy that arose from his rumored unscrupulous behavior in Georgia. Historians have struggled to explain why this successful evangelical organizer was so ineffective at either evangelizing or organizing in this first attempt. Many biographers have framed this rocky period, as well as other episodes in the romantic lives of John and Charles Wesley, with a familiar narrative of good men who were unwittingly snared by besotted women. Methodist historian Frank Baker suggests that the Wesley brothers were bound to find trouble in the Georgia colony, due to their bachelor status and their personal charms. Baker writes, "Both brothers suffered from the fact that they were earnest and eligible bachelors, becoming focal points for dissimulation, jealousy, intrigue, and gossip."⁶¹ Henry Rack confirms this sentiment in the title and content of his chapter on the Georgia mission, "Serpents in Eden." This title refers primarily to three women in Georgia, Sophy Hopkey, Beata Hawkins, and Anne Welch, though Hopkey is singled out as "the worst of all the serpents in [John Wesley's] Eden."⁶² The other "serpents," Hawkins and Welch, had reportedly caused Charles Wesley's early departure from the colony. According to Charles Wesley, Hawkins and Welch led him to believe that they had had adulterous affairs with Georgia's founder James Oglethorpe. When he tried to confront Oglethorpe about the accusations, the women reputedly recanted their initial accusations and made Charles Wesley the offender instead. Regarding these difficulties in Georgia, Rack concludes: "The whole episode suggests murky undercurrents of sexual jealousy and hysteria of which these idealistic and inexperienced clergymen were more or less innocent victims."⁶³ Wesley biographers have described the "pack of angry women"[64] in Georgia as "scheming," "petty," and "malicious," in order to dismiss the women's accusations against John and Charles Wesley in this period.

In some ways, historians have simply reflected the ambiguity that John Wesley, in particular, felt about marriage. Both Charles and John Wesley were at critical junctures in their lives, on the precipice of starting a new religious movement, and also considering whether they needed to be married or single to be effective religious leaders. In his parting words to Charles Wesley, Oglethorpe told him that he believed Wesley needed to marry to save himself future trouble, and he also thought marriage suited Charles Wesley and his spiritual mission. "On many accounts I should recommend to you marriage, rather than celibacy. You are of a social temper, and would find in a married state the difficulties of working out your salvation exceedingly lessened and your helps as much increased."[65] In contrast to his brother, John Wesley did not possess the same "social temper." A proper marriage would legitimize his social standing and his leadership of a religious group, but he was still uncertain. John Wesley was ambivalent about how central women were to his personal mission, even as they were increasingly important to the broader Methodist family.

In sum, the Wesley brothers were seemingly naive about the need to respect certain colonial power structures and inflamed the wrong people.[66] While the English colonists were jealously establishing favor with Oglethorpe and monitoring divisions of land parcels, some saw religion as superfluous, or worse, an obstruction to the colonists' economic success.[67] Overall, the Wesley brothers' rigid social and religious expectations made them ill-suited to the Georgia mission. The colonists accused John Wesley of being such a stickler for proper ceremony, titles, membership, and sacraments, which seemed so inappropriate in this hardscrabble colony, that they took him to be a Catholic in disguise.[68]

Yet America continued to influence Wesley long after he left Savannah. The most immediate effect of his Georgia mission and its disastrous final chapters was that it drove him to publish his first journals. In order to defend his excommunication of Sophy Hopkey, Wesley was compelled to print an account that emphasized the righteousness of his holy mission.[69] Long-lasting effects included Wesley's foundation of the social structure of Methodism, women's centrality to this structure, and Methodist attention to the ideals of missionary work.

Revivals in England and America

Despite the significance of the American mission to John Wesley's formulation of Methodist practice and thought, he left behind no sustainable Methodist organization in America. Methodist historians have tended to view American Methodism as taking root in 1766, when Wesleyan Methodist immigrants formed a significant, if small, society in New York.[70] Yet from 1738 to 1766, Methodism did exist in America, though it was mainly unattached to Wesleyan Methodism and under the leadership of George Whitefield. Whitefield, an ordained Anglican minister and fellow Holy Club member, picked up where Wesley left off his mission in Georgia. Whitefield arrived in Savannah on May 7, 1738, with some desire to cultivate the nascent Methodist organization there, but he observed "many divisions amongst the inhabitants."[71] The evangelical seeds had scattered, and it was difficult to see much obvious flowering left behind by the Wesleyan mission.[72]

Whitefield made successive preaching tours in America, attracting large crowds during his wildly popular tour of America in 1739. He preached to large interdenominational crowds everywhere he went, and he was widely known throughout America, England, and Wales.[73] His emotional, charismatic style of preaching was not altogether new to the colonies at this point. Whitefield followed in the footsteps of American revivalists like Jonathan Edwards and Gilbert Tennent, who were even more emphatic about Judgment, hell, and damnation than Whitefield.[74] And like Edwards and Tennent, Whitefield's theological underpinning was primarily Calvinist, emphasizing the unchangeable election of the saints and the burden of original sin.[75] Whitefield was a truly transatlantic itinerant, gathering large crowds on both sides of the Atlantic. In 1742, he reveled in the level of revivalism he had seen in England, Scotland, Wales, and New England, and he rhapsodized, "I believe there is such a work begun, as neither we nor our fathers have heard of. The beginnings are amazing; how unspeakably glorious will the end be!"[76]

Like Wesley, Whitefield had a sense of being a missionary in the colonial American arena, and he, likewise, saw it as part of his mission to work at converting African Americans. However, while evangelical preachers paid more explicit attention to converting slaves, some scholars argue that Calvinist theology naturally inhibited slave conversion through its emphasis

Figure 2. *Enthusiasm Display'd, or The Moor-Fields Congregation* (London: C. Corbett, 1739). George Whitefield is standing on two women; one has a mask and is named "Hypocrisy," and the other Janus-faced woman is "Deceit." Courtesy of the Library of Congress.

on the predestined elite.[77] The Church of England saw its missionary efforts through the SPG and the church's colonial establishment as working toward a "Humane and Christian system of slavery," which would do nothing to challenge slavery. Instead, Anglican pastors saw their mission as improving slaves' commitment to obedience and hard work through their sense of religious duty.[78] Whitefield, though critical of the SPG and the Anglican Church, operated within this sense of Anglican mission while in America. While Whitefield converted slaves, he directly promoted slavery by supporting the establishment of slavery in Georgia and by becoming a slave owner in the 1750s.[79]

While Whitefield and Wesley had both approached America with a sense of mission, their methods and their theological message were quite different. Whitefield's emphasis on the theology of predestination had caused some friction with Wesley. Contrasting with Whitefield's Calvinist views, Wesley espoused an Arminian emphasis on the potential for universal salvation or "free grace." As well, Wesleyan Methodists distinguished themselves from their Calvinist counterparts by searching ceaselessly for entire sanctification, a true assurance that one had reached a perfect, sinless state. In 1740, Wesley gave a sermon in Bristol where he declared that Calvinism implied that God abandoned people and incited the nonelect to antinomianism.[80] Unlike Wesley, Whitefield separated from the Anglican Church, openly criticizing its efficacy in America. He further charged that Anglican missionaries were "corrupt in their principles and immoral in their practices."[81] After his death in 1770, Whitefield's followers were folded into what became the predominant strain of American Methodism, Wesleyan Methodism. Despite theological differences, Wesley and Whitefield remained friends; the Wesleys and George Whitefield considered themselves a "threefold cord," working toward the same goal.[82] As perhaps a final testament to their friendship, Whitefield had designated Wesley to conduct his funeral.

Even while distinguishing his own movement from Whitefield's, John Wesley kept a close eye on the spread of American revivalism.[83] Wesley had read Jonathan Edwards's collection of New England conversion accounts, *A Faithful Narrative of the Surprising Work of God, in the Conversion of Many Hundred Souls in Northampton*, and Wesley was deeply affected by this collection. He drew parallels between American conversion experiences and those in his own circle.[84] Wesley not only admired Edwards's book, he reprinted it in London in the 1740s and 1750s.[85] As Wesley saw the connections between the experiences of converts in America and England, he began to conceive the scope of his mission as transatlantic, even worldwide. Surveying the numerous reports of large revivals in the 1740s, Wesley wrote, "Many sinners are saved from their sins at this day, in London . . . in many other parts of England; in Wales, in Ireland, in Scotland; upon the continent of Europe; in Asia and in America. This I term a great work of God; so great as I have not read of for several ages."[86]

Throughout the transatlantic world, the publication of conversion narratives exploded during the mid-eighteenth century. Sharing conversion experiences was an important way for evangelicals to connect to one another. Publishing conversion narratives served various functions, asserting both the universality of this experience and the common components evangelicals found in their journeys toward salvation. Conversion narratives provided Methodists and other evangelicals with the sense that their experiences were unique but not singular. This transatlantic network of writing created a spiritual community that crossed denominational and national boundaries.[87]

By the late 1730s, Wesley began to conceive of a religious community centered on the conversion experience, social discipline, and spiritual fellowship. In 1738, Wesley established the Fetter Lane Society in London; this society was cooperatively run with the Moravians. The society attracted converts, organized them into bands, and laid out the rules for social and religious discipline. Fetter Lane established the possibility of merging Moravians and Methodists in England, but, by 1740, John and Charles Wesley rejected this idea. The more radical elements of Moravian communalism and sexuality were problematic to the Wesleys.[88] But even more troubling was the theological divide between Methodists and Moravians. The Wesleys contended that the Moravians had antinomian tendencies, while Moravian leader Count Zinzendorf was bothered by John Wesley's insistence that it was possible to achieve Christian perfectionism, a state where one could no longer sin.[89] Moravians were also troubled by the enthusiasm central to Methodist conversion experiences: the noisy groaning, crying, and physical fits. Though Wesley had initially been somewhat skeptical of enthusiasm, by 1739 he had become convinced that enthusiasm was a true expression of the Spirit of God in the believer. Wesley had concluded this from seeing the similarities in physical responses to conversion, found in both Jonathan Edwards's conversion accounts in America and those he witnessed in England. He reasoned that these remarkable similarities meant the responses were legitimate.⁹⁰ Moravians countered that stillness was the appropriate response to conversion and that conversion was instantaneous, while Wesley thought this was not the only valid manifestation of conversion.⁹¹ With the additional and distinct step of sanctification, which offered to converts a final stage of sinless perfection, Methodists saw conversion as a longer process than that of the Moravians. The theological rift was evident in their different social plans as well. Wesley sought an evangelical society that was open to all, in contrast to the sort of bounded community that was necessary to reach Moravian goals.⁹²

In 1739, following Whitefield's lead, John Wesley began to preach in open air settings and established himself as an itinerant preacher.⁹³ Wesley had a sense of mission now and would not be a traditional Anglican minister, whose scope was bounded by a single parish. He wrote, "I have now no parish of my own, nor probably ever shall. . . . I look upon *all the world* as *my parish*"⁹⁴ He began to establish a group of itinerant preachers that would become a spiritual brotherhood. They would share poor pay, poorer conditions, and even mob violence to follow their sense of spiritual calling. Officially starting in 1744, Wesley began to organize a few ministers and a rapidly expanding group of lay preachers.⁹⁵ Itinerant preachers were predominantly lay preachers who had little formal training. But they were by no means without regulation. Wesley held control over their activities, prohibiting their administration of sacraments, and ordering itinerants into rotating circuits, ones he reassigned regularly. Preachers were expected to cover a large area, never staying in one community for very long; they coordinated and supervised the ongoing spiritual development of a set of communities. The basic structures of the laity, the classes and bands, were the local forms of Methodist organization. The preacher was the connection between these societies and the leadership, consisting of John Wesley and, eventually, the Conference of Preachers.⁹⁶

Wesley established an explicitly paternal system from the beginning.⁹⁷ He maintained control of many of the decisions on both the organizational level (preachers' circuits) and the personal level (marital choices). In 1766, at a conference in Leeds, he defended his power over Methodists by stating that Methodist followers asked for this sort of leadership. He stated that prospective preachers aspired to "serve me as sons and to labour when and where I should direct." In Wesley's self-defense of his centralized power, he maintained that his control was not tyrannical in that evangelicals willingly submitted themselves to it. He argued, "the Preachers have engaged themselves to submit . . . to serve me as sons in the gospel."[98] Wesley argued that the basis for his authority was voluntary, while the terms were compulsory and nonnegotiable, like the bonds of a natural family.

While Wesley's control seemed absolute in some realms, he also established important sources of power within the laity. In England and America, early Methodist societies included significant lay leadership and a considerable number of women. In Bristol, which was the center of Wesley's revivals, women were the predominant lay leaders. In 1742, in the London Foundery Society, women leaders outnumbered men by forty-seven to nineteen.[99] In the first decades of Wesleyan Methodism in America, women were likewise the largest group, outnumbering men by three to two in some areas.[100]

As Methodism became more established, bands and classes became the primary units of lay organization. As discussed above, bands were sites of close spiritual fellowship, based on the early models of the Holy Club and the first meetings in Georgia. Bands were usually single sex and formed of like-minded people from similar backgrounds and shared marital status, much like the Moravian organizations. The bands were supposed to foster intimacy, providing a comfortable space for sharing confessions of sins and self-searching.[101] The American Methodist superintendent Francis Asbury described bands as "little families of love."[102]

The classes, on the other hand, were the basic unit of official Methodist membership. Depending upon the area, they could be mixed sex or single sex. When an area was newly organized, the class might include all the Methodists from a particular community, and when the membership grew, the classes would become subdivided by different characteristics such as marital status, sex, and race. They were generally larger than bands, composed of usually a dozen members, and part of the economic undergirding of Methodism.[103] In class meetings, Methodists would relate conversion narratives and receive instructions on Methodist social interactions. Classes would be instructed on the rules outlined in the official guidebook for Methodist social behavior, the Methodist *Discipline*, including correct behavior, avoiding profanity, refraining from excessive conversation and conduct, and plain dressing.[104] To become a member of a class meeting, one had to be deemed fit for this select circle. This fitness was symbolized by the granting of a class ticket, which was a piece of paper that stated one's name and location. Proving one's mettle this way sometimes took months of regular attendance at preaching, prayer meetings, and interviews.

Preachers and experienced Methodists were the judge and jury as to a new Methodist's real intentions or seriousness. Many eighteenth-century Methodists describe the moment of acquiring their membership ticket as an essential step in their road to a rarefied spirituality.[105] Getting this ticket, this symbol and certificate of acceptance, meant joining a specific Methodist family that would include mentors and guides (brothers, sisters, fathers, and mothers) throughout each dedicated Methodist's life. Class meetings defined the basis for membership within this family, who was inside and outside this group. When Francis Asbury arrived in America in 1771, one of the first things he did was to be sure that the class meetings were made up of qualified Methodists and that outsiders were not allowed to meet with them.[106]

The bands, class meetings, and circuits were extra-institutional structures of Methodism that established its character as a social movement from the beginning. The people of Methodism were the basis for its organization. While many Methodists, especially those in England, might be nominal members of the Church of England and attend services regularly, Methodist social structures provided the backbone for their religious association outside of more traditional brick-and-mortar sites for worship. Aside from the central motivation for spiritual growth, the goals of the Methodist structures were social ones: discipline, identification, association, and fellowship.

While Wesleyan Methodism did not officially take root in America until the end of the Great Awakening, this wave of revivalism paved the way for the Methodist movement to come. Evangelical Baptists, Lutherans, Congregationalists, Presbyterians, and Moravians all had a hand in establishing the predominant evangelical message of new birth. In particular, Baptists paved an important path for Methodists in the South, where they used some similar elements of emphasizing emotional preaching styles and the centrality of rebirth.[107] Despite this wave of evangelical growth in America, Wesley waited a while to include America in his missionary plan.[108] In essence, Whitefield was the primary evangelizer and Methodist leader, underlining the Calvinist flavor of the First Great Awakening. Until the late 1760s, he seemed content to allow lay Methodists to drive the American Methodist movement. In the 1760s and 1770s, some Wesleyan Methodists began immigrating to America, and this seems to have prompted Wesley to advance his mission there.[109]

In the 1760s and 1770s, Wesleyan Methodism found areas of expansion, like the Delmarva Peninsula, where there were great numbers of English settlers and where the Church of England was established but not thriving.[110] The most significant growth took place in Maryland, Delaware, New York, and Philadelphia, where many Irish Anglican immigrants settled. David Hempton argues that these regions were ripe for evangelizing because "Methodism offered a more enthusiastic religion for Anglicans in an environment unsuitable to liturgical and moralistic refinement."[111] Methodists thrived in areas with strong Anglican Church establishment, because many Methodists were dependent upon and connected to the Church of England as their home institution. Methodists were routinely baptized in and often official members of the Church of England. They often attended their locally established churches, but met with Methodists outside those services. The Church of England offered sacraments and legitimacy to many English and American Methodists, especially prior to the 1780s. Methodism offered believers more than a sacramental home; it gave them a fellowship and way of life. Early Methodists felt strongly that real fellowship was essential to converting one's soul and to staying on the right religious path.

Certainly, Wesleyan convert Barbara Heck, an emigrant from Ireland, felt that a Methodist community needed to be established in New York to keep evangelical converts on the right path. In 1766, Heck helped light the Wesleyan Methodist fires in America. Heck and other immigrants, who had been converted during Wesley's Irish campaign, settled in New York City. One night in the fall of 1766, Heck interrupted a card game in another immigrant's home by seizing the cards off the table and throwing them into the fireplace. Heck was symbolically renewing vows to keep to the Methodist rules of avoiding trivial diversions and pointing out the fate of their souls if they kept at this; their souls would burn in hell, like so many cards in the fire. She also reportedly urged Philip Embury, a fellow Irish immigrant, to begin itinerating in New York.[112] Heck and Embury formed single-sex classes in New York City in 1766, and soon after there was a "modest Methodist community" in Philadelphia as well.[113]

The New York society was important in cultivating an early Methodist organizer and preacher, Thomas Webb. Captain Webb had fought in the Seven Years' War, converted to Methodism in England, and was very close to John Wesley, who encouraged his enthusiasm. He began preaching in various New York meeting spaces and organized a Methodist class in Brooklyn that balanced a mixed black and white membership. Heck, Webb, Embury, and other newly immigrated English Methodists built the first meetinghouse in New York City, and this was done largely without formal support from Wesleyan Methodists in England or leadership on Wesley's part. Captain Webb also ventured to other regions with new Methodist societies springing up throughout the middle colonies and upper South.[114]

During the 1760s, the promising religious field of America attracted evangelizing Methodists, since there were a number of denominations and a variety of new immigrants, especially in the middle colonies of New York, Pennsylvania, and Delaware. Unlike Methodists in England, American Methodists did not have to contend with a powerful and pervasive Church of England. While Methodists succeeded in some places where Anglicans were established, there were areas of America that were free of any religious authority altogether, and Methodism's evangelical itinerant system was well suited to exploit these open areas.

Alongside Irish and English immigrants, one of the primary groups of early American Methodist converts was African Americans. African Americans began to join evangelicals in significant numbers during the latter part of the Great Awakening, when the South saw its greatest revivals in the 1760s with Separate Baptists groups springing up in Virginia. Methodist meetings and revivals began sweeping the Middle Atlantic and the South in the 1770s and then surged strongly at the turn of the nineteenth century. During the initial expansion of evangelical religion in the eighteenth century, slave populations were expanding as well, which facilitated acculturation of English language and customs into African American populations. Given the concentrated populations of slaves in the South, the oftentimes remote location of slaves, and their understandable aversion to groups that emphasized formal religious education (such as the Anglican and Presbyterian churches), evangelical sects were better suited to converting African Americans.[115]

In the Revolutionary period, white Methodist preachers were especially ardent in their pursuit of African American converts, who, historian Don Mathews argues, "were often more responsive to the evocative Methodist preaching than were whites."[116] African Americans' increased attraction to evangelicalism had many causes, including the method and message of evangelicalism, its attention to spirituality, the primacy of the Bible, and congregational participation. Like evangelical revivals, traditional African spirituality was more participatory than traditional Christian churches; many African Americans contributed to the evangelical ethos of lay participation. The swapping of religious practices and influences between African

Americans and European Americans was an ongoing, collaborative process. From the 1760s and 1770s onward, influenced by African American participation, Methodists promoted a responsive, physical form of worship, which included crying, shouting, singing, and stamping.[117]

Evangelical leaders began to consider African American communities as a previously untapped arena for new souls in the competitive religious marketplace.[118] Robert Strawbridge, a gifted preacher who led Methodist societies in the upper South, had drawn a large number of African Americans to Methodist meetings in Maryland. In a society in Long Island that formed in 1768, black and white members were in exactly equal numbers. As Cynthia Lynn Lyerly writes, "Methodism was born in America as a biracial lay movement."[119] As Wesley's dream of African conversion was finally starting to be realized in America by the 1760s, it was remarkably different from the missionary ideals espoused by the Society for the Propagation of the Gospel. The SPG envisioned formal catechisms as the basis for inculcating faith among non-Christians, but African Americans did not respond to this formal teaching, nor had the Anglican Church been terribly effective at convincing slaveholders to allow them access to slaves.[120] While John and Charles Wesley initially saw African Americans as part of a wider and perhaps overly optimistic missionary evangelical project in the latter part of the 1730s, by the 1760s and 1770s, African American Methodists were central to the American Methodist connection.

Conclusions

The transcendence, sociability, and mobility of the Methodist organization were powerful ideas for African Americans. Slave and free African Americans could appreciate the transformative elements of conversion and transcendence of the physical world. The sociability of the Methodist family was a powerful element of association among African Americans and between white and black converts. The mobility of the itinerant preachers, particularly in the beginning of Methodist expansion in America, was central to its success at reaching populations that were not served by established churches. This was especially true for reaching slaves.

While the Wesley brothers did not see their time in America as an overwhelming success, it was clearly an important period for the birth of Methodism. From the 1730s and 1740s, when the Wesleys experimented with their missionary ideals, the transatlantic arena and its mobile populations were central to their formulations of Methodist practice. The early period of Methodism demonstrates its absorbent and ecumenical qualities. Methodists took in the social practices of religious meetings and experimented freely with various forms, keeping the bands and classes as central components in effective religious fellowship and as official forums for membership and discipline.

Early Methodists' social orientation formulated a tenet that was central to this group's success: while it drew the boundaries and discipline for belonging, it was also open to new members. It emphasized the certainty and benefits of belonging to this group, through having a ticket for class meetings and defining rules for living. They identified each other through these literal and material practices and by calling each other by family names. While their familial nature mattered, it was not a natal sense of belonging. One was not born into it; one had to earn it through commitment to true conversion and salvation. In many ways this is a profoundly eighteenth-century ideal, underlined by the universal promise of salvation. In the same way that true evangelical conversion pulled individuals out of their familial ties, conversion pulled individuals out of their bodily constraints and physical locations. Conversion made individuals members of a transnational and unearthly family, one in which members might not even meet in this world but were guaranteed to do so in the next.

Chapter 2

Loosening the Bonds of Family and Society

In the eighteenth century, the ideal Methodist convert was a young individual, someone who used her youthful energy to further evangelical growth. In Dee Andrews's meticulous survey of membership records in the Middle Atlantic region of America, she discovered a "prototype" for Methodist laity in the late eighteenth century: a woman who was sixteen to twenty-four years old, unmarried, and still living at home or making her living as a servant.[1] Reaching young men was also necessary for sustaining evangelical growth; the grueling pace and sacrifice of the preachers' circuit was seen as a young man's job. The prototypical circuit preacher Freeborn Garrettson joined the preaching ranks at the age of twenty-four, covering much of the Middle Atlantic and upper South, traveling over 100,000 miles from 1776 to 1793.[2] As young as many converts were, they had to consider their ties to their blood families when they joined the evangelical family.

Alienation from one's birth family was often a necessary preliminary step toward becoming a Methodist, especially from the late 1730s to the second decade of the nineteenth century. In their letters and journals, young Methodists regularly recorded the scorn and disapprobation of their families. Evangelical literature and fellowship helped these young converts through the pangs of separation from their previous lives, families, and friends. At the same time, anti-Methodist literature stoked the idea that there were two competing cultures in a young convert's life, one belonging to their natal family and tradition and the other to the strange ways of the Methodists. Early converts heard gossip and read pamphlets that characterized evangelicals as low class, deranged, self-serving, and false. As the first generations of evangelicals joined this group, they encountered social and familial opposition based on these negative characterizations of Methodism. Most Methodists did not become orphans in the literal sense, but many experienced profound distancing from their natural families as they joined a larger family of believers.

The erosion of familial bonds was both a stereotypical anti-Methodist critique and an accurate description of reality. In multiple pamphlets and journals, Methodists were charged with being antifamily, leading young, impressionable minds away from their normal dispositions.[3] In reality, Methodism did provide an impetus for separation from one's given family, and evangelical narratives illustrate the details of this separation. In these narratives, Methodists described their new religious ideas as a source of conflict in their families, and they further described real and symbolic ruptures between evangelicals and society as a whole. New converts changed their ways by dressing differently, associating with different people, and generally holding different values, many of which transgressed gender and class norms. Methodists encouraged one another to take up the cross, to suffer in seriousness against the obstacles of family and friends. In 1792, American preacher Stith Mead encouraged young converts to avoid their old irreligious friends, writing that a truly religious convert would

> not take pleasure in Company profane
> Who wishes to Adulterate and alter her name . . .
> Declaring she never her God will offend
> To be the Companion of a wicked friend.[4]

Dissent into Madness

One signal that others saw Methodists as a distinct and disturbing family was the regularity of association between madness and Methodism in the eighteenth century. This was not simply a fictional caricature, because some Methodists described themselves as truly consumed by the psychological trials of conversion. The first step in conversion was conviction of sin, which made some evangelicals merely melancholy. In others, awareness of their sinfulness caused them to act in ways that would seem insane—crying, trembling, groaning, talking to God, and displaying severe emotional swings. After attending a Methodist sermon, the young English convert Mary Maddern was awakened to her sinfulness, and she became convinced that she would go to hell. When Maddern discovered Methodism, she was a teenager. Soon after she attended her first meetings, her parents forbid her to go to any more, arguing that the Wesley brothers "had drove Many to dispare through [their pernicious] Doctrine."⁵ She seemed to confirm these rumors, when she left the Methodist meeting, "crying out what shall I do to be saved." She felt worse, not better, after successive sermons, and experienced several months of deepening depression. She went through several more months of feeling alternately at peace and in despair, which continued until she joined a band and felt some spiritual stability after a few months with that group.⁶ Her inconsistency and her attraction to a society that seemed to make her lose her senses alienated her parents and friends. The behaviors of evangelical children made their parents fear for their children's sanity, as parents saw firsthand the sort of depression that many Methodists described as the beginning stages of their conversion. This made Methodists seem dangerous and further produced an insider/outsider mentality that separated the believer from friends and family by a chasm of language, belief, custom, and culture that must have seemed unbridgeable at times.

Yet, American and British Methodists purposefully sought this suspension of the rational mind. If the believer truly felt the weight of his or her sinfulness, evangelical melancholy was a convincing sign of a convert's conviction. Benjamin Abbott, who was a farmer in New Jersey, became part of a Methodist revival in 1772. He wrote that traveling home one day he was suddenly struck with the idea that "as I was one of the reprobates and there was no mercy for me, I had better hang myself and know the worst of it." He denied himself all earthly pleasures, shunned his wife, avoided food, and had visions of the devil; he generally looked and felt awful. When he was born again after several days of being at the bottom, physically and mentally, it was a great relief to his family and friends as well as himself.⁷ This spiritual journey into darkness, visions, anxiety, and depression was part of a common stage in conversions. This period of conviction required the believer to wallow in his or her state of inherent sinfulness. For many, this meant reliving past sins as well as becoming acutely, painfully aware of the ways in which those sins were increasing daily. In fact, many Methodists never felt entirely free of this stage, since there were usually multiple backslidings in any Methodist's life.

Parents' worries were justified, according to anti-Methodist pamphlets that circulated in the eighteenth and early nineteenth centuries. In 1809, Leigh Hunt proclaimed that liberal British society agreed that evangelical conversion was the first step toward the madhouse: "The Arminian and Evangelical Magazines are full of the dying comforts of their disciples, but why do they not give us a candid account of those who die in wretchedness of mind? Why do they not give us a list of the Methodist lunatics throughout the hospitals of England? If they wish to terrify sinners, it is strange they should conceal that most alarming fact in their church-history. I returned a short time since from a large manufacturing town in the North, where I had an opportunity of inspecting the godly a little more closely than in the mazy multitude of London. . . . Those who were more seriously affected became either melancholy or mad."[8] Parents had reason to fear for their children's mental health, anti-Methodists maintained, if they became unmoored from their traditional religion and blood families to join with these dangerous fanatics. This widespread belief in Methodist-induced madness was so persistently circulated that Wesley felt it necessary to defensively claim the rationality of Methodists in the inaugural issue of the *Arminian Magazine* in 1778.[9] This magazine was published in London originally, and then in Philadelphia as well, beginning in the 1780s. The association between ardent religiosity and insanity was already fully developed in eighteenth-century Anglo-American society, drawing upon a deep well of associative images from the Puritan ascendancy and the explosion in enthusiastic dissenting religions of the seventeenth-century interregnum period.[10]

In the late seventeenth century, medical authorities declared "religious melancholy" a category of mental illness, alongside the more serious category of "religious madness" with its symptoms of delusions and hallucinations. Eighteenth-century physicians took the visions and dreams of evangelicals as proofs of insanity, committing people under the diagnosis of "Methodically mad."[11] Whereas early seventeenth-century dissenters risked being labeled as heretics and being legally persecuted, in the eighteenth century, dissenters risked being treated as mental patients. Anglican elites promoted this anti-Methodist view of mental health, in order to discredit evangelical religions.[12] This was not mere propaganda, because evidently doctors and parents took this association to heart. In the American South, some parents and spouses called for doctors when they saw the distressing effects of conviction on their loved ones.[13] English Methodists were disproportionately committed to insane asylums in the eighteenth century, counting for as much as 25 percent of Bedlam's inmates.[14]

While some concerned relatives deterred budding evangelicals with commitment to asylums and painful treatments, other parents expected the children to cure themselves, seeing religious melancholy as a self-inflicted state. Two young English converts faced similar responses from their parents in the face of their evangelical madness. Mary Bosanquet's parents told her to "rouse [her] Self out of that Low state."[15] Likewise, Hester Roe's mother described her daughter's madness as a prison of her own making. In some cases, parents and others used madness more as a metaphor than as a real diagnosis of young Methodists.

This supposed separation from sanity actually described a separation from families and their religious, social, and cultural traditions. The symptoms of the sickness, the insane grief and obsession of conversion, were also symptoms of disengagement from the moderate ways of a convert's familial faith. It had to be madness that forced sons and daughters to reject their upbringing and to prefer the company of Methodists to their birth families.

Dissent from Family and Society

Methodism was a religion of dissent during the eighteenth century, and this alone made it seem frightening to many people who were devoted to the Church of England. Despite the fact that John Wesley repeatedly avowed his allegiance to the Church of England and stated a desire to only supplement, not supplant, traditional worship, Methodism had all the markings of a dangerous sect. Its followers adopted a strange new language, one that had specific codes of discourse for addressing each other, for describing their leadership, and for shaping their emotions and religious fervor. At a profound level, Methodism seemed to provide young people with the tools to reject society and all of its customs. One of the persistent themes of anti-Methodist literature and everyday gossip in the eighteenth century was that Methodists simply did not know how to enjoy themselves. In their stringent adherence to austere moral and social codes, evangelicals rejected the commonplace joys of mainstream culture, according to their critics.

As diversions and entertainments increased in number, in theaters, novels, gambling houses, coffeehouses, and public houses, Methodists asked their members to abstain from these sorts of enjoyments. Methodists repudiated the normative social activities for young adults: dancing, gossiping, going to theater, dressing up, or being concerned with "trifling" things. Sometimes, in the accounts of young men, these behaviors included more serious sins, such as sexual indiscretions. For Virginian Stith Mead, who was twenty-two years old when he converted to Methodism in 1789, his religiosity flew in the face of his family's beliefs and practices. He had enjoyed dancing, fencing, card playing, and fine clothes prior to his conversion, but denounced them afterward. To his family members, these were innocent pursuits, sanctioned by society and culture. Yet Methodists, alongside Baptists, had specific rules about how members should behave, and these rules dictated strict ideas about moral behavior. Evangelical rules for behavior often involved a denial of gender-specific roles of masculine sociability, feminine socialization, or engagement in the fashionable world.[16] In 1738, John Wesley first set down the guidelines for Methodists in his *Rules of the Band-Societies*, and he went on to revise and republish these rules regularly during his lifetime; these rules became more commonly known as the *Discipline*.[17]

Alongside gender prescriptions, these rules also emphasized a plain way of life, wherein Methodists renounced much of the trappings of fashionable, excessive living and thereby any privileges of their class. As a broad directive, Methodists were enjoined to live as simply as possible and to help those in need. The Methodist *Discipline* emphasized the directive that its members practice frugality, spend their money only on necessities, and give the rest to charity. Wesley emphasized in various writings that holding money was not a problem, as long as it was not misspent. Followers were expected to give excess income to charity for the support of less fortunate Methodist members.[18] Upper- and middle-class Methodists, like Stith Mead, Mary Bosanquet, and Hester Roe, emphasized the differences from their familial culture, by dressing more plainly, working harder, and avoiding social occasions.

By adopting the specific codes found in the Methodist *Discipline*, Methodists seemed to abruptly discard the values and activities of their birth families. Evangelicals countered the traditions with which they were raised, and they sent waves of disapprobation toward their unconverted parents, siblings, and friends. An anti-Methodist pamphlet charged: "It is not only the pomp and vanity of the world which [Methodist preachers] denounce, but the whole world itself, abstractedly considered, with all its enjoyments and attachments, from dancing, song-singing, and spectacle, to the happy frolic of youth."[19] As this writer describes, evangelicals' antisocial behavior looked like a rejection of humanity altogether. In the accounts of young Methodists, they commonly voiced the need to dissociate from their peers, either because of their friends' explicit anti-Methodist sentiments or their irreligious activities.[20]

In the 1790s, Stith Mead often separated himself from his family in order to conduct prayers in secret, and this was a point of derision for his family members. He did not always pray alone, though, and made repeated efforts to convert the rest of his family. He was successful with one brother, Samuel, but the rest remained unconvinced. His uncle Nicholas Mead announced that "he would have no more praying," after Nicholas's wife started to respond to Stith's efforts. Despite his labors, the Mead family continued their enjoyable social practices, and as one sister remarked, she "did not see the necessity of giving up all the pleasures of the world."[21] Later, Stith Mead wrote a series of letters to his father aimed at awakening his father and siblings. His brother Samuel, who had been on the path of conversion, had recently died, and Stith Mead was afraid that his father had led him spiritually astray before his death. Stith wrote his father a scathing letter: "Father, the Indulgeance of Fidling and Dancing, has ever been your beseting Sin, and I fear will be your final and Eternal Ruin; do you Continue to Send your Children to the dancing Schools or Indulge them to attend the balls? If so you are training them up for the DEVIL to make them an heir of Hell-fire."[22] Mead declared he was not afraid of the threat of disinheritance, weakening this incentive for filial obedience. Yet, even while telling his father he would burn in hell, Stith Mead signed his letters "Your dutiful Son in Jesus Christ."[23] Mead's father continued to resist his call for conversion, but he did leave his son a sizable inheritance.[24]

Narratives of Separation

The personal sense of psychological transformation shared by Methodist converts appears in their autobiographical narratives. The conversion narrative was the central genre in the rise of evangelical print culture. The spread of Methodism relied on its models, which were transmitted through conversion narratives. These narratives exemplified the ways in which conversion changed individual lives and showed the extent to which entering the Methodist family was transformative, socially and culturally.

The importance of autobiographies and biographies to evangelical culture cannot be overemphasized. Building on the Puritan tradition of commonplace books, daybooks, and spiritual memoirs, eighteenth-century English and American evangelicals actively promoted the accounting and recounting of one's spiritual life.[25] Privately, many Methodists recorded their daily experiences in journals and diaries that were later published or used for biographical sketches. Private reflection was the cornerstone of evangelical experience, and Methodists were ceaselessly contributing to narrative production as a group. These autobiographies became exemplars, which individual evangelicals would apply to their own lives.[26] Converts treated published and epistolary religious narratives much like personal advice from a family member. They wrote about these spiritual paragons in their letters and journals, and they condemned themselves for not living up to their examples. These autobiographies bound the culture together, across many miles, to produce translatable models of behavior and modes of religiosity that bound the transatlantic family.

As models of experience, evangelical narratives were particularly helpful in leading converts through the periods of transition, from their unawakened self to their converted self. Often these autobiographies were clearly organized around the (re)production of religious experience, framing the key moments of one's life in terms of religious awakenings and transgressions. As the genre of conversion narratives developed through the eighteenth century, certainly the replication of language and emotional accounts became evident; by the middle of the nineteenth century, these narratives were obviously mimetic.[27] Yet, while the genre was still in its infancy in the eighteenth century, conversion narratives tended to include autobiographical detail that made the accounts highly individualized. These life stories were recounted in numerous journals and daybooks and through individual conversion narratives, which were written originally in letters and then published in pamphlets and magazines. Charles Wesley, in particular, was a great solicitor of conversion narratives. Laywomen responded volubly to his requests, and many noted the particular time and care it took them to write this sort of account, some demonstrating a painful lack of familiarity with writing altogether. Through these apertures, one can see the common patterns of language and custom in early Methodism and the emergence of a new sort of family.[28]

Methodist conversion narratives followed similar stages in describing converts' steps toward the Methodist family and away from their birth families. In these narratives, women and men went through the initial religious pangs of alienation from their old ways as they felt the conviction of their sins. In the next stage, they individuated, by separating from their old friends and family and more securely forming their own sense of spiritual expression. In the final stage, they rejoined a family, which was their evangelical family. These stages of alienation and individuation were similar to anthropological notions of separation, liminality, and reintegration.[29] Conversion narratives were central components in the formation of modern religious identity. As the eighteenth century witnessed an unprecedented expansion of mobility that loosened individuals from the traditional strictures in many ways, the conversion narrative was a way to reconstitute their sense of self and their new identities as religious converts. Religious historian Bruce Hindmarsh asserts, "Religious experience became, therefore, far more voluntary and self-conscious, and far less a matter of custom or givenness, as women and men were presented with alternatives. In this context the turn to spiritual autobiography played a crucial role by allowing believers to negotiate an identity that could no longer be merely assumed."[30]

In the primary stage of alienation, Methodists valorized the image of the lone saint struggling through multiple obstacles to realize his or her religious life. There is a strong theme in early Methodist literature that associates patient, Christ-like suffering with increasing godliness. Many early Methodist narratives feature the figures of the stalwart individual and the precocious child saint. The journals of Methodist women in particular reveal the difficulties that many early converts faced when attempting to join this group. Methodist women, more so than their male counterparts, tended to focus on this departure from their birth families. Their accounts make clear that the spiritual calling of Methodism tended to be individualized, which not only alienated relatives, but also transgressed the gender codes of eighteenth-century England and America. Women's entry into Methodism was a phenomenon of particular concern to English and Anglo-American society.[31]

Some women framed their journey toward Methodism as a continuation of their moral upbringing, but more often the call to religiosity was ignited by an impulse from within. This heightened the individuality of spiritualism within the account and made each woman the central actor in her own conversion. Men were expected to take distinct paths for themselves in young adulthood, but women had to justify this individuation. In the surviving literature of conversion narratives, Methodist women were more likely to root their spiritual lives within their childhoods than their male counterparts were. In these portraits, women describe themselves as following their own, particular callings of religiosity, which often pitted their wills against their parents'. As young women, they described this disobedience as always balanced by their desires to be dutiful daughters. Yet, Methodists, who felt that their callings had divine origins, could justify even the most flagrant filial disobedience.

Separation from one's parents was not a requirement for becoming a

Methodist, but this was a persistent theme in autobiographical accounts of childhood. In some cases, the convert phrased this separation as a necessary weighing and shifting of priorities, the inevitable realization that the divine authority had superseded earthly ones. Hester Roe, for example, framed her conflicts with her mother as instances in which God permitted and encouraged her to disagree with her mother's wishes. Methodists referred to the multiple passages in the Bible that state that a Christian's devotion to God should supersede any concerns about family and friends. At a turning point in Mary Bosanquet's individuation, she proclaimed that loving her parents more than God was now inconceivable and that she had to accept their disapproval. Bosanquet cited the example of Jesus, who asked his disciples to give up the ties of family, saying "he that loveth father and mother more than me is not worthy of me."[32] Eighteenth-century biblical commentator Matthew Henry interpreted this passage as an acknowledgment that disciples should expect persecution and avoid the concerns of the world. This directive is similar to the commandment to worship no other idols before God, and Methodists interpreted this commandment as a caution against idolizing people by allowing them to become more important than God. In Elizabeth Hayden's narrative, she wrote that she had worshipped her mother. In 1789, she recounted, "Neithr of my Parents were in the narrow Way, and my Mother whom I idolized, was very tender and Affectionate (and many Years I had to wean me from my Idol)."[33]

Through exposure to religious literature and practice, children garnered the right to be spiritual authorities over their parents, inverting the parent-child relationship.[34] In a letter to Charles Wesley in 1738, Mrs. Clagget wrote about her experience of being converted by her daughter, who had been secretly attending Methodist meetings. At first, she opposed her daughter's evangelicalism, until the mother was converted by the combination of seeing Charles Wesley preach and listening to her daughter. She admitted to the curious inversion of finding her daughter spiritually wiser than herself. Clagget wrote, "[A]t about 13 [she] seemed utterly to have renounced the World and gave her Selfe wholy to God. I know See what before I had no notion off how far she has been made Instrumental to the bringing about my own Salvation, She everyday watched for opportunities of Shewing me the Danger I was in by being too Anxious about Temporal things whilst I neglected the one thing needfull, telling me that she desired not to be Rich or great, at the Hazard of my Eternal happiness."[35]

This story of a mother's eventually joyful conversion under her daughter's spiritual leadership was rare. More commonly, parents strenuously objected to their children's evangelical conversion. As a result, young evangelical converts struggled with how to frame their relationships to their birth families. Converts could justify their seemingly rebellious behavior toward their parents by claiming that they owed their ultimate obedience to a higher spiritual authority. The theme of obedient disobedience within conversion narratives marked the sense that Methodists grappled with the conflict between the rules and customs of their birth family and the alternate codes and behaviors of their religious family.

The narratives of three young Methodist women, Mary Bosanquet Fletcher, Hester Ann Roe Rogers, and Catherine Livingston Garrettson, recount a common theme of alienation from their birth families, as they joined in the mores and customs peculiar to their new evangelical family. These women were educated enough to create coherent narratives of considerable length and were prominent lay leaders of the eighteenth-century Methodist movement. They represented the exemplars of aspiration so precious to the wider family of transatlantic evangelicals. Mary Bosanquet became a leader within Methodism, influential in her control of a major Methodist center and known for her power as an exhorter and preacher. Hester Roe and Catherine Livingston were never as prominent as Bosanquet, and never as close to the Wesley brothers. Yet, in their own way, they were also extremely important. Livingston encouraged the establishment of Methodism in upstate New York, an arena that would become more important to Methodists as the nineteenth century progressed. Roe's published narrative became exemplary of the struggle of evangelical women and circulated throughout the English Atlantic world.

These narratives establish common stages that new converts would experience when joining Methodism in the eighteenth century. Their narratives follow a process of deconstructing the old codes of the birth families and joining a new family as a convert through their "new birth." With slight variations, these narratives trace a common path to the new family: (1) a realization of difference, which can begin at an early age or in the teenage years; (2) recognition of an alternate religious life, resulting in conversion; (3) conflict and alienation from the ways of their birth family; (4) isolation within their birth family (becoming the lone, suffering saint); and (5) leaving their old family to join with the new family.

Figure 3. Mary Bosanquet Fletcher, engraving by John Chester Buttre, ca. 1855–85. Courtesy of the Drew University Methodist Collection.

Mary Bosanquet's Narrative

Mary Bosanquet Fletcher (1739–1815) wrote in her manuscript autobiography that she had felt, as a precocious four-year-old, that "god heard prayer."[36] By the time she was five years old, she began to distinguish between sinful and good behavior and wondered about the fate of her soul.[37] From the beginning, Bosanquet felt different from other members of her family, who attended the Church of England but had little zeal.[38] In 1746, she discovered Methodism through her sister and their servant, and Bosanquet dramatically recalled the moment of recognizing the alternative to her natural family's religious practices: "I well remember the very Spot we stood on, and the words She Spake, which tho we were but a few minutes together sunk so deeply into my heart they were never after Erase. My reflections were suited to a child not 7 years old. I thought if I became a Methodist I was sure to be saved and determined if Ever I could get at this people whatever it cost I would be one of them."[39]

Later in her childhood, she set about to conform her life to evangelical norms. This behavior marked her as different from her three siblings, and her parents were often perplexed by her strangeness and disobedience.[40] She recalled her mother's chastising words: "that girl is the most preverse creature that ever lived, I cant think what is come into her."[41] Bosanquet continued to frame her childhood journey as a rebellious and isolating process, separating her even from the sister who had introduced her to Methodism. Her elder sister never converted; instead she married in 1754, leaving Bosanquet without a religious ally in the family.

Throughout her teenage years, Bosanquet sustained her evangelical ambitions. Her parents fired the Methodist servant and hid religious tracts from Bosanquet, who began to feel like a lone, suffering saint. In 1755, Bosanquet continued to glean evangelical ideas from family friends and literature, and she abstained from going to the theater, a frequent family activity. Her father attempted to dissuade her, remarking that she acted as if "all dress and company, nay, all agreeable liveliness, and the whole spirit of the world, is sinful."[42] The family was based on a large estate in Leytonstone, Essex, and they frequently traveled in a fashionable circuit of bucolic resorts and urban entertainments.[43] They had asked her to endure public entertainments quietly, "to do as they did and not bring reproach upon them in a Strange place. This seemed a very reasonable request—but alas,

I could not comply; for the Spirit of the worlds was contrary that of Christ."[44] She wrote that she was afraid of "snares," which in Methodist code refers to both the public traps of entertainment and trifling diversions, as well as the more intimate traps of romantic love.

Methodists often felt the tension between obedience to their blood family and the demands of the new family. This tension was particularly difficult, because Christianity promoted filial obedience as a central commandment yet also encouraged following individual conscience in spiritual matters. Bosanquet reflected on this central quandary between individual religious yearnings and filial obedience, when she wrote about conforming to the dress required of her class, despite her desires to dress more simply for religious reasons. "I plainly saw the throwing of dress would be to my relations a great trial—I loved my parents, and it hurt me to disoblige them—I sought for arguments to quench that little Spark of Light wich was kindling in my Soul. Conscious they could not see in me my Light—and knowing that obedience to parents was one of the first dutys—I did so far quench it that I put on again many of the things that I had thrown off.—my acquaintance took much notice of me, and I was so afraid of Losing their good opinion that I had no power to reprove Sin, or even to refrain from joining in Light or trifling conversation when in company."[45] It is clear from Bosanquet's narrative that there was much more at stake than outward conformity to familial culture. Bosanquet equated this small acquiescence to losing her religious sense of self.

Bosanquet's writings also confirm that evangelicals sought their new family as the final step into a new life. When she was with her old friends, it was harder for her to be religiously authentic. Thus, instead of partaking in the usual fashionable pursuits of her age, she searched for a religious life and family of like-minded souls. In 1758, Bosanquet found her new family when she began boarding in London with a company of single Methodist women, including Sarah Ryan and Sarah Crosby.[46] She wrote about the London Methodists: "The more I saw of that family the more I was convinced Christ had get his pure Church below . . . whenever I was from home this was the place of my residence and truly I found it to be a little Bethel."[47] Taking these friends as her real family signified the point in the narrative where she experienced significant dissonance between her old family ways and the new family. The new family members prided themselves on simplicity, not finery and elaboration, and fiery religiosity over conformity. And these new friends were both from lower classes than the Bosanquets; Sarah Ryan and Sarah Crosby simply subsisted in their roles as housekeepers and secretaries for Methodist preachers.

This decision must have vexed her parents, who saw her deepening entanglement with the evangelical world as a sort of madness. Clearly her parents viewed her London evangelical society as more Bedlam than Bethel; they blamed Methodism for her "strong nervous fever—they thought it all arose from some trouble of mind I would not own—and told me one day if I did not rouse my Self out of that Low state my head sho[u]ld be blistered and I should be shut up in a dark room." They also threatened to place her in an insane asylum.[48]

Mary Bosanquet's relationship to her parents became strained as she became more and more embedded in the culture and customs of her new Methodist family. Her parents worried that Bosanquet would be a bad influence on her brothers and convert them to Methodism.[49] When she came into a small, but adequate, inheritance of one hundred pounds per year at the age of twenty-one, she recognized this could support her new life. She already had plans in mind, then, when her father sat her down to discuss her future and told her, "there is a perticular promise I require of you, that is, will you never on any accation Either now or hearafter attempt to make your Brothers what you call Christian." Her father clearly saw evangelicalism as a madness that could be contagious and hoped that his daughter would not infect her brothers. Bosanquet wrote that in her response, "I answered Looking to the Lord—'I think Sir I dare not consent to that.' He replyed then you fo[r]ce me to put [you] out of the house."[50] In recalling this flagrant disobedience, Bosanquet emphasized that God's ultimate authority superceded her parents'. Joining with Methodists allowed Bosanquet to challenge her father in ways that would not have been possible otherwise. In these conflicts between household and religious authority, Methodists felt that familial authority was secular and temporal, while divine authority was absolute. After many weeks of increasing familial tension, one day her mother ordered a coach to carry her daughter away from home.[51]

It was important to Bosanquet, in constructing this autobiography, to write about the ways in which her religious rebellion was justified within an alternative culture and code. Bosanquet reported that on her first night as an "orphan" (though she was twenty-one), she lay awake in her new bed, and "I looked on my Self as lying under a deep reproach—and was ready to tremble at the thought of being thrust out from under the Othority and protection of My father's roof. But I remembered that word he that loveth father or mother more then me is not worthy of me."[52]

The tangled lines of affection and economics persisted between Bosanquet and her parents through her young adult life. In 1763, she thought about taking a vacant farmhouse on her property in Leytonstone, a mile from her family's house, in order to hold Methodist meetings there.[53] As an adult, Bosanquet had struck a peace with her parents. She visited them, and they were satisfied with her life, as long as she was living her new life at a distance from them. She sought divine assistance as to how she could preserve this peace while drawing dozens of evangelicals to preach and pray near her parent's house. "Those words again presented 'he that loveth father or mother more than me is not worthy of me.' "[54] In 1763, when she decided to go through with her plans to live near them, her parents were surprisingly equanimous in their assent to this plan, but her father "added with a Smile 'if a Mob Should pull your house about your ears I cant hinder them.' "[55]

Bosanquet had made a deeper peace with her parents before their deaths in 1767. While her father had left her a diminished inheritance because of her refusal to marry when she was younger, her mother increased this on her deathbed. Bosanquet and her mother spoke of those "formal trials" in an affectionate manner, and Bosanquet recalls, "I found much love to her of consequence much pain, She Express a tender kindness towards me in her illness."[56] But even as her parents were facing their final moments, Bosanquet admitted her mind was often elsewhere. She was thinking of her new family circle: the religious orphanage she had begun, and the woman she called her "Spiritual Mother," Sarah Ryan, who lay close to her own death in the bed and home they shared. Eighteenth-century people shared beds with friends of the same sex when necessary, but their sleeping arrangements may have been part of their choice to live plainly, claiming no more space than necessary. Sharing a bed also most certainly marked the intimacy of their chosen relationship; they were inseparable until Ryan's death in 1768.[57]

Bosanquet's narrative reveals the ways in which converting to Methodism created rifts in many families during the eighteenth century. Bosanquet found connections, extended family, and friends, who drew her toward her new spiritual life and into a new family. She found a new sense of belonging in a very different kind of family that allowed her to remain single throughout her young adult life, when her primary bonds were with fellow Methodist women.

Hester Ann Roe's Narrative

Hester Roe (1756–93) was also an English Methodist, but her entrance into the Methodist family was very different from Bosanquet's, and, by her account, included an extended period of separation from her birth family before she was free to become a full member of the Methodist family. Like Bosanquet, Roe was a prominent Methodist layperson whose piety was renowned in Wesleyan Methodist circles. In the nineteenth century, her autobiography became a sensation, in both the secular and religious print realms in England and America, going into multiple printings and versions.[58] She compiled the autobiography from personal journals, to tell the story of her early years and the beginning of her attraction to Methodism. Her writings served as a model for many nineteenth-century American women; she was well known and beloved to nineteenth-century readers who admired her story of piety overcoming temptations and family pressures, an autobiography that was as dramatic as a romantic novel.

Roe grew up in Macclesfield, a small town near Manchester, England, in a small, close-knit family with only one other sibling who survived to adulthood, a brother who left home in his early teens. Her father, an Anglican minister, had died when she was young, and Hester was left to take care of her mother, who was frequently ill. Roe's family had a servant and was never particularly troubled financially, but her family was simply comfortable in comparison to the upper-class stratum of the Bosanquets. Just as the familial situations of these two women were very different, their cultural situations were also dissimilar. Bosanquet's world revolved around southern England's fashionable arenas and the sheltered estate of Leytonstone, while Roe's world was the provincial town of Macclesfield in the North of England. North England became an increasingly important arena for the Methodists in the latter part of the eighteenth century. Manchester was the capital of the industrial North and the engine for England's launch into the industrial age, with factories and mines springing up throughout the North. As well, Methodists were able to capitalize on the population growth and lack of institutionalized religion by drawing up new itinerant circuits as these industrial centers became ripe fields for new converts.[59]

Roe described her childhood as one marked by unremitting filial duty

Figure 4. Hester Roe Rogers, engraving by John Chester Buttre, ca. 1871. Courtesy of the Drew University Methodist Collection.

and, like Bosanquet, precocious spirituality. She highlighted her moments of spiritual awakenings: when she was visited by the devil as a child one night after forgetting to pray, and when she had a dream, during her frivolous teenage years, that she had died and saw the awfulness of the hell that awaited her, only to be forgiven by God.[60] As a teenager, Roe realized she was different when she began to exhibit an innate seriousness, despite her teenage flirtation with dancing and parties. In her autobiography, much as in Bosanquet's, her path to Methodism was marked by inevitability and the isolation of this individualized calling. Like Bosanquet, she risked much in converting to Methodism. In her journal, she highlighted the gulf that existed between her birth family and the Methodist family; the former was familiar and safe, but the latter was fairly exotic and dangerous. As a teenager, Roe heard others compare Methodism to Catholicism. The word on the street confirmed that both religions produced false piety and imitations of prophecy. She heard that "they deceived the illiterate and were little better than common pick-pockets."[61] Echoing the themes of anti-Methodist literature, her friends warned her that Methodism perverted people's minds; it made some presumptuous and unbearable, others insane. She also heard that they were incredibly antisocial, caring only for their own members.[62]

All of these voices of public and private condemnation followed her to her first Methodist meeting in the early 1770s, when she heard Reverend David Simpson preach on the sinfulness of dancing and other diversions. For Roe, unlike Bosanquet, the stages of discovering this alternate religiosity and discord with her family were greatly compressed. Upon hearing Simpson, she immediately set about to shred all her "fine caps and clothes," cut her hair, and commit herself to rooting out her intrinsic sinfulness. Her friends were stunned and her mother, horrified. Her mother told Hester that she "thought I was losing my Senses."[63] Like Bosanquet's mother, Mrs. Roe likewise saw madness in her daughter's behavior.[64] Mrs. Roe's initial response was even stronger than Bosanquet's parental censure. Hester Roe wrote in her autobiography, "I knew if I persisted in hearing the Methodists I must litterally give up *all*. My mother had already threatened, if ever she knew me to hear them—She would disown me—Every friend and Relation I had in the World—I had reason to believe would do so also—I had no acquaintance even among the Methodists to take me in—nor knew any refuge to fly to but my God."[65] Roe felt estranged from her family's ways almost immediately, and she started going to prayer groups and reading evangelical literature in secrecy. Her mother insisted that converting to Methodism meant losing her blood family, but she had no new family yet, so she felt the need to keep her evangelical life hidden from her mother for some time. When her mother discovered her daughter's clandestine life, "a flood of persecution opened upon me—but in that time of need, God raised me up a friend in my Uncle Roe which kept my mother from turning me out of doors. Yet what I suffered, sometimes thro' her tears and entreaties, and at other times her severity, is known only to God."[66]

Though Roe did have a sympathetic uncle, she became increasingly isolated within her family. Her relatives coordinated a campaign to turn her away from Methodism, but Roe outtalked them all. Her mother resorted to subtler means of pressuring her to leave Methodism; she tried taking her daughter out of town for an extended trip. Instead of joining in the social outings, Hester literally refused to dress the part and insisted on staying home to pray several times a day. "[I]n a little time finding all their Efforts in vain, they began to let me Alone—only I was made to understand, I had now nothing to expect from my Godmother as to temporal things, this however weighed nothing with me."[67] Roe emphasized that economic pressure was an ineffective tool on her. In fact, in the ultimate act of obedient disobedience, she inverted this threat of economic sanction by offering herself as the house servant, much to her mother's horror. Her mother allowed her to go to Methodist meetings in exchange for cleaning the house, "believing I who had never been Accustomed to Hard Labour, would soon be weary and give it up."[68] Roe had less to gamble with than Bosanquet, but the stakes were still high in terms of comfort and familial support. Roe cited the large body of Methodist literature and John Wesley's work on sanctification, in particular, as aids during this difficult period of isolation. It was this literature, she insisted, that helped her endure living and working as a servant, incurring her mother's prolonged and pronounced displeasure.[69]

In fact, the hardships she endured seem to have been incentives toward Methodism, because they fed her self-image as the lone, suffering saint. Roe wrote, "[S]he has been Sever with me—yet Glory be to god my Soul is at peace—I know these Crosses are for my good and the happiness I enjoy in God, more than repays my Soul."[70] Even as her widowed mother attempted to enforce her social conformity, Roe insisted that her true self was inaccessible to her mother. She wrote, "My Mother insisted on my going with her to dine and drink Tea with her at an uncles—and I was not Suffered to attend Preaching Morning or Night—but I had secret intercourse with my God which none could hinder."[71] Roe began to grow further and further apart from her mother by beginning new friendships outside of her family's social circles and taking up a spiritual life that she did not share with her mother.

Eventually, Roe's secret life won out, and her mother allowed her to become a member of the Methodist family, albeit grudgingly. Roe's biography became a Methodist model for disobedience and refusal to participate in frivolous ungodly company at any cost. Her willingness to give up her class comforts, to become a servant rather than go against her spiritual calling, was a hallmark of the religious sacrifice necessary for converts. Roe marked her alienation from the norms of her family by upending them completely and becoming their servant. Persevering through suffering her mother's persecution sealed Roe's fate as a member of the Methodist family. She rejoiced, "I now am enrolled by Name among thy Dear People."[72]

Catherine Livingston's Narrative

Although Catherine Livingston was across the ocean and living in a remarkably different setting from Roe or Bosanquet, Livingston's narrative demonstrates the striking similarities between the conversion narratives of American and English Methodists. Livingston (1752–1849) was born into a large, prominent family in New York. The Livingstons were well established with extensive landholdings in upstate New York, where their name is still as prominent as the houses they built on the banks of the Hudson. Catherine Livingston's mother brought a considerable landholding of her own into the Livingston clan, and Catherine's father was a judge.[73] Catherine Livingston would become widely regarded as a leader of Methodism in New York State, a distinction her family could not have wished for her. Like Bosanquet and Roe, Livingston was well loved by her parents and reported a happy childhood. Her parents adhered to traditional churches; her mother was a Dutch Calvinist, her father an Anglican, and the children were raised in both traditions.[74] In 1775, her father died suddenly when she was twenty-three, and the family went through considerable upheaval during the Revolutionary War, when the British set fire to her family home of Clermont. However, the Revolution did not merit mention in her spiritual autobiography, which she wrote in 1817.

As a young woman in elite circles, Livingston had a full social calendar,

Figure 5. Catherine Livingston Garrettson, engraving by John Chester Buttre, ca. 1863. Courtesy of the Drew University Methodist Collection.

reporting invitations to no fewer than five balls one week. Like Hester Roe, she realized her difference from others in her family when she was a teenager. Livingston, though, always had a sense that she lacked fulfillment in the circuits of her class: "If the smiles of the world and the pleasures of it could have bestowed happiness, I should certainly have enjoyed it, but no, there was something wanting, and a dear friend, who was also an inmate in the same dwelling, and myself would sit up after returning from brilliant balls, and gay parties, and moralize on their emptiness, till it became burdensome to accept of invitations."[75] An awakening followed the death of her sister-in-law Margaret Livingston in 1785, when Catherine Livingston began to read the Bible more and socialize less. Livingston reported in her autobiography that she began to withdraw from her family as well, because she was not sure if they would understand her religious ardency. She was isolated, much like Bosanquet at times, because she had no Methodist circle to enter. As a result, she went back to the social realm of her family, attending balls, parties, theaters, and the Anglican church.[76]

In 1787, she felt a true conversion where "[a] song of praise and thanksgiving was put in my mouth—my sins were pardoned my state was changed; my soul was happy. In a transport of joy I sprang from my knees, and happening to see myself as I passed the glass I could not but look with surprise at the change in my countenance. All things were become new." Livingston captured in her diary the sense of new birth, as she saw the world with different eyes and felt transformed. She shared her conversion with her mother who seemed happy for her.[77] Like Roe, she avoided all social gatherings in earnest, discarded her frivolous clothes and trimmings, and opted for only serious clothes and serious pursuits.

Much like Mary Bosanquet, one of Livingston's key entries into Methodism was through a servant. A housekeeper gave her a copy of Wesley's writings, "so that I ever claimed him for my spiritual father. And I often thought of writing, to let him know how much I was obligated to love and honor him. These books had opened to me the way to get religion and the only way to keep it when attained."[78] Her true family, Livingston claimed, was not found in her family's house, but in the books and narratives circulating through the transatlantic Methodist family. In 1787, Livingston sought increasing solitude, and she took to writing an account of her spiritual life. In the first pages she prays that she can "put on the whole 'Armour of God,' Having my loins girt about with Truth and having on the Breastplate of Righteousness."[79] The imagery of war was significant. Not only did

Livingston feel combative toward the omnipresent sinfulness and temptations of living in this world, but she also felt like a warrior who stood alone in this fight, because she was at odds with those nearest and dearest to her, her unconverted family and friends. Because she lived at a great distance from the nearest Methodist society, Livingston had no alternate family around her. Yet she entered into a virtual spiritual family by imbibing their literature and following their practices by praying, isolating herself, reflecting, and writing in her spiritual diary.

Like many Methodists, Livingston worried that her newfound religiosity and its deep psychological effects appeared as insanity to outsiders. She reported mood swings, alternating doubt and joyfulness in her spiritual state. One day in December of 1787, Livingston wrote of waking in a good mood as usual, thinking happily of her relationship to God. Then, after she took a walk and began some self-examination, she found some long-established faults, vanity and selfishness. "Instead of praying to that Great power, Whose Hand is ever near to help those who confide in Him, I prayed that He would lay me low, low in the Dust, before Him, that He would shew me myself, and encrease my dependence upon Him. Presumtuous Wretch!"[80] Her happiness disintegrated over the course of the day until she felt herself at the very bottom, "deform'd with Sin, Naked, Helpless, Worthless, beyond the power of Language." She wrote, "the terrors of the Law, and the Arm of a Just Judge; appeared to be lifted up to strike a Guilty Wretch. . . . Was it any wonder my poor Weak reason, was on the point of deserting its mansion forever!—My Actions, and language I knew were those of a Frantic Bedlamite."[81] In this passage, she wrote of feeling isolated, and she poignantly described the sensation of losing her reason. She wrote with surprising self-awareness of being on the edge of suicide.[82]

Livingston's stage of isolation was more profound than Roe's and Bosanquet's because of the lack of Methodists in her area. From late 1787 through the following year, Livingston relied on private prayer, Christian writings, and her diary to substitute for Christian fellowship. Livingston spent more and more time alone in her room by the end of 1787. She found solace in reading; both the Bible and John Wesley's *Journal* comforted her with examples of Christian persecution and isolation more severe than her own.[83] She still had a few friends whom she counted as "Christian" and capable of "serious conversation," and she circulated in her old network occasionally. She wrote in late December of 1787, "I spent some Hours in that trifling manner, which is usual in gay circles, and was glad in the evening to find myself at home after a short ride. I retired to my Room that I might find Him without Whom, this World, and its highest enjoyments, is barren and incapable of bestowing one moments gratification."[84] The world outside did not contain God; Livingston felt the divine presence only when she was alone, in private and undisturbed. The Methodist family offered divinity in a social circle, one that she was without. That night she read in the book of John a justification for separating herself from irreligious folks and finding the "Children of God" and "the love of Brethren," as opposed to "the love of the World."[85] Livingston privileged her virtual evangelical literary family above the blood family. In her location, on the frontier of Methodism, an area of upstate New York that held few Methodists, she had few personal associations with Methodism. Like many early converts, she was an itinerant soul, looking for a place to land. Itinerant preachers also found themselves isolated at times, preaching to nonbelievers, traveling a solitary life. The conviction of the isolated, suffering saint was unparalleled in Methodist literature—this was the mark of a true saint. It also exemplified the transatlantic family. Even when they were not physically connected, they found each other through evangelical language. In this case, by reading Wesley's words, Livingston connected herself to the pervasive, well-published community of transatlantic saints.

Livingston's familial feud did not come to a head until her mother forbade her writing for a period of three weeks in late March and early April of 1788, to try to end her increasing solitude. When she took up the pen again on April 15, 1788, she wrote, "Twenty one days have elapsed since I was commanded to shut this book. I see and adore the wisdom and tender love of my beloved Master: The incidents that have taken place in that interval, I could not have written, without the greatest violence to my feelings. And God in Mercy spared the recital. Suffice it to say; I have been lead thro' fearful, distressing scenes:—But God will I doubt not make me a way to escape."[86] After this entry, her passages tended to be briefer, responding to the restrictions her mother placed on her time in spiritual solitude.

During 1788, her family continually pressured Livingston to spend more time with relatives and in public, while depriving her of the freedom to worship alone. She had less time for her personal devotions, and more time was occupied in business, family affairs, and chores. Altogether, she noted resignation over the conflict with her family.[87] She conceded that her introspection did result in her emotional detachment from them.[88] Livingston withstood steady pressure from her family to quit her spiritual quest. For much of 1788 and 1789, her family had strictly barred her from writing in her diary.

When Livingston wrote again, in April of 1791, she had become part of the Methodist family. The occasion for her resumed writing was "to relate the death of my Father in Christ [John Wesley]."[89] She had joined with Methodists officially in 1789, when she started the first Methodist class in the Rhinebeck area of upstate New York. She would soon make her membership in the Methodist family more official still, by leaving her family home and marrying the Maryland preacher Freeborn Garrettson in 1793. Livingston's narrative confirms some common experiences in joining Methodism, ones she shared with Bosanquet and Roe: a sense of isolation from one's normative social circles, the psychological rupture of conversion, and the reliance on models found in evangelical literature and in life. Even more so than Bosanquet, Livingston was initially isolated and drew from her transatlantic Methodist family primarily through evangelical literature, not a personal network.

Conclusions

Livingston, Roe, and Bosanquet shared a similar path to religious adulthood. Because their identification as Methodists required a level of alienation from the values and customs of their parents and relatives, their separation from the parental bosom was much more than the usual rites of adolescence. Parents did not see becoming a Methodist as simply a matter of exercising one's personal religious choices. As the anti-Methodist literature made clear, there was much more at stake. Methodism could forever alter their children's senses, drive children insane, distort their moral compasses, or just make them insufferably self-righteous.

Early conversion narratives exemplify the extent to which Methodists saw separation and distancing from their parents as a first step in their religious paths. What is also apparent from conversion narratives is that loosening the familial bonds for religious reasons often entailed class and gender transgressions, alongside repudiating one's birth family and customs. These intertwined strands of rebellion provided a path of self-realization for young people in the eighteenth century. Religious rebirth created new identities for evangelicals that were distinct from their natal familial cultures. Evangelicals claimed a distinctive kind of authority, one that challenged parental authority, while being careful to maintain certain standards of obedience to one's parents.

Many young converts emphasized their sense of being alone in the world, and this marked their liminality and suspension between the old and the new families. It was important for evangelicals to see themselves as orphans before they could take on a new set of familial relations in their adoptive family. For Methodist converts, the ultimate father was now God. This isolated Methodists from their particular family bonds, but it also brought them into a new connection. As Stith Mead wrote to a young woman who was facing parental opposition,

> He'll a Father to the Fatherless be
> And be the widows God
> If friends and neighbor you reject
> Put your trust in the Lord
> And he will never you neglect.[90]

This rebellion against parental authority included economic sacrifices in some cases. American leader Francis Asbury ventured that it was "a mere miracle, for a Methodist to increase in wealth and not decrease in grace."[91] Presumably, the inverse was true: becoming poorer made one increase in grace. By becoming Methodists, both Roe and Bosanquet forfeited inheritances and gifts from relatives, a sacrifice that seemed integral to joining the faith. Methodism was associated, through oral and print culture, with the working class; this association was used as a cause for both criticism and praise. Anti-Methodist writers characterized evangelicals as the illiterate dupes of a manipulative organization. In Methodist literature and practice, godliness was associated with self-sacrifice.[92]

Bosanquet believed that the working class naturally achieved a higher spirituality. Her romantic views of working-class spirituality were revealed in her attempts to locate poor Methodists, who would be better spiritual guides than the rich ones she knew.[93] Perhaps finding Sarah Ryan, a working-class woman who became her evangelical bosom friend, satisfied this desire for Bosanquet to find a purer spiritual guide. For the upper and middling classes of Methodism, imitation of working-class dress was essential to spirituality, as confirmed by all of the narratives. The narrow way did not include silk clothes, feathered caps, or beaded purses; trifling pursuits for women included shopping and displaying finery. This emphatic plainness further bound Methodists together as a visibly recognizable family.[94]

Through these maneuvers, declassing became linked to degendering for Methodist women. Plainness also exemplified one of the many ways in which Methodists transgressed eighteenth-century gender codes. Roe sought to express her ardent spirituality by chopping her hair short and shredding all of her fine clothing. This was an act of ultimate rebellion for Roe, signaling her rejection of the usual path for genteel young women, much as Bosanquet had. They refused to maintain class distinctions that would have allowed them to mix in society and find a suitable spouse. This was another way of not adhering to social customs, but it also signified sheer madness to Roe's mother. To family and peers, not conforming to societal and gender codes seemed like a form of insanity. In refusing to mix with society, more generally, the young adherents in all these accounts pronounced themselves exempt from the standards for their sex. But only by throwing off their previous clothes and sinful ways could converts prepare themselves to be born again. In addition, these women were challenging the gender codes by simply being rebellious instead of compliant to their families' wishes. When Livingston evoked the imagery of readying for war in order to fight the challengers from her friends and family, she employed a traditionally masculine sensibility to express her sense of isolation.

Stith Mead provides an example of how Methodist conversion challenged norms for masculinity as well, as Mead was compelled to forgo his inheritance and birthright when he took up preaching. In addition, he condemned the normative modes for southern male culture, including gambling, drinking, dancing, and other diversions, and he firmly and publicly rebuked his father and brothers for participating in these activities. He gave up the comforts and security of his natal family culture, but this seemed necessary in order to cleanse his soul of pernicious influences and be born again. When Methodists were born again, they joined a new family and a new culture, the Methodist family.

Chapter 3

The Best of Bonds: Joining the Methodist Family

When Susannah Designe wrote to Charles Wesley in 1742, she proclaimed, "I find greater ties Both of Love and Duty to your Brother and you than my natural parents after the flesh."[1] While not all Methodists would state this exchange of families in such bald terms, all evangelicals joined a new family when they converted. Methodist laity typically described their relationships to their religious brothers, sisters, mothers, and fathers as the "best of bonds."[2] These bonds were employed in various stages of their lives, through conversion, commitment to a religious life, courtship, marriage, childbirth, and death. These family ties bound Methodist structure, promoting a religious association that went deeper than common worship space and practice. On the interpersonal level, these bonds allowed individuals to construct a new sense of family, one that included many more chosen family members than blood relations.

During the eighteenth century, various economic, social, and cultural forces confirmed the primacy of the nuclear family, alongside the rise of romantic, love-based marriages.[3] At the same time, English and American evangelicals moved in a seemingly opposite direction toward an expansive familial association. By formulating religious bonds that often challenged or competed with the "natural" family, they expanded eighteenth-century families to include chosen, unrelated family members from within the religious ranks. In this family, they replicated the titles, emotions, and supports of the nuclear family structure.

Broader secular and religious networks of association contributed to new familial practices and embedded individuals and nuclear families within larger sets of connections. The friendships, kinship bonds, and intimacies that eighteenth-century people forged with one another expanded upon the nuclear family. These broader connections tended to submerge, or, as Naomi Tadmor puts it, "blur" the nuclear family.[4] Furthermore, the developing concepts of romantic love, placed within the context of the Methodist family, took on a more complex hue, shaded by ideas of divine love and the fraternal love between members of the religious family.

The family as the basic unit of English society was extremely important through the early modern period. As Michael MacDonald and Terrence Murphy write, "The family was the atom of English society, and sentiment was the force that bound its particles together."[5] MacDonald and Murphy emphasize that "[a] person without a family was in a sense not a person; one's status and role in the community followed from one's role in the family."[6] The central importance of the nuclear family to early modern English society underlines the radical nature of the formation of the Methodist family as an alternative family. It also helps us understand why the Methodist family constituted itself along the lines of the nuclear family, with all the same titles and roles. At the same time that Methodists emphasized the central roles of the early modern nuclear family, they de-emphasized the core nucleus of the married couple. Through the promotion of celibacy and the focus on fraternal bonds, the early Methodist family diminished this key component of the nuclear family.

The Bonds of the Nuclear Family

The nuclear family, the normative household of a couple and their offspring, has been in existence since the early modern period. At the same time, that nuclear family was not identical to the one we see in contemporary England and America. There were numerous mutable factors, including the permeability of households, the emotional relationships between family members, and proximity of friends and kin, which have influenced the meaning of "family" quite profoundly from the sixteenth century into the modern period.

When historians have focused on the quality of intimacy and emotional arrangements of the family, they have seen a significant difference between modern and premodern families.[7] In the late eighteenth and early nineteenth century, qualitative markers emerged in the modern family: the ideas of emotional closeness, the focus on children within the family, and the idealization of a strictly private realm for the nuclear family. In describing what is particular to the Victorian sense of family that dominates family culture in the nineteenth century, historians have often focused on the emotional intimacy that ideally existed between parents and children. As well, the nineteenth century witnessed the emergence of a private domestic sphere that allowed the nuclear family to segregate itself from society.[8]

Part of defining this strict division was to separate the nuclear family members from intermediaries within the family, such as extended family members and close friends. One of the key differences between eighteenth-century families and contemporary families is the importance of intermediaries in the family. When one analyzes the emotional relationships within eighteenth-century Anglo-American families and marriages, one can see that these families were not nuclear in the way that we understand that term today. One can see that the relationships between children and mothers were not exclusive and that there were a number of other adult kin who figured centrally in children's lives.[9] Similarly, when examining the emotional relationships within European families, one finds that the broader networks of associations and kinship modified the presumed insularity of the early modern nuclear family.[10]

The Methodist family provided a number of adults who would figure centrally as fictive kin for other members of the family, becoming like assumed family members or intermediaries within the nuclear family. That aspect of expanding the sense of family and encouraging the permeability, not the enclosure, of the family made it appear as though Methodists were working against the nuclear family. Yet, Methodists underlined the emotional connection between their family members in a way that became the hallmark of affective, emotional relationships in the nineteenth century.

Structures of Family

Methodist "families" operated on a number of different levels, and these levels overlapped, providing layers of meaning to the concept of family for each Methodist. One could describe the model for the Methodist family in terms of concentric circles, although the relational lines were not as well defined as that picture would imply. The personal lines of the chosen, intimate family acted as a sort of nuclear family, while the larger, looser connections of religious figures (prominent laypersons, exhorters, and preachers) formed an extended family. The larger circle of secondary family

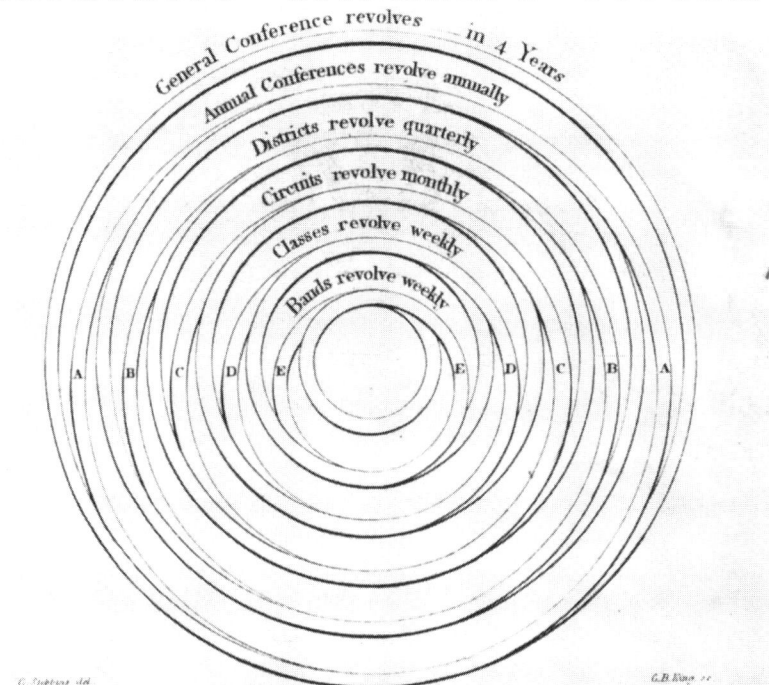

Figure 6. G. Stebbins and G. King, *Methodist Itinerant System,* broadside (New York: John Totten, ca. 1810). Courtesy of the Rare Books Division, New York Public Library, Astor, Lenox, and Tilden Foundations.

consisted of visiting preachers, occasional exhorters, and epistolary relationships. Through their promotion of religious models in print culture, Methodists enacted yet another layer of family.[11]

The bonds of family were often articulated as individual friendships, but they were also encouraged by certain defined structures within Methodism. The powerful circularity of Methodist structures was an important symbol for evangelical practice and organization. This circularity reinforced the sense of constant community, as well as a regularity of religious associations. In the early nineteenth century, a broadside titled *Methodist Itinerant System* displayed this concept by showing Methodist religious structure as an interlocking series of widening circles, resulting in an upward spiral. This circular metaphor was used on each level, from the circuits that revolved monthly to the most encompassing circuit, the General Conference (the meeting of all ministers and preachers). Since each circle fed into the next, the sense was that Methodist structure enabled a constant connection from its basic believer to its most exalted leader. Furthermore, it showed the necessity of regulating time, a persistent theme in Methodism, in order to reinforce regularity, structure, and purpose.

The smallest circle in the *Methodist Itinerant System* was labeled as the bands meeting, surrounded by the next circle which was the class meeting, both of which the chart described as revolving (or meeting) weekly. The lay circles of the local bands and classes were the most intimate, basic level of Methodist association. As discussed in Chapter 1, the establishment of a chosen circle of religious intimates grew out of various evangelical influences, including Wesley's encounter with transatlantic Moravianism. It was essential to the Methodist sense of family, and this level of family was where members held each other accountable to their religious commitments.

The most basic level of family was knit together by the next level of Methodist structure, the circuit. The "circuit" (also called a "round") described the actual circle that each itinerant male preacher traveled in the course of approximately a month, visiting individual communities of believers. Traveling preachers rode the circuits, tracing connections between isolated communities and, sometimes, families of believers. This circle was drawn through a flow of letters, regular visits, and material support that went between the preacher and the evangelicals of his round. Each preacher relied upon the members of his circuit to support him with food, lodging, and supplies, as he traveled from town to town, rarely, if ever, visiting a blood family member. Preachers also drew this familial circle in emotional terms, which they maintained by writing to members of their circuits, even after being reassigned to new circuits.[12]

On the broadest level, eighteenth-century Methodists participated in an expansive print culture of evangelicalism from which they drew support. As exemplified by the conversion narratives of Bosanquet, Roe, and Livingston, personal stories were frequently circulated and helped to draw the connections between the broader Methodist "connexion." Methodists found models for their lives in published biographical accounts in magazines, pamphlets, and books. Evangelical Christianity arose at the same time as an explosion in the variety and availability of popular forms of print, and evangelicals used and benefited from published accounts in an unprecedented manner and scope.[13] This literal exchange of material imposed another level of circularity for evangelicalism, providing a network of instructions, biographies, and language. By circulating these biographical materials, individual preachers (from the Wesley brothers to the regular itinerant preachers) and exhorters (men and women who led prayers and did some preaching) helped to draw the larger connections, outside their circuits, between Methodists over a wide area in the transatlantic world of evangelicals.

Methodist leadership, though, was ambivalent about social attachments and the extent to which they hindered or enriched religious life. The basis of itinerancy, for example, required preachers and exhorters to travel extensively, repeatedly starting and halting associations with fellow Methodists. The demands of the circuit often compelled preachers to spend no more than one or two days in any given place, greatly limiting the chances of forming meaningful ties with the people in their rounds. This limitation of stationary, local bonds was, in fact, the point of a circuit. Preachers could also expect their circuits to change from year to year. Preachers in the "Conference," a group that met regularly from the 1740s onward, determined the general business of their area and decided the assignment of circuits.

The itinerancy was the basis for Methodist leadership, and the preachers considered itinerancy to be the highest calling. This was in part because of the sacrifice it necessitated, not the least in terms of one's relationships to family and friends. As the enthusiastic preacher James Quinn wrote, "Methodism itinerancy, as a system, has hitherto had no place for loungers, and may Heaven forbid it ever should, and let all the people say, Amen. This plan calls for men to cut loose from the world, and cast it behind. Let us have the men who are constrained by the love of Christ, moved by the Holy Ghost—men who can walk hand in hand with poverty, for twice twenty years; then leave their widows to trust in the Lord, and their fatherless children to be provided for and preserved alive by him."[14] At least as Quinn envisioned it, the Methodist ideal replaced individual families with a large extended family, headed by God. Quinn's vision of a holy fraternity presumed that their divine calling and this fraternity, not Methodists' own nuclear families, would meet the economic and emotional needs of individuals, especially itinerant men.

Forsaking the traditional ties of family and marriage as support systems, traveling preachers relied upon the kindness of Methodist strangers, who would become their surrogate families for much of their adult lives. Itinerant preachers depended upon the bonds within the Methodist family, which compelled Methodist men and women to open their homes and offer sustenance at every stop of the circuit. While travel might have disrupted certain relationships, it made others necessary. American preacher Stith Mead commented on one host family: "I don't suppose my own parents would be kinder to me than what they are; I am well provided for by the friends."[15] After preacher Jeremiah Norman stayed with his hosts "Old Brother Harris" and his wife in August of 1793, he said that they were truly a father and mother in Israel, and echoed Mead's sentiments: "if I had been their own Son they could not use me better."[16] Preachers relied upon their circuits' families, particularly the women of those families, to provide their necessities. Instead of preachers' wives doing these crucial chores, mothers and sisters on the circuit patched their shirts, cooked their meals, and nursed the preachers when they were sick.

In return, preachers developed sincere attachments to their host families. Jeremiah Norman worried that the Harrises, living in Norman's circuit in the unsettled backcountry of Virginia, would be uncomfortable in their waning years living in this physical and spiritual wilderness, much as a son would worry about his parents' isolation. In 1796, the young Methodist itinerant William Spencer wrote about the people in his North Carolina circuit, "I have Fathers and Mothers, Brothers and Sisters, houses and Lands in great Abundance."[17]

In their accounts, early Methodists frequently described the choices they made between their "family of the flesh" and their "family in Christ." Like circuit preachers, laypersons relied upon their connections to others in the Methodist family. The first generation of Methodists rebelled against parental religious traditions, and they counted on the surrogate evangelical family for emotional, financial, and religious support. As the previous analysis of narratives showed, the emotional upheaval of conversion was often a painful stage before the convert's assimilation into a new life. Leaving the old family behind was not necessary or even officially sanctioned by Methodist leaders, but there were official and unofficial structures that helped Methodists through this rough transition. A convert could rely on the regularity with which Methodists met to pray and support each other in class meetings and band meetings to fill the gap left by the former activities and intimacies of their birth families. The people and organization of Methodists provided a safety net for converts who created a new identity for themselves apart from their "natural" parents and family.

Joining the Methodist Family

Methodists created a new family circle, one that bore many of the markings of a traditional family, while innovating in some important ways. When eighteenth-century Methodists joined this group, they took on new roles. The Methodist family often referred to itself as the "connection," or "connexion," terms that came to be employed more often in the eighteenth century to refer to extended kin, as well as nuclear family members. The term "connection" was opaque, since it was unclear in definition and flexible in application.[18] In fact, all nuclear familial and kinship terms were remarkably flexible in their use during the eighteenth century. Even the most basic and seemingly natural identification "Mother" could refer to any number of women who filled a maternal role. Historian Naomi Tadmor confirms the flexibility of nuclear family titles, arguing that "[t]hese extended-nuclear usages were indeed so common in seventeenth- and eighteenth-century England because, contrary to any simplistic anthropological account, the language of kinship was used not only to describe relationships by blood and marriage but also to signify social relationships and moral duties. . . . The recognition of these relationships by naming, therefore, was an announcement of status and a possible undertaking of obligations. Solidarity, consideration, duty, and support could be expected, even if not given."[19] Evangelicals employed this "extended-nuclear" framework when assigning the kinship roles to their fellow converts. While these titles may seem confusing in their multiple and varied applications, they carried the expectations, duties, and sentiments of their associated familial roles.

This "extended-nuclear" framework was already familiar to eighteenth-century African Americans, before they became Methodists. The flexibility of evangelical familial structures found particular resonance with African Americans, who likewise employed familial language to describe close friends. African Americans used the terms "brother," "sister," "mother," and "father" to denote a form of extended kinship within slave communities. Herbert Gutman found that African American familial naming patterns kept slaves embedded in the "enlarged kinship group," particularly through the use of "fictive kin."[20] In the face of the tremendous challenge to maintaining African American nuclear families, slaves were able to knit together a wider net of associations that provided a durable fabric for family life.[21] In some ways, the extended kinship patterns of African Americans provided a link to older African practices that stressed the larger kinship networks, outside of the nuclear family.[22] Like the wider Methodist family, African American Methodists in particular used the terms of family or "fictive kin" to imply a sense of communality of experience and to provide economic, social, and cultural supports that were missing. Unlike white Methodists who actively sought the liminality of making themselves like orphans in order to join the evangelical family, most African Americans had the very real experience of familial loss, which the extended evangelical and slave families could assuage to some degree.

On an institutional level, Methodists established alternatives to traditional domestic spaces, which enabled the mobility of transatlantic Methodists. Methodists were sometimes literally adoptive, through shared living situations, evangelical boardinghouses, and orphanages. Throughout England, in particular, there were a number of key evangelical homes that provided common way stations for Methodists; preachers would stay there on their circuits, and laywomen and men often found temporary homes there as well. Mary Bosanquet Fletcher's home in Madeley was renowned for always hosting a number of rotating Methodists. Fletcher often described her house in Yorkshire as though it were a sort of Methodist hostel: "our House is Like a pilgrims inn, and needs much Care to Chuse and refuse in many points."[23] Catherine Livingston Garrettson's home in upstate New York served a similar function. It was a popular place for Methodists to stay, usually while traveling to circuits in northern New England or Ohio in the late eighteenth and early nineteenth century. In North Carolina, preacher Edward Dromgoole's family hosted many Methodists throughout the late eighteenth and early nineteenth centuries. John Wesley's base in London, the Foundery, served as a central stopping place from the late 1740s until Wesley's death in 1791. The Foundery became a home to some Methodist women, through employment as housekeepers and other domestic workers. These were points of refuge plotted on the maps of England and America, which laid out possible places to settle, at least temporarily, and be welcome as a member of the Methodist family.

Methodists also created more formal refuges, by starting orphanages in the eighteenth century. Methodist leadership began the tradition with George Whitefield's orphanage in Georgia in the 1740s and John Wesley's school and orphanage at Kingswood. When Sarah Ryan's niece Sarah Lawrence lost her mother at age four, Mary Bosanquet employed her and eventually treated her as an adopted daughter.[24] Bosanquet had adopted many children before Sarah, through the auspices of her orphanage. In the house that she inherited in Leytonstone in 1762, Bosanquet began her orphanage (with assistance from Sarah Ryan, who had also helped to administer Kingswood). Bosanquet called her orphanage "the Family" and went into debt to support it.[25] "The Family" included many children of all ages, as well as adults, mainly widows. In 1768, she moved her family to the Leeds area of Yorkshire, in order to broaden her service. Bosanquet did not marry until well into her forties, but her early years were devoted to raising children and forming a familial compound with her friend and spiritual mother, Sarah Ryan, as well as other Methodist women, including Sarah Crosby and Ann Tripp. Bosanquet stated, "I have a great family." In just five years, her house had become home to thirty-five children and thirty-four adults, as well as a hospital, school, and source of charity to many others.[26]

Outside of these formal structures, Methodists had other means of formulating a sense of family. Methodists called each other by familial names, giving each other the status and personal relationships of family members. The predominant relationship in the evangelical family was that of sister and brother. Members never received official titles, although the use of "brother" and "sister" as terms of fellowship in evangelical circles became remarkably pervasive. Whereas the Puritan sense of family was deeply hierarchical, the early evangelical family was explicitly egalitarian. Puritans equated church with family, but the evangelical sense of family was extra-institutional. In the South, evangelical Baptists found a "cohesive brotherhood" that contrasted with the formal structures of Anglicanism.[27] Like the Baptists who replaced the terms of "reverend" and "father" with "elder," Methodists did away with the class of priest as a separate and elevated category.[28]

Methodist historians have emphasized the brotherly aspects of Methodism as promoting egalitarian roles for men. For instance, American Methodist historian Russell Richey describes the fraternal bonds between Methodist itinerant preachers, and he argues that the term "fraternity" defined early Methodist culture. Richey maintains that Methodism's fraternal model threatened the reigning ethos of domesticity, by promoting a celibate class of single men in the itinerancy.[29] Henry Abelove, analyzing English Methodist culture, likewise emphasizes the bonds between members of the same sex, especially the fraternal nature of the preachers.[30] At the same time, men were not only brothers but also fathers, as I discuss further below, mitigating the exclusively egalitarian idea of fraternal bonds. As well, women's prominence in Methodism tempered the masculine nature of the itinerant fraternity, while not entirely negating the fact that the fraternal order of preachers was the group's ruling body. Itinerant preachers spent many days of the year in constant interaction with, not the fraternity of preachers, but families and sisters, who supported their itinerancy in their circuits. Sisterhood was important and crucial to the growth of early Methodism, since Methodist women were the majority of the laity as well as the majority of the lay organizers in the early years of Methodism.

Fathers, Mothers, and Babes in Christ

When individuals converted to Methodism, they described themselves as being born again, a phrase contemporary evangelicals still commonly use. In the eighteenth-century context, though, this was a relatively new idea. Eighteenth-century evangelicals commonly talked about becoming a "babe," emphasizing the sense of newness and wonderment of spiritual rebirth. Many converts noted this sense of being a "babe" at other stages in their lives as well, when they returned to this enviable religious state. This sense of newness was multivalent: it marked a stage of impressionability and malleability, in opposition to the hardened ways of one's sinful preexistence; it signaled a sense of innocence and freeing oneself from a dangerous nature; it described a sense of helplessness, weakness, and abandonment to one's fate; it signaled an abnegation of self, a lack of ego and pride; and it marked a new timeline for one's soul, a place where one could begin again, with new guideposts and new guides.[31]

Many Methodists talked about themselves as "young Babes in Christ" or as a "newborn Babe," especially when relating their narratives to ministers like Charles Wesley. Early narratives from the 1740s to the 1760s are rife with this imagery. In this context, these phrases signaled the idea that as a babe they were soliciting the care of the father, Charles Wesley. This becomes particularly clear, as one evangelical writes to Charles Wesley: "O Dear Sir Revered father in Christ Remember me in your Prayers," and then in the next line writes, "I Beg Leave to Subscribe My Self one of Your young

Babes in Christ."[32] Many women in particular used that last phrase as the standard closing for their letters to Charles Wesley.[33]

Both laymen and laywomen described themselves as babes or children of God, employing an infantilizing language in letters and narratives, and they also frequently addressed preachers as "fathers." This relationship of father to child was strongly linked to conversion moments. But the relationship was also invoked when Methodists described other rites of passage (such as sickness, deaths, childbirth, and marriage), when a preacher provided a eulogy, gave advice, or visited their family. Charles Wesley, in particular, was often thanked for his "fatherly" advice or instructions. Since he was happily married and had a number of children, unlike his brother John, his role as counselor often took a more personal tone.[34] No doubt, laymen and women believed he would have a more sympathetic ear when it came to the demands of family life. The term "father," like other familial terms in Methodism, was never entirely fixed. Someone could be a father to some, a brother to others. For instance, African American preacher and leader Richard Allen called preacher Benjamin Abbott "a father and a friend," because Abbott was both an advising elder and a preaching brother.[35] Not every preacher took on fatherly roles and became fathers to other Methodists. Only a few select Methodist men, like the Wesley brothers and American leader Francis Asbury, were given the title of "father" frequently. The title "father" was not usually a personal assignation between two intimates; it sometimes described a relationship that was more official than intimate, as "father" was reserved for someone who was in superior rank and spiritual development to the "child." It indicated the degree to which the father was expected to teach and guide the child, because there was a significant gap in knowledge and spiritual position.

The parental role of ministers, particularly prominent ones like the Wesley brothers, was intertwined with the parental imagery that surrounded God in Methodist writings. Methodists were particularly fond of using phrases in the Bible that evoked the divine in familial terms. Conversion narratives often cited a particular passage: "For as many as are led by the Spirit of God, they are the sons of God. For ye have not received the spirit of bondage again to fear; but ye have the Spirit of adoption, whereby we cry, Abba, Father. The Spirit itself beareth witness with our spirit, that we are children of God: And if children, then heirs; heirs of God, and joint-heirs with Christ; if so be that we suffer with him, that we may be also glorified together."[36] This passage from the book of Romans speaks to the

Arminian process of conversion and became a key source in many Methodist writings. People could leave their sinful natures behind and become adopted into a new spirit of living, a new family that shared their religious experience. In this vein, in many early narratives Methodists described themselves as being or becoming children of God. They identified one another this way, as belonging to the same family, often delineating lines of suitable relationships and communications. As children of God, they had all the benefits of family, the sense of community and commonality, as well as the rights of inheritance. If they were a family, Methodists reasoned that they deserved to share in the rewards of the next world, together; by linking their fortunes, one to the other, they all shared the same fate of salvation.

For example, in 1740, Ann Martin described her conversion experience to Charles Wesley by writing that she prayed to God as a father and received the "spirit of Adoption, crying Abba father." She wrote that she now wanted to be "as a little child beg[g]ing to speak plain" and she dwelled on the filial relationship between God and Jesus.[37] Joseph Carter very similarly paraphrased this biblical passage when describing the first contact he had with Methodism, when a young carpenter apprentice preached to him on this subject. Later when he felt that moment of conversion, he again related it in familial terms: "I burst out a Crying, and Laughing, and Dancing, and Jumping about the Room, that any one if they had seen me, would have thought me' Craze. I then knew that God was my father, and I could Cry Hear Father, my Father abba Father!"[38] In these descriptions, believers felt a closer, more palpable sense of their conversion by familiarizing the divine.

Methodists particularly sought the affections and blessings of those who seemed to exude holiness, preachers or gifted female exhorters who had experienced sanctification. One preacher whose approval was highly sought was Charles Wesley, who had solicited a large collection of conversion narratives, in which converts took great care to craft letters that would assimilate them into the Methodist familial framework, by making the most prominent preachers responsible for them as their parents.[39] In many conversion narratives, writers used this familial language to draw a web of interconnectedness between themselves as children of both the divine father and the preacher father. Ann Martin appealed to Charles Wesley's affections, writing that the preacher George Whitefield "was the first Instrument in drawing me to the Son of his love but you I must own as my Spiritual father."[40] In 1740, Mariah Price similarly wrote to Wesley that he was instrumental in her conversion calling him "my own father" and "father in God," as well as giving herself the title of "your own dau[gh]ter in God."[41] In 1766, Ann Davis also used the term "Daughter in the Lord," and she used this familial assumption as a springboard for talking about Wesley's wife and her recent childbirth, her own illnesses, as well as her doubts about being forgiven for her past sins.[42]

Select prominent women garnered the terms of spiritual mother, "Mother in Christ" or "Mother in Israel." The term "Mother in Israel" probably originated in seventeenth-century English Quaker circles, where the title denoted a woman who had achieved a certain spiritual stature.[43] Evangelical Baptists and Methodists adopted the title in the eighteenth century and called the most spiritually advanced sisters by this name. A distant Methodist might call a prominent woman they had never met a "Mother in Israel" as a signal of the fact that they had revered her from afar, perhaps by reading her accounts. A "Mother in Israel" was not only a model of piety. Women garnered that title by being active cultivators of faith in others, by spreading their spiritual teachings to their Methodist "children." Methodists frequently called Mary Bosanquet Fletcher a "Mother in Israel"; she earned this title by nurturing the growth of Methodism in England. North Carolina preacher William Spencer called Mary Gordan his "Mother," because she was a mentor and perhaps a patron, as well.[44] Significantly, Methodists did not envision "Mothers in Israel" as domestic figures. Methodist literature did not outline specific roles for domestic duties, the raising of children or the making of an evangelical household before the mid-nineteenth century.[45] "Mothers in Israel" were noted for the passion of their piety and the ardency of their faith.[46]

Mothers in Israel were much more common on the English side of the Atlantic and less prevalent among American Methodists. Mothers in Israel were often preachers or spiritual leaders on par with male preachers, and, simply put, American Methodism had fewer female leaders and preachers.[47] In the post-Revolutionary Middle Atlantic region, for example, there was only one female class leader in Philadelphia and seven female class leaders in New York in the 1780s. By 1795 in New York, there were no female class leaders.[48] The contrasts between the official leadership roles of English and American women had much to do with the differences in how Methodism took hold in each area. When English Methodism was beginning, its institutional presence was the Church of England. Officially, preachers were men, and some, like John and Charles Wesley, derived their authority from their positions as Anglican clergymen. Women were given supplemental roles, and they excelled as lay exhorters and preachers who complemented the official worship within the Church of England. English Methodism relied heavily on its extra-institutional domestic spaces, where women had a fair amount of power. In contrast, American Methodism began to take hold in the 1760s, and within only a couple of decades, the Methodist Episcopal Church established itself as a denomination that was separate from the Episcopal Church. In this way, the size and scope of their mission was remarkably different, and the fast-growing American Methodist Episcopal Church confirmed its legitimacy through male leadership. Further, the great need for preachers in the rapid growth of American Methodist membership provided a practical point for reserving class leadership as a training ground for male preachers. In the 1780s and 1790s, women's power had a direct inverse relationship to the size of the American societies; as American Methodism grew, their voices diminished.[49]

Still, American Mothers in Israel did exist, even if they were less published and less prominent than their English counterparts. In the *Arminian Magazine* and the *Methodist Magazine*, American Mothers in Israel read the accounts of English Methodist women, like Hester Roe Rogers and Mary Bosanquet Fletcher, and they doubtless aspired to be like these model Mothers in Israel.[50] American women were less likely to have the title of Mothers in Israel, but they were leading and exemplifying this ideal through being exhorters, supporting itinerants, and, in select cases, leading class meetings. Exhorters expounded on the most important parts of the sermon and made personal appeals to the congregants. For men, exhorting was a stepping-stone to itinerancy; for women in America, it was the highest order and accorded them a pseudo-preacher status.[51] After one woman requested the right to preach, Francis Asbury told her to "[s]peake to all the sisters, aged and young, rich and poor. Pray with them, preach to them powerfully in companies." In this instance, he clearly outlined an acceptable role for gifted female speakers—they could urge piety among other women, but not in mixed-sex settings.[52] In the nineteenth century, some women left the mainstream Methodist Episcopal Church, in order to preach in splinter groups.[53]

Women's leadership was somewhat stronger in the African Methodist Episcopal Church, which formed in 1807, and African American women staked out more explicit claims to leadership. In the 1820s and 1830s, independent female preachers, such as Jarena Lee and Zilpha Elaw, emerged within the African Methodist Episcopal Church.[54] Jarena Lee published her autobiography and justification of women's preaching in 1836, after Bishop Richard Allen reluctantly granted her the title of traveling exhorter.[55] While African American women were not given official leadership roles in the church, they had more meaningful, active lay roles in church business and lay leadership than their white counterparts.[56]

In the eighteenth and early nineteenth centuries, English Methodism offered striking examples of female preachers and their leadership, especially compared to American Methodists' dearth of female leadership. In the earlier years of Methodism, Wesley disavowed female preaching altogether, not wanting Methodism to be associated with radical interregnum groups like the Quakers, who promoted female preaching.[57] Yet, English Methodist women often began preaching spontaneously, citing it as God's will and justifying it as a calling. Sarah Crosby was an itinerant preacher who held several sessions of public and private preaching every week. In the 1760s, Wesley began to shift his position on female preaching, commending multiple female preachers for their talent and zeal.[58] At the same time, he often curtailed their absolute freedom to preach, counseling women to not preach too long or too loud. In 1769, he cautioned Crosby to exhort for no more than five minutes at a time, and to "keep as far from what is called preaching as you can." Instead, Wesley instructed Crosby to call her activity a "prayer meeting."[59] In 1771, when some Methodist preachers were complaining that Sarah Crosby had overreached her role, he bolstered her authority to preach. He wrote, "I think the strength of the cause rests here; on your having an extraordinary call; so I am persuaded has every one of our lay-preachers; otherwise I could not countenance his preaching at all. It is plain to me that the whole work of God termed Methodism, is an extraordinary dispensation of His providence. There fore I do not wonder, if several things occur therein which do not fall under ordinary rules of discipline." Wesley called Crosby "My dear Sister" and signed his letters as "Your affectionate Brother," and both titles sought to enfold her in the brotherhood of preachers, a privilege extended to select Methodist Englishwomen.[60] She was a mother on par with the father of all Methodists.

Designating Crosby's preaching as an "extraordinary calling" meant that Wesley only approved of female preachers in certain exceptional cases, and he also shied away from giving them the title of preacher. At the Annual Conference in 1787, Wesley confirmed that Sarah Mallet could be a "preacher in our connexion, so long as she preaches the Methodist doctrines and attends to our discipline."[61] Female preachers, though, were certainly never included in circuit plans or asked to join the leadership bodies of preacher conferences. After Wesley's death in 1791, a more conservative leadership fairly stifled these Mothers in Israel. In the early nineteenth century, female preaching was disavowed, but some English preachers, Mary Wiltshaw, Sarah Eland, Ann Carr, Margaret Adams, among many others, spoke publicly, if not officially, as Methodist female preachers. Female preaching flourished outside of mainstream Wesleyan Methodism, in the fringe sects of Methodism, through the nineteenth century in England.[62]

However, preaching was not the only way that a Methodist was recognized as a "mother." In more intimate relationships and closer spiritual tutelages, a senior woman could become a "spiritual mother" to another member. Bosanquet called Sarah Ryan her "Spiritual Mother," a title that implied the affinity they felt for one another, but it also evoked a particular apprenticeship. She met Sarah Ryan in 1760, when Bosanquet was first mixing in the London Methodist circles and Ryan was a housekeeper for John Wesley. Ryan had helped introduce Bosanquet to the Methodist inner circle. While they had little in common regarding their class and culture, the spiritual connection Bosanquet described seems to be the overriding factor in their close relationship. She wrote, "The more I conversed with Mrs. Ryan, the more I discovered of the glory of God breaking forth from within, and felt a strong attraction to consider her as the friend of my soul. I told her the past sins, follies, and mercies of my life, and received a similar account from her."[63] Ryan was a spiritual mother in that she counseled Bosanquet, an intimate and important role for Methodists. Bosanquet formed a relationship with Ryan very soon after becoming a Methodist, and she depended upon Ryan to guide her through her new life. Bosanquet reflected, "I considered her as a Mother and like the other young women desireed to a lot me my Rules and imployment or at Least to assist me in the c[h]oice of them."[64] Bosanquet and Ryan had a mutually beneficial partnership, due in part to their class difference. Whereas Bosanquet had money and multiple connections outside Methodism, Ryan provided practical knowledge, economical advice, and evangelical connections.[65] As Bosanquet took on more and more responsibilities in running an orphanage with Ryan, she found herself bewildered by housework.[66] Ryan, who was born into poverty and had been a servant all her life, was no stranger to these practicalities and was an invaluable resource in managing the orphanage.

Bosanquet and Ryan remained inseparable until Ryan's death; John

Wesley called Bosanquet and Ryan "twin souls."[67] In 1768, as Ryan was dying, she asked Bosanquet to move her to Bosanquet's bed: "My dear I want to lay in Your Arms once more for the last time." Bosanquet reassured Ryan, "my dear we shall be one forever—She answered with difficulty—'there is no doubt of that—no doubt of that!' "[68] Bosanquet fell into a deep depression for a year after her mentor's passing. Yet, Bosanquet was comforted by dreams of Ryan mothering her still, sharing in her emotional trials and helping her to understand her own spiritual destiny.[69] Ryan and Bosanquet were so close that after Bosanquet married John Fletcher, he told her they were a "threefold cord."[70]

John Valton, an English preacher, also wrote extensively in his journals about a woman he described variously as his "Spiritual Mother," "Mother in Christ," "Companion," and his "Souls friend," who was a married woman named Mrs. Edwards.[71] He was raised a Catholic, and, following a stint in the army, his military connections had introduced him to Mr. and Mrs. Edwards in 1764. Mrs. Edwards was apparently more pious than her husband, and she introduced Valton to Methodist society and became his spiritual tutor. Valton described the particular closeness he felt to her when her death seemed near: "Good God what were the emotions of my soul to see her in that State. I prayed that God would not separate us, but cut short his work in me, and admit me her Companion [this is crossed out] in to the Realm of Bliss, whither I thought she was hastning."[72] It is clear throughout his diaries that this relationship was one of great intimacy and importance. His diaries betray the quasi-romantic attachment he felt to his Spiritual Mother, much like the relationship between Bosanquet and Ryan.

In the case of Valton and Mrs. Edwards, however, the third person in the relationship, Mr. Edwards, was not happy to be a threefold cord. He apparently did not share his wife's feelings for Valton, and when she was sick, Mr. Edwards barred Valton from his wife's sickbed. Mr. Edwards attributed his wife's illness to Valton's inflammatory religious talk and circulated rumors that Valton was insane. Mr. Edwards may have suspected that their relationship was adulterous. Valton, in turn, accused Mr. Edwards of "growing cold" spiritually, which was a serious accusation in evangelical circles.[73] Valton, who had a love of the dramatic in writing his narrative, described his pain on being separated from his spiritual guide: "I was never to see my Friend more. Silence will most emphatically express what I suffered in being debarred from meeting my Friend! The Friend, that was Gods instrument to convert me! I was now seperated from my Friend! My

Guide and Acquaintance! We took sweet counsel together and walked in the ways of the Lord, but now, I am like a Pelican in the Wilderness and Owl of the Desert, I watch, and am as a Sparrow on the House Top."[74] Whichever bird he was, he was a lonely one without Mrs. Edwards. He wrote in his diary plaintively, "How can One be warm alone"?[75] After this tumultuous period, his diaries described her in less romantic terms, more strictly as a spiritual parent. It is safe to infer that Mr. Edwards halted the increasing intimacy of this spiritual pair. Mr. Edwards felt threatened by the way in which Methodist fellowship allowed an unrelated man to insert himself into their marital relationship.

In the phase that followed, the relationship of Valton and Mrs. Edwards evolved away from that of mother and son, as Valton rebelled against Mrs. Edwards's maternal spiritual watch. The disharmony between them reached a climax, when he wrote, "We hardly ever meet but to hurt one another. I plainly said to my Friend that I desired we might not ever meet but keep from one Another. I feel my Love for her almost expired, but indeed it commenced from our [spars], 'I was ever saying or doing something that was not right.' Let me say no more, I know that what passes between us tear my Soul to pieces, between Bounden Gratitude to her and Duty to my God, I know not how to act."[76]

Valton described the flexible possibilities of these familial relationships in Methodism, wherein a son could become a father by improving himself spiritually. In September of 1765, Mrs. Edwards decided there should be a shift in their relationship and begged Valton's forgiveness for her judgment of him. In this passage he crosses out the standard "Mother" in describing her, which makes sense in light of her speech (as he records it):

> How was I surprised when my Mother Mrs. E. on the 14th came to me and said, She could not have peace till she told me that God had chose me her Son to be her Father, that She had declined it for several days, but at last it was so strongly impressed on her mind, that God had said on her objecting I will send by whom I will send, to be her Guide thro Sanctification; go and tell him to what I have called him it will strengthen him and be of service to him. She told me that, some reproofs that I had given her often, had been of the Greatest Service to her tho' Nature would not suffer her before to tell me so. My Reproofs and way of Life had been more Service to her than all the Sermons she had ever read or heard.[77]

In this passage, Mrs. Edwards provided the definition of the spiritual father; he was expected to lead the way in spiritual sanctification, to provide reproofs, and to be a guide to his children. Part of any Methodist preacher's job, particularly itinerant preachers, was to use their time wisely in providing personal spiritual counseling to the women and men on their circuit. Methodist fatherhood included intense spiritual and emotional responsibilities within the Methodist family. In this way, Methodist fathers were more than just the patriarchal head of the family. Yet, as Valton's example demonstrates, Methodist fatherhood included significant patriarchal tones. Valton described Edwards as suddenly submissive to him, humbly following his lead. This was God's will, according to Valton, because her submission gave him strength to become a preacher, and, as a preacher, he was less likely to acknowledge a Mother in Israel, since he aspired to be a father himself.

It is significant that as Valton became more devoted to his religious calling, he outgrew, to some degree, his relationship with Edwards and began to form others. Simultaneous with the dissolution of this relationship, he took on a "daughter" in Sister Healey. She was likewise married, and she was clearly his spiritual tutee. He became her guide through the process of conversion. In another interesting example of complex familial syntax, he often referred to her as "my Dear Daughter Sister Healey."[78] While Healey was a "daughter" in that she needed Valton's spiritual leadership, she was also "a sister" in that she offered him comfort and advice when he needed it. In general, Methodist family titles were flexible and voluntary, and in this way they undermined the sense of fixed hierarchy implied by parental titles.

Brother and Sister, Brethren and Sisters

By far the most widely used familial terms in Methodism were those of "brother" and "sister." While they never presumed the terms "father" or "mother" for themselves, Methodists called themselves "brother" or "sister." Among the laity, "sister" and "brother" were commonly used terms to distinguish Methodists from others, but they designated more than simple membership in this group. In many cases, the terms carried associative meanings that were meant to spark certain actions and reactions.

In the letters exchanged on both sides of the Atlantic, Methodists employed sibling terms of affection very frequently, as a common mode of address between members, regardless of their status within the group. The most important meaning attached to this title was simply that of belonging. While it was often an innocuous form of address, it also clearly signaled a reinforcement of cohesive group identity. Some Methodists used these sibling terms to reinforce a wayward soul, to incite a feeling of indebtedness, or to imply a common understanding of the terms addressed in the letter. In the same vein, the omission of a familial title occasionally signified a person whose identity was primarily outside the group or one who had not experienced a full conversion.

The other important valence attached to the terms "brother" and "sister" is that of egalitarianism. The ubiquitous use of these terms denoted the basic message that Methodists were all equal. This egalitarianism was true on a spiritual level, in that even preachers were on the road to sanctification, like any other brother and sister in the Methodist family. These terms of equality saw particular power when applied between black and white members of the family, as these ideas of shared kinship and equality transgressed the norms of Anglo-American society. When southern preacher William Colbert called the members of a black Methodist society "my good black brethren," the term of evangelical brotherhood shed its quotidian associations and became a statement about the bonds that surpassed not only blood but stark societal racial divides.[79]

Preachers were brothers within the institution of Methodism, and they were the only members of the group whose familial title was official. Preachers were automatically brothers to one another and it was de rigueur for preachers to address one another in brotherly terms. Preachers felt a deep identification with one another, as they were uniquely bonded in their common deprivation of material comforts and the pursuit of wayward souls. This sense of commonality and affection found perfect manifestation through fraternal expressions. In 1793, American preacher John Metcalf wrote to Stith Mead, whom he called his "Brother" and "fellow Sufferer." He confirmed, "You are my Bro[the]r whom I love with a pure love, fervently, in the Bowels of Jesus."[80] Yet, his brotherly bond was not a simple declaration of love. Metcalf specifically employed this brotherly language in this letter to convince Mead that he should accept his current circuit assignment and not write to the people in Metcalf's circuit, where Mead longed to preach. Brothers invoked their spiritual familial bonds to stress the necessity of toeing the line and submitting to a higher authority. In this case, Metcalf strove to convince Mead that, though he wanted a different circuit, it was his brotherly duty to accept the authority of the Methodist leadership that had assigned these circuits.

Preachers did not simply use these bonds to manipulate others into submission; they had significant, intimate bonds with each other. Asbury made this intimacy an official policy within the body of American Methodist preachers by instituting "covenant brothers." Asbury designated pairs of itinerants to be spiritual guides for each other. In this brotherhood, itinerants would pray for each other at the same time every day and write to each other at least every two weeks.[81] American Methodist preachers were also encouraged to travel together in some cases, which made this brotherhood a less distant relationship.

This familial language delineated larger distinctions of gender and seniority in Anglo-American society. For instance, "brother" and "sister" certainly held different casts, while Methodists used both terms to emphasize connection and commonality. The title of "brother" had more of an official valence, partially because, in the case of men, it could be used to distinguish the laity from the preachers. Female laity did not have any such distinction in adopting the title of "sister." In some cases, it accentuated the senior status of a person, her embodiment of a certain spiritual level, as well as her role as an exhorter, but in many cases a sister was simply a regular member of the Methodist connection.

There was a class dimension to these titles as well, since "brother" and "sister" implied an egalitarian element that supplanted the honorifics of "Lady," "Lord," "Mr.," "Mrs." and "Miss." For a number of the upper-class members of this group, the honorifics of "Mrs." and "Miss" persisted through their conversion and spiritual attainment. Lady Huntingdon, the major benefactor for Whitefield's missions, never became Sister Huntingdon. Many Methodists still called Mary Bosanquet Fletcher "Miss Bosanquet" or "Mrs. Fletcher." This was more pertinent for female members of this group; the male members found it easier to shake their former titles and become brothers. For instance, the Wesleys, also raised as members of the upper class, were more often referred to as "Brother," primarily by the "brethren" of preachers. At the same time, both Charles and John were often referred to in fatherly terms by the laity and preachers, de-emphasizing their brotherly roles in some cases.

Men had the brotherhood of a fraternal community, but Methodist women also had a sisterhood within Methodism. The words "brotherhood" and "fraternity" are of course deeply gendered, but accurate for describing the core Methodist ethos. In fact, when a group of English Methodist women wanted to describe their sense of unity and spiritual purpose, they called themselves the "Female Brethren."[82] This moniker illustrates the difference in status between brotherhood and sisterhood. Within Anglo-American society more generally, the idea of sisterhood was not as pervasive as brethren or brotherhood.[83] The plural of a religious "sister" and the correlate to "brethren," "sisteren" or "sistren," was rarely used after the sixteenth century. As well, within the Methodist family, the Methodist brothers had the fraternity of preachers to reinforce their brotherly identities. Sisters had no official designation, and a group of sisters had no readily available official identity. And so the most prominent of Methodist female preachers in the area of Leeds, England—Ann Tripp, Sarah Crosby, Elizabeth Hurrell, and Sarah Stevens—banded together and called themselves the "Female Brethren." It was oxymoronic perhaps, but the term was meant to denote the fellowship, unity, and prominence of this group. These women had traveled and preached extensively, around London and in the northern areas of Leeds and Manchester, earning themselves a renowned place in evangelical circles. Even though the Female Brethren were not considered part of the official Methodist Conference, they had considerable influence. When the Conference convened in Leeds in 1789 and voted to station the prominent minister Adam Clarke to the Leeds circuit, the Female Brethren sent a counter petition: "Dr. Clarke was learned, but he was dull." Although Clarke had been outwardly supportive of the Female Brethren, they succeeded in overturning his appointment.[84]

Conclusions

Eighteenth-century Methodist conceptions of the family had troubling implications in the wider Anglo-American world. Literature from both anti-Methodists and Methodists alike described a rupture of normal relations, behaviors, genders, and even basic psychological constitutions. This rupture opened the way for a new order of family and social arrangements within dissenting communities. The bonds of the Methodist family assuaged the painful process of conversion. Methodists banded together as though they were orphans in need of a family, and in this way they joined the greater evangelical family as equals who were equally dispossessed. This sense of family came out of Methodism's mode of belonging, but depended upon the individual's sense of being orphaned or unmoored. They stripped themselves of the stability of traditional religious identities and willingly took on a state of constant doubt, want, and hunger in their spiritual lives. In their spiritual vulnerability, all evangelicals promoted the sense of melting the hard edges of their previous existence, becoming like a child, and then finding a new identity. Methodists created a family through this shared sense of spiritual marginalization.[85]

Paradoxically, the Methodist family was based on both the traditional, natural unquestioned bonds of the nuclear family and the voluntary bonds of contract. The Methodist community was made up of many individuals who chose to enter it and formed a fictive family. In many ways it was very different, though, from a natal family in that all of its members joined through their own volition and merit. Membership was intentional, and members had to prove themselves worthy throughout their lives.

The new order called for unity in emotions, material support, and all of the affections of a family. The ongoing nature of Methodist conversion had the potential to be an unbridled, uncontrolled experience, but the structures of the Methodist family kept these original and wild impulses within a certain controlled environment. Methodists enjoined their brothers and sisters to alter their discourse and behaviors. Members within bands modeled behavior to one another as "little families of love." In this manner, the family was a way to reconnect and discipline the potentially disturbing aspects of conversion. In practical terms, for believers who had to turn away from their birth families when converting, the Methodist family provided the support that was painfully missing. The eighteenth-century Methodist family did not entirely supplant blood families, but it did provide the comforts of having a very expansive set of relations, who confirmed their primary commitment to their spiritual lives above all else.

Chapter 4

Religious Ecstasy and Methodist Sexuality

> One would suppose, to hear the perpetual anathemas which their preachers pour forth against *this world*, that GOD had given us no reason for a smile throughout his whole beautiful creation. It is not only the pomp and vanity of the world which they denounce, but the whole world itself, abstractedly considered, with all its enjoyments and attachments, from dancing, song-singing, and spectacle, to the happy frolic of youth, the electric sympathies of social pleasure, the love of woman for herself and her virtues, and lastly, the love of all mankind. Doubtless the Methodists love their wives purely for the glory of GOD, and have entirely renounced that worldly passion called natural affection: every thing must be done for GOD's glory.
> —Leigh Hunt, *An Attempt to Shew the Folly and Danger of Methodism*

In 1809, Leigh Hunt railed against Methodists, condemning them as inhuman in their opposition to pleasure.[1] Eighteenth-century Anglo-American society viewed Methodists as the new Puritans in many ways. Satirists used this evocation to disparage Methodists as fanatics, highlighting the political and social danger they posed to society.[2] They derided Methodists' supposed avoidance of any worldly pleasures, portraying this group as a family that separated itself from the ways of the world. This portrayal reveals the significance of Methodist conversion of young people in the eighteenth century; only a strange, sexually obsessed sect could pull people away from their birth families and culture.

Evangelicals themselves often talked about their abnegation of general society and customs. Baptists and Methodists were in agreement that true religiosity meant avoiding some of the sexual and social customs of their contemporaries.³ In their own narratives, Methodists like Catherine Livingston and Stith Mead wrote about distancing themselves from "irreligious company" and displaying great caution in forming social relationships. When Hester Roe shredded her dresses and ribbons, she not only signaled to her family that she was a serious Methodist, but she also opted out of the normal courtship customs of her class.

Historians, as well, have made a connection between Puritanism and Methodism in terms of social outlook and sexual practices.⁴ Lawrence Stone in his study of the English family argued that Methodists were Puritans' direct heirs in repressiveness: "both sides stressed the enforcement of patriarchy and obedience, and the crushing of the libido."⁵ E. P. Thompson argued that both Puritanism and Methodism were links in the chain that kept the English lower classes trained to the wheels of capitalism and that English Methodism was part of a broader campaign to discipline the working class toward a moral work ethic and a repression of sexual behavior.⁶

While Methodists were supposedly the heirs to Puritan views of sexuality, their eighteenth-century critics also claimed that their repression cloaked secretive, promiscuous practices. Though mainstream Puritan groups were less likely to be accused of secretive sexual practices, radical Puritan sects often garnered suspicion regarding the sexuality of female followers. Similarly, according to anti-Methodist literature, deviant sexuality and misled women were the primary social outcomes of the evangelical movement, and this signaled the movement's radical threat to society. Anti-Methodist authors argued that the religious ideas themselves were dangerous and led to sexual transgressions; evangelical practice was obsessive, ecstatic, and sexual in nature. One pamphlet exposed the story of a "female saint, who had a child during her husband's absence." The Methodist woman reportedly gave a lame, sanctimonious excuse for her adultery, saying, "Lord help us, we are indeed subject to great wrestlings with the wicked one."⁷ Methodist practices provided a cloak for unseemly behavior, and Methodist language was employed to excuse great sins. In 1807, an anti-Methodist tract commented on evangelical unity as something essentially sinister and cultish. Author Joseph Nightingale purported to tell the inside story of the Methodists. He cited extensive rituals, prayers, and lore as proof of his firsthand knowledge. Nightingale quoted hymns and poems that he insisted were used for indoctrination. These verses were proof of the insidious effects of the closeness of the Methodist family, "When we consider the cementing tendency—the uniting influence—of these meetings, and these hymns, need we be surprised, Madam, at the union and increase of the Wesleyan Methodists? Here is every thing to warm the imagination—to inspire the affections—to engage the hart. All the generous passions of the soul, and all the tender sympathies of love are here invited to share the sweets of benevolence—the mystic pleasures of devotion."[8] His discourse on the "passions," "tender sympathies," "rapturous delights of present enjoyment" led the readers to imagine an incestuous family, which was a repeated charge against Methodists in the eighteenth and early nineteenth centuries.

Satirical cartoons and writings lampooned evangelical women as sexually vulnerable and preachers as sexually exploitative, depicting camp meetings and love feasts as the settings for an orgiastic mix of sex and religion. This body of literature emphasized the interdependent idea of evangelicalism's power and women's susceptibility to this power. Suspicions often followed itinerant preachers as they trooped from town to town, attracting accusations of sexual deviancy and duplicity. Women were common targets of anti-Methodism, because they were the majority of evangelical converts in the late eighteenth and early nineteenth centuries.[9] A widely held perception was that women were leading their families into new, delusional religious and moral spheres. Anxiety about the possible disorganization of the traditional family and the inversion of traditional hierarchies was at the root of many attacks on Methodist preachers and converts.

Anti-Methodist publications were not isolated ravings, but part of a burgeoning anti-Methodist movement in the eighteenth-century Atlantic world. The phenomenal expansion of printing presses during the eighteenth century spurred this war of words. Richard Green, a nineteenth-century cataloguist, found a deluge of these anti-Methodist pamphlets; over six hundred survived from the eighteenth century.[10] Many anti-Methodist authors were ministers, primarily from the Church of England.[11] Much of their criticism was aimed at Methodist preachers and reflected a fear that Methodism was formulating an internal attack on the Church of England. Anti-Methodist literature was largely published in England but distributed in America as well.[12] These publications came in pamphlet form, in books, and in journals. In particular, the *Gentleman's Magazine*, which was popular on both sides of the Atlantic, featured prominent satires of Methodists from the 1730s through the 1780s.[13]

Anti-Methodism formed a wide and popular strain in society, which found outlets in the press, but also in significant anti-Methodist violence. There were physical attacks and even mobs that railed against Methodism throughout the eighteenth century in America and England. In America, these attacks intensified during the Revolutionary period, as Methodists' presence in the colonies increased, and Methodists were judged guilty of Tory political beliefs by association with John Wesley's pro-monarchical writings.[14] Anti-Methodist anger and violence continued in America through the beginning of the nineteenth century, including mob attacks and disruptions of religious meetings, particularly in the South and backcountry regions.[15]

The criticism aimed at eighteenth-century evangelicals was part of a larger Anglo-American cultural tradition that sought to neutralize political and religious dissent with accusations of sexual deviancy. In 1754, one anti-Methodist writer, George Lavington, compared Methodism with Catholicism and a wide variety of enthusiastic dissenting religious groups when he asserted, "'tis observable in *Fact,* that a *Multiplicity of Wives,* and promiscuous Use of Women, has been the *Favourite Tenet* of most Fanatical Sects."[16] In seventeenth-century England, Quakers, Ranters, Baptists, and other interregnum religious sects were objects of malicious sexual slander. Critics lampooned their religious discourse and associated this language with abnormal sexual proclivities.[17] In seventeenth-century America, Quakers and dissenting Puritans, particularly female members of these groups, were also common targets of sexual innuendo.[18] In the eighteenth century, opponents skewered Moravians and other Pietists, accusing them of sexual profligacy.[19] According to their detractors, dissenting groups perverted the natural sexual order and overthrew monogamy for polygamous or adulterous practices.

The actual sexual practices of dissenters seemed to have no bearing on the criticism leveled. Even in cases of conservative sexuality, as with Catholic priests, critics charged that the repression of natural desire manifested itself in secret acts of perverse sexuality. Many evangelicals, including Methodists, were generally conservative in their sexual practices, encouraging sexual continence.[20] Baptists in America, alongside Methodists, discouraged licentious socializing, including gambling, drinking, dancing, and other forms of entertainment. Eighteenth-century Baptists were particular objects of scorn for their repressive influence on the imbedded social practices of the South.[21] Dissenting religious practice was the common element in all of these cases of religio-sexual slander. Additionally, these dissenting groups shared common characteristics in attracting large numbers of female believers and in using expressive language.

Methodists provide an interesting example of the collusion of sexual and religious criticism. Unlike Moravians, eighteenth-century Methodists never published manuals on sexual practices or sexual religious iconography; comparatively, Methodists were quite tame.[22] Also unlike Moravians, Methodists never sought to create separate Methodist settlements; they lived within communities and families that held different, often conflicting, values. It is perhaps because of Methodists' popularity and their integration into the community that they sparked so much criticism.

Yet, casting Methodists as sexual misfits was not a figment of imagination or an image that the Church of England created simply to suppress dissent. Methodist practices were indeed easy to interpret as sexually extravagant, because evangelicals chose ecstatic and sensual language to describe their deepest religious experiences. The particular nature of Methodist fraternization contributed to this public picture of sexual deviance in dissent. The closeness that Methodists found with one another and the distance that this sometimes put between converts and their birth families made it seem as though this religion had a stranglehold on its adherents. Methodists introduced a new language and familial organization, which appeared as secret codes to outsiders.

Evangelical language and bodily religious practices were the most contested and specific points of criticism from those outside the group. While the evangelical conversion experience grew out of the larger Protestant emphasis on conversion, eighteenth-century evangelicals gave the act of conversion a different dimension. Evangelicals were tremendously concerned with the state of their souls, and they used expressive language to continuously assess their current state of conversion, and therefore their ongoing knowledge of God's will and God's presence.[23] Evangelical language reflected a new physical reality as well. Evangelicals dramatically recounted their experiences with God, and they detailed their physical responses to divine contact, such as trembling, groaning, sighing, crying, transporting, exclaiming, shouting, and singing. Evangelical religious worship was livelier and noisier than services in the standing churches. Outsiders saw their physical language and manners as excessive and far too sensual. Sensual was the point of it, though. To evangelicals, their senses were the primary instruments for calibrating religious experiences. Having their senses overwhelmed; enjoying rapturous, heavenly views; tasting aspects of divine wonder; feeling joy and tingling in the presence of God—these were all evidence of God's ongoing presence in their lives. The Methodist openness to sensual aspects of religiosity was part of the eighteenth-century rise of sensibility. In fact, the rise of Methodism and sensibility, 1740–1840, are coincident.[24]

Sensibility encompassed a large cultural shift in Anglo-American society. The growing web of sensibility influenced multiple spheres of activity, including the increased acquisition of goods, the refinement of manners, the further definition of polite society, the rise of the novel, and the increase in romantic marriages. The idea of sensibility arose from a post-Lockean "receptivity of the senses," a skill to be trained, to heighten one's consciousness. In the late eighteenth and early nineteenth centuries, sensibility also became the bedrock for reform movements, since it opened one's sensitivity to the suffering of humanity. As well, sensibility became instrumental in the growing orientation toward domestic spaces in the same period.[25] The coincident rise of sensibility and evangelicalism resulted in a reformation of manners, sexuality, and marriage.

Anti-Methodism and Religious Enthusiasm

The anti-Methodist movement mounted a fierce response to this transformation of emotional, sexual, and familial expression and behavior. While anti-Methodist writers leveled many false charges, the accusations were a response to real Methodist practices. In anti-Methodist literature, one of the most disputed elements of Methodism was its enthusiastic religious experience, which outsiders saw in the sudden, transformative waves that overcame Methodist revivals.[26] Methodists were not the originators of religious enthusiasm. The idea of excessive religiosity and the desire to distinguish between true and false prophecy existed well before the eighteenth-century evangelical revivals, and in the eighteenth century criticism mounted against evangelicals of every denomination. Charles Chauncy, an anti-revivalist writer and New England Congregationalist minister, described enthusiasm as a physiological disorder, caused by an overexcited imagination where passions triumphed over reason. Scottish philosopher David Hume described enthusiasm as an absence of rationality and morality, which allows the enthusiastic person to excuse a host of immoral behavior through supposedly divine inspiration.[27] When critics denounced Methodist religious practice by calling it "enthusiastic," they meant that it was emotional, irrational, and relied on false claims to inspiration and revelation. Methodist preachers whipped up emotion in their followers, allowing laypeople to become "self-appointed visionaries."[28] In 1755, Samuel Johnson defined "enthusiasm" as the "heat of imagination," and the "enthusiast" as "one who vainly imagines a private revelation; one who has a vain confidence of his intercourse with God."[29]

Methodist enthusiasm was dangerous, because it relied on the idea of believers having close, personal relationships with the divine, a concept that seemed heretical to many Christians in the way it humanized God. As one satirist argued, "[T]he greatest scoundrel has nothing to do but to believe, in order to enter at once upon the privileges of an Archangel: he is immediately favoured with divine visions, and interferences, and sweet experiences ... in short, he cannot take a beefsteak or a walk, he cannot stumble upon a stone or a dinner, he cannot speak, look, or move, without interesting the Divine Being most actively in his behalf."[30] Critics lampooned Methodists as self-important fools, who imagined themselves as central to the divine universe. Generally, the Protestant Reformation brought about a more personalized relationship between believer and God and made individual faith a central concern. However, fellow Protestants criticized Methodists for presuming intimacy with God and making God into a humanistic entity, prone to whimsy and favoritism.

The most popular anti-Methodist work was a print by the prolific eighteenth-century satirist William Hogarth. This piece, titled *Credulity, Superstition, and Fanaticism: A Medley* (the original draft was called "Enthusiasm Delineated"), appeared in 1762, and Hogarth shows a preacher (probably Whitefield) expounding to an unruly congregation.[31] The preacher holds up puppets of the devil and a witch, and his wig has flipped up to reveal a monkish tonsure—he is a papist in disguise. The frenzied hordes below him are a confusion of bodies and idols. This satire portrays Methodism as a form of Catholicism, exhibiting the same supposed extravagances, idolatry, and trickery.[32]

When Hogarth's print was published in the 1760s, it rode a wave of popular anti-Methodist sentiment. In 1760, Laurence Sterne had published *The Sermons of Mr. Yorick*, which took Methodists to task for their enthusiasm, which he described as their pretense at having a real "intercourse with the Spirit of God."[33] Methodists attempted to separate their honorable practices from these spurious satires. John Wesley wrote to his brother Charles in December of 1762, to describe a London Methodist meeting, which included "horrid screaming, and unscriptural, enthusiastic expression."[34] He quickly set about to correct the misbehavior that had flourished,

Figure 7. *Credulity, Superstition, and Fanaticism: A Medley*, engraving by William Hogarth (London, 1762). © Trustees of the British Museum.

he reasoned, due to inadequate local leadership. In 1765, the Methodist Conference defined a number of disciplinary rules, including the prescription that love feasts last no longer than ninety minutes and that they should end by 9 p.m. These new regulations were a direct answer to the taunts that Sterne and others directed toward Methodist practice.[35]

John Wesley and other Methodists were understandably defensive at the charge of enthusiasm, but Wesley also defended the strong, vibrant practices of faithful Methodists.[36] Methodists believed that divine intervention was possible and perceptible and that loud, bodily responses to conversion were sincere responses to the Holy Spirit working within individuals.[37] Methodist practices were part of wider evangelical turn toward more expressive worship. Methodists drew upon Moravian practice in instituting hymn singing at the center of their worship. Charles Wesley's hymns were instrumental in building a new poetic spirituality. Methodists were physically demonstrative in a way that many evangelical Baptists and Presbyterians were as well, making their joyful transports, their sighing, exclaiming, clapping, and exalting normative elements in religious worship.

Love feasts and watch-night services were two evangelical practices that raised considerable anti-Methodist criticism. Both were originally Moravian forms of worship, which Wesley had borrowed and somewhat altered. These services were held outdoors or in private homes. In the love feast, Methodists would typically take communion, pray, sing hymns, collect for the poor, and share religious experiences.[38] In 1740, Wesley started watch-night services for the coal miners of the Kingswood area, offering this nocturnal worship as a godly alternative to spending their evenings in alehouses. The watch-night service consisted of singing, praying, exhorting, and preaching for a number of hours. Wesley meant to establish it as a monthly practice, always at full moon to keep the meeting well lit. In America, this service often supplanted times of traditional drunken revelry, like New Year's Eve and Christmas Eve.[39] The setting, timing, and naming of these meetings opened them to criticism from anti-Methodist writers, who were quick to portray the practices as sexually immoral.[40] One writer accused love feasts of being nothing other than orgies, hidden under cover of the night:

> *There* Saints, *new-born*, lascivious *Orgies* hold,
> Meek *Lambs* by *Day*, at *Night* no *Wolves* so bold,
> There the *new Adam* tries the *old one's* Fort,
> And *Children of the Light* in *Darkness* sport.

> Together wanton pairs promiscuous run,
> *Brothers* with *Sisters, Mothers* with a *Son*:
> *Fathers*, perhaps with yielding *Daughters* meet,
> And *Converts* find their Pastor's Doctrines sweet;
> *Pure Souls* are fir'd by *Love's* divinest Spark
> And *Paradise* is open'd in the *Dark*.[41]

This author's image of "wanton pairs" of incestuous brothers and sisters, mothers and sons, and fathers and daughters demonstrates the disruptive nature of the Methodist family. The natural outcome of forming a new family with few blood relations was confusion of sexual and religious activities. The intimacy of the religious family combined with lack of strictures against incest within that family would yield the obvious sexual confusion. Despite lampoons of this practice, love feasts and watch nights occurred on both sides of the Atlantic in the late eighteenth century and well into the nineteenth century.

In the American context, enthusiasm was generally more acceptable and more widely expressed, owing in part to the influence of African American members. As Methodism spread throughout America in the late eighteenth century, African Americans were at the forefront of developing evangelical religious practice. African Americans expressed enthusiasm in its dual meaning, as a deep sense of religiosity, as well as a "noisy," bodily expression of spirituality. Jeremiah Norman, in his North Carolina circuit, often wrote about African American Methodists in his journals, where he reported a distinctive style of worship. In 1796, he exhorted near Halifax, North Carolina, where "[t]here was a Large collection of Black People. Not many whites . . . the Black People began to make some considerable noise . . . [a fellow exhorter] was Last in the Dusk. he stamped most [happily]. Some times Raised his foot even with his waist [then] Brought it to the floor of the Pulpit with all the force he was [master] of."[42] The exhorter followed the lead of the African American congregants' enthusiasm, by improvising a stamp in response.

As increasing numbers of African Americans found a home in evangelical traditions, they influenced Methodist practice. Some African Americans found that African religious experience resonated with evangelical spiritual communion with the divine, as well as with the central idea of individual conversion.[43] Increasingly, African Americans innovated upon Methodist practice to include more physical and enthusiastic practices, such as call and response, stamping, clapping, and hymn singing. Preacher James Meacham wrote in his journal of hearing slaves participating in a watch-night meeting in July of 1789: "Some time in the Night—I judge near the Middle watch—I awaked in raptures of Heaven by the sweet Echo of Singing in the kitchen among the dear Black people (who my Soul loves). I scarcely ever heard anything to equal it upon earth. I rose up and strove to join them."[44] For the most part, Methodist preachers responded to the innovations of African American Methodists, by following their lead and commending their deep sense of religiosity.

Evangelical Anglican leader Devereux Jarratt had been concerned about African American singing, which, he worried, "led to emotional 'excesses,' but Francis Asbury counseled that as long as proper attention was paid to Methodist rules, ecstatic emotion could well accompany proper practice."[45] While some preachers were confused about how to receive the different emotional and physical styles of African American worship, the leadership did not officially discourage their enthusiastic practices.

The Space of Methodism and Physical Enthusiasm

As satirists with a drafting pencil were quick to depict, evangelical spaces lacked social order. Hogarth's *Credulity, Superstition, and Fanaticism* emphasized that evangelicals made the sacred space of a church (even the Church of England) a chaotic place. Looking at Hogarth's print one can almost smell the sweaty heat of bodies pressed together and excited by evangelical preaching. Hogarth depicted Methodists standing in the pews instead of sitting. They seemed to flail about, each to his or her own tune. Bodies filled the aisles and sat directly under the pulpit. These were not respecters of the church, and this scene would have certainly offended Anglican worshippers.

People's homes were a common space for prayer, meetings, and exhortation among eighteenth-century Methodists. While they were certainly not the first religious group to do so, Methodists depended on evangelicals' homes for a wide variety of religious purposes. Methodists, alongside their Baptist competitors, frequently used private homes as places to host itinerant preachers for meetings, prayer, and overnight stays on the circuit. The privacy of the home and the irregularity of the outdoors as places of worship underscored the ways in which Methodism challenged traditional boundaries, presuming the place of the family in the home meetings and eschewing the traditional church/parish structure in the outdoor assemblies.

In America, anti-evangelicals criticized the itinerant method for its disavowal of traditional local nodes of power, especially the church and the seated minister. One of the main critiques of American Methodism was its rootlessness. Anglican ministers portrayed the established parish ministers as the only respectable religious leaders, who provided, in historian Timothy Hall's words, "steady reliable points of reference by which the community's members could situate themselves in a bounded, hierarchical, patriarchal social universe. Itinerancy threatened to unleash disruptive influences that would draw away the community's unsteady members by 'a kind of sympathetick Power.'"[46] Spatial instability led to social instability.

Extra-institutional space was an effective arena for evangelicals, though. Open-air meetings allowed evangelical Methodists, Presbyterians, and Baptists to improvise around the lack of institutions in the sparsely settled southern and western areas of America. By the nineteenth century, mainstream Methodists began to establish institutional spaces, including churches and meeting halls, but Methodism still thrived in the home meetings and open-air assemblies such as camp meetings. Camp meetings, originating in America around 1800, were evangelical open houses, where people would gather to hear a particular preacher or a series of preachers expound in an open-air setting, usually a clearing in the woods (where attendants would camp in order to participate in praying, preaching, and singing from sunrise to sunset). The popularity of camp meetings directly contributed to Methodism's first overwhelming success in the early nineteenth century during the Great Revival in Kentucky, Tennessee, and Georgia.[47] In this arena, mobile populations could travel to meet up with other evangelicals in great numbers and in areas where they would not have a standing church to define the space and culture of religious worship.

Like love feasts and watch-night services, camp meetings invited criticism. The openness of the setting, lacking the usual strictures of church comportment, encouraged the emotional responses of evangelicals. Many contemporaries wrote about the indelible images that these meetings produced, of men and women swept up by the tides of religious emotion.[48] The popularity of camp meetings in America spawned a number of lascivious cartoons depicting Methodist meetings as displays that were chaotic and overly enthusiastic. Women, who were the majority of followers, were

Figure 8. *Camp-Meeting*, lithograph by Hugh Bridport, based on an earlier nineteenth-century print by Alexander Rider (Kennedy & Lucas Lithography, ca. 1829). Courtesy of the Library of Congress.

shown as swooning and generally becoming highly emotional, while the men, unaffected, used the occasion to fondle and court the attending women.

Camp meetings signaled a difference between American and English Methodist attitudes toward enthusiasm that arose in the early nineteenth century. English Methodist leaders feared that camp meetings were sites of irregular behavior, and they put English Methodists' newfound denominational respectability at risk. The issue of the camp meeting split the Methodists on each side of the Atlantic when the British Methodist Conference proclaimed in 1807: "It is our judgment, that even supposing such meetings to be allowable in America, they are highly improper in England, and likely to be productive of considerable mischief: and we disclaim all connection with them."[49] Camp meetings were too popular to outlaw in America, and they were well suited to the mobile, underchurched populations of American expansion following the Revolution. In England, they were both less necessary and less desirable to the well-established Methodist leadership in the early nineteenth century.

Religious Enthusiasm and Gender

In Hogarth's *Credulity, Superstition, and Fanaticism*, a man and woman fondle each other just below the pulpit (see Figure 7). Prominently featured in the foreground is a thermometer to measure the crowd's level of enthusiasm. The thermometer registers the degrees of false evangelical belief, from lukewarm through "Love Heat," "LUST," "Extacy," "Convulsion Fits," "Madness," and finally "Raving" (which was termed "Revelation" in Hogarth's original drawing). One of the clearest examples of enthusiasm is the woman collapsed on the floor, giving birth to a line of rabbits. This figure is an obvious allusion to Mary Toft, a young rabbit breeder who lived in Surrey and created a sensation when she claimed to have given birth to over a dozen rabbits in 1726. While she quickly confessed that these bunny births were actually hoaxes, many were dismayed at the fact that a large group of doctors and the public had taken her claims seriously. Hogarth and others emphasized that this incident revealed that English society was ripe for mass delusion, and women were at the center of such chicanery.[50]

The idea of female moral and spiritual vulnerability was not new to eighteenth-century readers. One can find the roots of this characterization in the early modern period, when medical manuals warned against female susceptibility to any number of evil hosts.[51] Early modern Anglo-Americans believed that women's bodies were the protectors of their souls and that their perceived physical weakness made them more susceptible to both divine and satanic influences.[52] This view of women's permeability extended to their emotions, religiosity, temperaments, and physical states. As historian Phyllis Mack writes, "The sponginess and porosity of the female physiology . . . meant that she might experience difficulty in separating her powers of rational observation from her emotional or biological impulses. Since there was no strong inner scaffolding, no reliable central core or conscience, her mind was easily permeated not only by outside influences but also by her own strong inner drives. Thus, a feeling of anger might seep involuntarily into the soul and pollute her religious ideals; heretical beliefs might seep into her bowels and engender lust."[53] In the eighteenth century, the belief in women's heightened sensibilities suggested that women's senses were likewise more open and receptive to influences, both good and bad.[54]

Anti-Methodist authors described female evangelicals as vulnerable and very open to suggestion. Women's susceptibility accounted for both the danger and popularity of evangelical religion. Critics argued that evangelicals took advantage of women's weaknesses, as women easily confused sexual and religious enthusiasm.[55] Enthusiasm and its association with heat implied a state of being that was reactive and open. Much like the characterization of femininity, enthusiasm sprang from people with no solid core, who were much too flexible and fanciful. With religious enthusiasm, there was a tendency toward the imaginative over the rational faculties. Feminine religiosity had the same problem—it was associated with openness to the real and unreal, rational and irrational, good and evil, in too equal measure with no guiding rational faculty to discern the improper influences.

In the Revolutionary period, the association between feminine religiosity and emotional reactivity became a justification for excluding women from the political sphere, where citizenship depended upon balanced reason and hardy temperament.[56] The femininity of evangelical religion, in contrast to the eighteenth-century masculinity of British and Anglo-American military prowess and rational citizenry, associated evangelical men and women with weakness. Enthusiasm led believers to abandon the roles they would have held as citizens and made them dangerous to the social and political order. In the Revolutionary and post-Revolutionary era, the role of women, as wives or mothers, revolved around their stabilizing and supportive influence on the men in their family, their husbands and sons. In contrast, evangelical women were either married women who acted like single women or single women who were in the vulnerable stage between daughter and wife. At the base of many critiques of Methodism was the accusation that it threatened to overturn the accepted gender order, which was integrally tied to familial order. Heightened enthusiasm led to a further weakening of religious patriarchy, as women were tempted to give up their true feminine qualities, including their chastity. As the anti-Methodist publications were quick to assert, Methodist women were not safeguarding the patrilineal nature of the family if Methodism tempted them into sexual transgressions. Further, they failed to safeguard the economy and intimacy of the nuclear family against outsiders, if they joined with the Methodist family.

Anti-Methodist writer Leigh Hunt vividly recounted the first waves of

English religious revivalism in the 1740s and 1750s. According to Hunt, during this period religious ardor became like sexual catnip to women. He wrote, "The levees of Whitfield and Wesley used to be crowded with young women enquiring about their sensation; and a number of grown females, widows, &c. were always coquetting in a song-of-Solomon way with these illustrious fathers. There is a kind of military ardour in such Defenders of the Faith, which has the effect of a co[c]ked hat and a sword upon the female bosom; and on the other hand, the soft admiring nature of the 'lovely Saints' renders them so many objects of worship to the spiritual Champions of Christendom. A black coat now-a-days disputes the power of gallantry with a red one."[57] Methodists encouraged women to probe their "sensations," which the writer juxtaposed with the flirtatious language of older women, to imply that these were not religious sensations, but physical, erotic ones. He mocked the idea of spiritual leaders like Whitefield and Wesley fashioning themselves as "illustrious fathers," since these fathers encouraged romantic images of themselves and seduced widows.

Numerous illustrations and drawings portrayed the besotted female follower and the calculating preacher. In a 1776 drawing, *The Continence of a Methodist Parson, or Divinity in Danger*, the well-dressed, well-coifed, and well-fed preacher (perhaps Whitefield) is flanked by two female followers (see Figure 9). The older woman is pulling him toward the church, but he ignores her in favor of the younger woman who is leading him to the public house. In case the implication is unclear, the public house is named "The Old Goat new Reviv[ed]." Another set of illustrations, published in the English periodical *Town and Country* between 1775 and 1784, included a series of portraits of young evangelical women and preachers in pairs. The portraits that emerged in 1775 included a "Pious Preacher," clearly John Wesley, and "Miss D——ple," a young and pretty follower (see Figure 10). In 1775, John Wesley's wife, Mary Vazeille Wesley, had just left him for the final time, accusing him of infidelity. The illustration and accompanying article in *Town and Country* imply that Wesley had a relationship with a beautiful follower, who was the daughter of an important attorney. This article confirmed the rumors and Mary Wesley's contention that he was more interested in his female followers than her.

If women were susceptible, they were also largely passive in their fate as victims of religious seduction, according to most commentaries. Anti-Methodist tracts reproduced, in word and image, this idea of the female follower and the exploiting preacher. In *The Methodists, an Humorous Bur-*

Figure 9. *The Continence of a Methodist Parson, or Divinity in Danger* (London: R. Sayer and J. Bennett, 1776). Courtesy of the Lewis Walpole Library, Yale University.

Figure 10. *Miss D——ple; The Pious Preacher* (London: A. Hamilton, 1775). Courtesy of the Lewis Walpole Library, Yale University.

lesque Poem (1739), Methodist women were typified as easy prey, and preachers, as lechers:

> What *Maid* wou'd not be holy kist?
> Or who her *Teacher* can resist? . . . .
> In those soft Moments, (all the Soul unbent)
> The Maid on heavenly Joys intent,
> Who could withstand the pleasing Proffer,
> Or withstand the pious Lecher's Offer?
> Say wou'd she not in her *New Birth*
> Know some Part of her *Heav'n* on *Earth*?
> Then warmly push the am'rous Play—
> A *Devotee* is soonest won—
> —Who feels more *Passion* than a Nun?—[58]

Methodist women were not setting out to seduce their preachers in much of the anti-Methodist literature; Methodist language, religious practice, and duplicitous male followers seduced them. Perverted evangelical religious ideas and religious ecstasy led women into unwitting sexual relationships. As another anti-Methodist poet phrased it in 1778: "With *Man of God Priscilla* shares her *Bed,/ By Christian Love* to *Prostitution* led."[59]

Anti-Methodists explicitly extended the early modern idea of women as prime candidates for religious delusion, due to their naturally open natures. Hunt argued, "we may see directly what influence the body has upon this kind of devotion. . . . The female sex for instance are acknowledged to posses the greater bodily sensibility, and it is the women who chiefly indulge in these love-sick visions of heaven."[60] Because women were more physically liable and possessed greater tendencies toward sensibility, they more readily absorbed the enthusiastic language of Methodism. In a similar argument, Hunt sought to inspire repugnance for Methodist language by assigning it to the ignorance of the lower classes, confirming a common anti-Methodist characterization of evangelicals as disproportionately uneducated and poor. He typified both women and poor folks in general as having no control over their rational faculties, and he claimed that Methodists plumbed and promoted, excited and exploited this irrationality.[61]

The anonymous author of an amazing novelistic pamphlet, *The Story of the Methodist-Lady, or The Injur'd Husband's Revenge* (1770), billed this tale as an exposé of how the Methodist economy of sexual power worked.[62] The narrative warned potential female converts against Methodist rakes who were "[b]aits laid for their Virtue, cover'd with specious Pretensions to Religion and Sanctity."[63] The main character, Theodosia, was a Devonshire woman who had been happily married for ten years before joining the local Methodist band. The group "gave her, unhappily, an Occasion of satisfying that Passion so often dangerous to the whole Sex."[64]

The woman's attraction to Methodism was framed as sectlike and dangerous from the beginning. Her first act of "Methodical madness" was a very generous donation to the Whitefield-like leader. The notion that Methodism drained men's finances by converting their wives was a popular theme in the anti-Methodist press.[65] The second, more troubling sign was her inattention to her wifely duties. Prior to conversion, she had found time for charity work and maintaining social connections; after conversion, she spent her entire day "in Closet Conversation with the new converted Brethren, and in listning to the Instructions of her new Guides. The Affairs of her Family were neglected, and nothing of any Moment transacted in it without the Consent and Advice of her spiritual Director."[66] Methodist women rearranged their priorities after joining the group. Their religious duties supplanted their household ones. Her new guides, men and women in the Methodist family, replaced her husband's authority.

The downfall of Theodosia came when the "Captain" entered the Methodist family under the guise of a repentant sinner. His true aim was not spiritual redemption but sexual union with Theodosia. "In a Week or two he soon learn'd the Trim of these new Saints, and that a wonderful Love and Freedom subsisted amongst the Members of the Society. This was sufficient to determine him to become one of their Number. He was a good Mimic, and in two or three Days Observation, learned their Phrase, Cant, and demure Look."[67] Like romance, Methodism subsisted on an imitation of manners and gestures that seduced unsuspecting women. To welcome him into the group, "[t]hey saluted him brotherly with a holy Kiss," which the author claimed was standard Methodist practice.[68] This account highlighted the supposed vulnerability of Methodists, who became intimate with each other in their meetings. In this account, the intimacy extended to physical affection, which was, in fact, not a feature of eighteenth-century Methodist meetings. Yet, the implication is clear; if members were spiritual intimates, other forms of closeness were sure to follow, and nonbelievers like the Captain could easily take advantage of Methodists' closeness to exploit these members.

The pamphlet charged that Methodists imprudently allowed men and women to mix together. Theodosia became the rake's tutor, and they had daily private meetings.[69] The Captain quickly converted their friendship into a sexual relationship, which the author argues was the natural outcome of unhealthy, religiously obsessive Methodist relationships. The author describes this slippery slope of singular religious affection: "They pretended to imitate the Angels, and adore one anothers Perfections without Distinction of Sexes. . . . Thus a Squeeze of the Hand, an amorous Hugg, a wanton Ogle, or a luscious Kiss, which when used by Men of the World, indicated a lascivious Desire, amongst the Saints had not such Ideas annex'd to them; they were only Simbols significant of the inward Workings of the pure Spirit of seraphic Love."[70] The Captain managed to convince Theodosia that sex was the perfect expression of their religious ardor. After many months of religious, extramarital sex, she found herself pregnant. This was particularly problematic, because she had stopped sleeping with her husband shortly after her conversion.

The gruesome conclusion to the story was that the husband surprised the couple in the act, and the husband pointed a gun at the Captain and forced him to castrate himself. The surgeon who later attended the poor Captain served as the supposed key witness to the story. Whether a true or sensationalist account, it follows the generic moral novel by describing the unrepentant rake, hell-bent on a virtuous woman's destruction for the sheer pleasure of it. Methodism was an accomplice to the rake in this story by providing all the hallmarks of a safe, loving family with none of the security. After all, Methodist classes were composed of unrelated men and women, and the story suggests that this was an easily exploitable breach. While exemplifying themes found in eighteenth-century moral novels, including the susceptibility of women, it also reveals some truths about how Methodism was perceived by eighteenth-century society at large. Anti-Methodists contended that the confusion of religious and erotic passions, central to the Theodosia story, was a normal, frequent occurrence in Methodist bands and meetings. Eighteenth-century Anglo-American society interpreted the closeness of the Methodist family as intimacy and secrecy that impinged on the sanctity of female sexuality.

Language and Religious Sensuality

Anti-Methodists were especially critical of the ways that evangelical language suggested intimacy and sensuality. Some of this language, most notably that of female adherents, tended to employ embodied, ecstatic imagery in recounting aspects of the divine. Historian Cynthia Lynn Lyerly has explored the ramifications of early Methodist women's language, and she describes its advent within the particular context of the American South. This discourse, Lyerly argues, provided an outlet for women in this heavily patriarchal culture.[71] However, this language of sensuality was also found outside of the American South, throughout the transatlantic evangelical world, where it produced a similar shock to patriarchal sensibilities.

The anti-Methodist writer Leigh Hunt considered the sensual language of evangelicals to be so widespread that it would be familiar to his British readers in 1809. He lampooned the language of Methodist women in detail, noting their particular fondness for sensual writings in the Bible. Hunt asserted:

> The language of these women is so entirely earthly, that in general if you change the name of the object, you might think their devotion addressed to a mere lover. . . . Thus they ransack the whole vocabulary of Love for expressions suitable to their sensibilities: and GOD is addressed with a familiarity at which a modest Christian would shudder. Every thing is full of love, desire, flames, sweetness, charms, and enjoyments; GOD is the Husband of our souls, the *mystical marriage*, the *fruition that pains with pleasure*: JESUS CHRIST is the *dear* JESUS, the *sweet* JESUS, the *sweet and beautiful* Saviour, the *fairest among ten thousand*, who makes us *sick with desire and longing*: the Methodists perpetually talk of *lying in his bosom, gazing on his face*, and being *filled with the fullness of his love*. Is this a Christian or a Mohamedan Paradise?[72]

Hunt charged that the way that Methodist women talked about God was closer to a secular romance than religious devotion and clearly violated the boundaries of submissive female sexuality. Their language was "all body" and not enough soul; their chosen images were too embodied, physical, and "earthly." Hunt's readers would have been familiar with his parting shot at Methodism, associating evangelicalism with the supposedly rampant sexuality of the Middle East.[73] A "Mohamedan Paradise" translated Methodism into an exotic, alien identity. The particular association with a Middle Eastern image allowed the reader to imagine, as satirists confirmed, that male Methodist leaders were attracting a harem of female followers.

When Leigh Hunt wrote that Methodist women's writings were "full of love, desire, flames, sweetness, charms, and enjoyments," he might have been reading the personal letters published in Wesley's *Arminian Magazine*. First published in London in 1778, the *Arminian* was a monthly periodical, which John Wesley edited.[74] By the end of the eighteenth century, the *Arminian Magazine* was printed in Philadelphia as well, and Methodists circulated digests of this publication throughout America and England. In its pages, Methodists talked about God in terms of earthly love, and they talked about earthly relationships in terms of divine love, particularly their relationships to Wesley and other preachers. Many evangelicals, women especially, used the Song of Solomon, or as Hunt would say, "coquett[ed] in a song-of-Solomon way" to describe God. This text was an interesting choice, since it was a disputed contribution to the Bible and a love poem. When giving her conversion narrative to Charles Wesley in 1742, Hannah Hancock used the rich, fecund images from the Song of Solomon: "[T]hen I fou[n]d much sweetness with God and grate power over Sin I could then Say with Solomon I Sat under his Shadow and with grate Delight and his Fruit was Sweet to my taste—I Could then say his left hand was under my head and his Right hand doth Embrace me." In the same letter, she also described hearing John Wesley preach and the resulting vision that Jesus "mett me while I was a grate way of[f] he Run and fell upon my neck and kissed me with the Kiss of peace."[75] In both passages, the convert used physical terms for their religious sensations, and her descriptions of physical affection denoted a sense of satisfaction about her spiritual salvation.

Decades later and across the ocean, Sally Eastland corresponded with the esteemed southern Methodist preacher Edward Dromgoole, who had itinerated in her area of Virginia. In 1790, Eastland wrote to Dromgoole, "I feel encouraged, tho a child to speak to one of the Lords annointed, and dear Brother the topic is Jesus and his Love, but oh my feeble pen it, fails; it, fails, my unskillful hand falls short here; I cant tell much, but one thing I can tell I love to be hearing of him, and when I hear from Him, some times all my poor [heart] desolves in love, in some of his love visets to my poor Soul of late, He's left me as it ware help less on the ground, ah sweet momentes, how fain wou'd I faint away in his arms, and never [be] a sinner more."[76] Sarah Jones also lived in Virginia in the late eighteenth century and wrote in one enthusiastic, feeling account of her religious experience. "O! all flesh, O! dust and ashes, O! angels and men praise the Lord, for his love endureth for ever!—Excuse my passion for it is genuine.—Rolling, rising, burning love. I believe every drop of my crimson life is turned into love. Oh. Lord what I feel! Oh! That my dear Jesus would cut short years, and months, and hours, and overleap time, that I might behold him face to face, for there is enough in him to busy the love of all this world, yet how few adore him with all their heart.—I can hardly write—do pray bear with me."[77] By the 1790s, Sarah Jones, Sally Eastland, and other evangelicals had emulative models of ecstatic language that emerged from the transatlantic circulation of the *Arminian Magazine*. In addition, circuit preachers and exhorters circulated these expressions to a wide field of evangelicals on both sides of the Atlantic.

Wesley published letters from his past correspondences, including ones written by his mother, Susanna Wesley, and prominent English female exhorters. Many of these women had corresponded with John and Charles Wesley in the 1740s and 1750s and had no idea that their letters would be published thirty years later in the *Arminian*. Many letters contained sensual imagery and intimate allusions that the authors may not have intended for a wider audience. Sarah Perrin wrote wistfully, "O that my soul was a thirst for God, and my whole heart panting after him."[78] Perrin's passionate language exemplified how many Methodist women described their ecstasy and romantic longing for God. When Mary Thomas died in 1763, according to an account published in the *Arminian*, "Jesus personally manifested in her heart, and she cried out—'Christ is mine!' . . . Then she sung praise to him that loved her, and bought her with his own blood. . . . ' 'Tis but for Christ to speak the word, and I am gone. I only wait for that word, "Rise up, my love, and come away." ' "[79]

The preponderance of ecstatic writing by women provided fodder for anti-Methodist tracts. Additionally, some Methodist histories have contended that Methodist women were besotted with the Wesley brothers, John Wesley in particular. Methodist preachers were probably attractive in many ways to their followers, but there is scant evidence of any sexual relationship. Still, according to Methodist historian Henry Abelove, the casting of the minister as seducer was not so far from the truth; John Wesley used his sexual charisma to entrance his followers, male and female.[80]

Abelove's main contention is that this sexual charisma gave Wesley a considerable amount of power over the laity. Abelove underscores the importance of John Wesley to the success of Methodism, describing him as "seductive and monopolistic," especially in his relationship to Methodist women.[81] According to Abelove, Wesley projected a mixture of upper-class refinement and sexual charisma in order to garner the love and deference of female adherents in the competitive world of eighteenth-century evangelicalism.[82] Abelove's analysis of Wesley's seductive powers as the primary Methodist shepherd gives him a central role in the denomination's success and tremendous power over the laity. In reality, evangelical culture was a sprawling transatlantic network of major and minor saints, hallowed literature, and intense fellowship, all of which influenced and retained converts. Even in describing John Wesley's ideals or directives, one cannot presume a clear translation from edict to lay practice. The laity found exceptions and bent rules, without directly rebelling against Wesleyan imperatives, especially those regarding friendships, sexuality, and forming families. Furthermore, reducing the relationship between Wesley and female Methodists to seduction further ascribes a sexual desire to religious expressions and relationships and dismisses religious yearnings as essentially sexual. Methodist men and women sought close relationships with John Wesley and other preachers, as they hoped to draw their own souls into the close network of the Methodist family, in order to insure their religious development and ultimate sanctification.

Sarah Perrin, whom John Wesley described in the *Arminian Magazine* as "my Housekeeper at Bristol, and a Mother in Israel," wrote a particularly interesting series of letters about her relationship to the Wesley brothers, employing this sensual evangelical language. In October of 1742, she described her own spiritual state and reflected on John Wesley's ministering: "These words of our Lord have been comfortably brought to my mind of late: *Ye shall know them by their fruit: do men gather grapes of thorns, or figs of thistles?* I know, the fruit of your Ministry has been sweet to my taste, and strength to my soul. Therefore I have great confidence in you, and can speak freely, although we differ in some things. O my Brother, how have I wished such Ministers were in every Parish in this Nation! It would make it easier for Dissenters to join with you."[83] Perrin used strikingly bold language to describe his ministry, despite their differences in class, status, and age (she was only nineteen when she wrote this letter to the Methodist leader). Perrin's childhood as a Quaker undergirded her audaciousness in claiming spiritual authority.[84]

In Perrin's letters, which appeared in the *Arminian* in 1778, she claimed authority for herself, while describing her attachment to John Wesley. In her correspondence, Perrin revealed her confidence in the righteousness of her behavior and her relationship with Wesley.[85] However, it did seem as though Wesley, or another Methodist, warned Perrin against being too stridently affectionate toward him. In her next letter, she wrote, "Since I have writ last, I have had a caution given me, not to write so freely; because my Affection has been misinterpreted; lest it should hurt the Cause of God. But I cannot see, if we feel Love and Thankfulness for the Blessings we receive from your Ministry, why we should refrain from speaking of it, whilst the World are so ready to open their mouths against you. That we shall always find more Nearness to some souls than others, I am firmly persuaded. . . . Therefore I think, as my Soul prospers, the same Love, I have always espressed, will increase. . . . My heart is knit more and more unto you."[86] Perrin acknowledged that anti-Methodists might be ready to seize upon women's love of the Wesley brothers as improper, but she justified her enduring affection and its expression. In her letters, Perrin sought to cement her association with the Wesleys and to confirm her sense of belonging to this family, of their mutual ownership in the same spiritual fate. While her language was sensual and daring, it underscored the urgent emotional need she had to be a part of this affective family.

Perrin conducted a voluminous correspondence with both John and Charles Wesley, writing at least fifty letters to Charles, always with eloquence. In 1749, John Wesley recommended her as a suitable match to Charles Wesley.[87] Soon after, Charles Wesley married another woman, Sarah Gwynne, and Sarah Perrin married another Methodist preacher in 1750. By the time the *Arminian* came out in the late 1770s, John Wesley was a venerated elderly churchman, confident enough to print letters that might have once seemed too amatory, potentially hurting "the cause of God." Yet, the Methodists were still vulnerable to attack in this latter period; anti-Methodists were in full form in the 1780s, imputing scandalous sexual behavior to Wesley and his followers in an ever-growing body of scurrilous pamphlets.[88]

Love and the Methodist Man

Ecstatic language was the ideal for Methodist women, who commonly described Jesus as an embodied lover, someone who kissed and caressed the believer. In distinction, Methodist men tended to describe God in terms of fatherly affection, still bodily, but not as romantically imbued as women's language. However, some men adopted this language of love when describing God and their feelings for their ministerial leaders.

In the 1780s, John Matthias described seeing the preacher John Dickins walking with another preacher in New York: "when I [fastened] my eius upon tham I love'd them and if they had spock to me at that time, I du Know from my presind feeling it wold have over come me and for all I know I should have cried for mercy."[89] Matthias felt overwhelmed by the spiritual path that lay ahead of him, while he was still early in the process of conversion, and he conveyed the power that preachers held over some laypersons. His language described the sensation of being struck, much like feeling love at first sight, when he saw the powerful preacher John Dickins.

In the 1750s, John Hutchinson frequently wrote to Charles Wesley in ways that could easily have been mistaken for a lover's words. He wrote to Wesley of the ecstatic love he felt for him, whom he found "dearer to me than Life," and he exclaimed, "my Heart is ready to break that Providence has allotted me to be So far Separate from you."[90] In one letter, he observed a decline in correspondence from Wesley and jealously urged him to "write to me often and love me more, let no new convert be my Rival, continue your loving Kindness unto me and admit no one to have a greater Share in your Affection." In the same letter, Hutchinson described his jealousy in detail: "I have been broken hearted ever since your Departure. What yielded me most Ease was the Thought of hearing from you which I impatiently waited for, upon first Sight of your Letter my Heart leaped for Joy, I have read it over Times without Number, but cannot find your accustom Manner of writing ([which] was), dear Johny, dear youth, etc. etc. . . . I desire I may cease to breathe when I forsake you, you are dearer to me than myself."[91] Charles Wesley warned Hutchinson not to invest so much in this relationship, but Hutchinson refused to relinquish his idolatry of Wesley. He insisted, "[A]s to my Love I think it is of the right sort and such I hope as was betwixt David and Jonathan. I dremt last night of being with my dear CW and I don't know what is the matter with me all this Day, I feel my Heart so exceedingly enlarged towards you, in so much that I think I could almost pull out my own Eyes to do you Service."[92]

Hutchinson alternated between portraying their relationship as something brotherly and something romantic. These two models were not mutually exclusive; Hutchinson believed this single-minded devotion would endear him to Wesley and demonstrate the seriousness of his religious commitment. Hutchinson cited the model of David and Jonathan, as many Methodists did. By patterning their friendships on the selfless, singular bond between these Old Testament figures, Methodists evoked the ways in which the righteous bonds between godly people should overthrow natural family bonds. Jonathan had sacrificed the love of his father (King Saul) and his rights to the throne in order to prevent his father from killing David. Jonathan did this "because he loved him as his own soul," and he felt an intense, instantaneous dedication to David.[93] The feeling was mutual; after Jonathan's death, David laments, "thy love to me was wonderful, passing the love of women."[94] On the one hand, Jonathan and David formed the ultimate religious friendship, based on a foundation of unshakable commitment to each other, a covenant of shared religious ideals. On the other hand, their bond was singular and romantic in many ways. Methodist friendships often blended these ideas of shared religious commitment and romantic attachment.

Itinerant preachers developed deep bonds with one another, and they melded divine and romantic imagery together when they described these attachments. When Henry Smith fondly remembered the closeness he felt to his fellow preacher John Kobler, he wrote, "O how often we have retired together from some log-cabin to a lonely place for private prayer, and embraced, and wept over each other's necks, and sometimes shouted aloud for joy, that we were accounted worthy to suffer a little in the cause of Christ!"[95] Kobler inspired preacher Stith Mead to write poetry:

> Although we ride so far a part
> I love you in my very heart . . .
> O Could I see your Solemn face
> I'd take you in my arms embrace[96]

Kobler and Stith were paired as "covenant brothers," but Stith expressed that bond in openly sexual terms, proclaiming, "I love you with a pure love fervently. . . . I dream of you; I dream of Embracing you, in the fond arms of Nuptial love, I dream of kissing you with the kisses of my Mouth. I am Married to you; O that I could see you and spend a few moments in Heavenly Converse together."[97] Invoking the idea of marriage between itinerants is definitely unusual in preachers' correspondence, but itinerants felt wedded to one another, since they were sharing lives of religious commitment and physical discomfort.

By writing frequent letters, Methodist brethren formed singular relationships, even though they served separate and often distant preaching circuits. Perhaps Mead was responding to the isolation and the lack of physical contact on the circuit. There is also a distinct possibility that Mead was expressing a real sexual attachment to Kobler. The Methodist itinerancy certainly attracted some men who were willing to forgo marriage because they were not interested in romantic relationships with women. In general, the same sex bonds between evangelicals were emphasized by the same sex groupings of preachers and bands. While anti-Methodists fretted over the mixing of opposite sexes in the camp meetings and love feasts, the quotidian intimacy of same sex bonds were overlooked by the anti-Methodist press.[98]

The Evangelical Body and Sexuality

Despite this erotic language, Methodists were tame in comparison to their Moravian brothers and sisters. Methodists generally avoided explicitly sexual imagery or language, unlike eighteenth-century Moravians, who equated Christ's side wound with a vagina in many detailed illustrations.[99] Overall, there is little historical evidence of preachers like Mead and Kobler or converts like Theodosia and her captain consummating sexual relationships and exploring their "bonds of love." Yet, their exclusive bonds, intimate meetings, and ecstatic expressions fueled sexual interpretations of their religious practices. The fear that Methodists might insidiously steal away members from within families and communities, particularly the women of those communities, vexed some contemporaries. The sexual attraction explained why good women left loving families to go into the suspect Methodist family.

In their own narratives, many Methodists expressed extreme caution about amatory relationships. Methodists agonized over the consequences of falling in love and getting married. Many young evangelicals, like Hester Roe, saw their religious calling and sexual, romantic desires as opposed to each other. It was not merely a question of morality; the ambivalence that evangelicals expressed over social relationships in general led them to question the usefulness of sexual relationships in particular. Like the opposition that some converts felt between their birth families and their spiritual family, Methodists also reconsidered forming singular ties, because these ties might draw them away from the general bonds of the spiritual family. The nonevangelical world was ready to condemn Methodist sexuality as loose and immoderate, yet Methodists themselves wrote many cautionary narratives about the danger that surrounded bodily temptation.

Documenting the cases of sexual behavior in eighteenth-century Methodist writings is, of course, difficult; what surfaces in letters and journals are carefully worded phrases, penned for posterity. Yet, glimpses of sexual practice can be found, primarily in men's writings and occasionally in women's writings as well. Converts employed adoring, sensual language to describe their feelings toward fellow Methodists, but one can only speculate whether there were any sexual relationships to match. All we have is the language of love in these letters, not the actions. In their published narratives, their generally chaste writings about sexuality form a conscious rebuttal to the derogatory representations of Methodist licentiousness.

Anti-Methodists drew the association between sensual language and Methodist sexual immorality, but how can we extrapolate behavior from this language? John Wesley's wife did suspect sexual relationships were behind Wesley's voluminous correspondence with women. Wesley had hoped that the marriage would eradicate "the prejudice about the world and him."[100] He expected his marriage to quell scurrilous rumors about affairs with Methodist women, but ironically, his wife actually contributed more fodder to the swirl of accusations. Mary Vazeille Wesley wrote feverish notes to her husband about his alleged infidelities, intercepted mail from female followers, spied on him, and complained about his private meetings with female Methodists. There are even reports that she beat him in frustration over these alleged affairs, and ultimately her suspicions of his infidelity prompted her to leave him in 1758 after seven years of marriage.

Male converts customarily confessed to a sinful past as preludes to their conversion narratives. For example, when Thomas Cooper wrote to Charles Wesley in 1741, he described awakening to the sin of his past, when he had gone "horing drinking dansing plays and such vice as youth is prone to." Yet, he also wrote that recently he had felt "Lust and uncleness Come upon me as a flud and such filthey dremes as I am a shamed to menshon." He repented these persistent transgressions, but despite his best intentions, they continued.[101] Women would also include allusions to a youth of thoughtless gaiety, dances, and other diversions, which they now avoided as Methodists. They also commonly expressed shame over having taken pride in their good looks or to having attracted attention from men. In all cases, women talked about sexual temptation in a vague manner and in the past tense, occurring before conversion.

English preacher John Valton frankly confessed to his journals the confusion and lustfulness he felt toward fellow Methodists, especially as he was beginning to preach in 1767. He described that once he had such "violent Temptations to Lust, insomuch that I have stood sweating when I have been near a Woman, fearing least I shoud be forced to take liberties."[102] During a visit to a sick Methodist, he was aroused by the sick woman's embrace and her naked arms. On another evening, a woman visited him on spiritual business, and her "Cloak being thrown by, Her Whole Neck was bare. I had not the presence of mind to reprove her. When She was gone," Valton confessed, "I *thought* I felt a Sinful desire," confirming the need to note even the mere suggestion of sin.[103]

Of course, eighteenth-century diaries and journals were very vague regarding sexual behavior. Interspersed with reports of the sermons they preached, the people they met, and the miles they rode, preachers often commented on the state of their souls. However, their language was somewhat cryptic when describing their sinfulness. Sometimes, they would simply write that they felt "some temptations." Jeremiah Norman, an itinerant in North Carolina, often wrote in vexingly circumspect terms, as he did in August of 1794: "I still see my flesh and spirit are opposite parties."[104] Another favorite phrase of Norman's was "my Flesh Clogs my Spirits."[105] William Ormond, also a preacher in North Carolina, wrote after a series of troubling dreams, "My flesh is an enimy to my soul."[106] Still, it is safe to extrapolate the sexual meaning behind certain passages found in preachers' journals. When writing in 1796, Norman made a cryptic reference to a sexual transgression: "For my part my Flesh had no rest. & Spirit was disquited with in me. I hope to get the disquietude remooved by means of my good Friend. & the Letter I wrote this Afternoon. if Jezebel remains in the house of God. I am fully [persuaded] that there will but Little good done. if I have done wrong in this thing. O Lord. give me to see my [error]. . . . I feel my Body relapsing. I am unfit for any [Business]."[107] Norman's relapsed and unfit body mirrors the division of flesh and soul that Ormond reports in his journals; both likely referred to sexual desires and masturbation.

While Methodist preachers were troubled by sexual thoughts and actions, they noted a general lack of sexual inhibition among their flocks, especially in the South. In the 1790s, American preachers complained about how few new people were converting to Methodism. Preachers wrote about religious fervor leveling off everywhere and a deadening or growing deficit of believers in many places.[108] In the American South, clergy and itinerant preachers described the religious disaffection, sexual licentiousness, and debauchery of manners in the people they met. Preachers complained of some southerners' disregard for marital bonds and legal sanction for sexual activity, but also improper manners, dress, and language. Historian Richard Godbeer relates the specific sexual history of the South to the lack of religiosity these preachers encountered: "Unmarried, serial and bigamous relationships occurred in all the North American colonies, even in New England, but they were much more prevalent in those regions of British America where the guiding hands of minister and magistrate were ineffective or nonexistent among white settlers."[109] This problem of regulating the sexual behavior of colonists began in the seventeenth century, well before Methodists ever set foot there, when sex ratios, settlement patterns, and the lack of religious establishment in the southern colonies led to a looser standard for social behavior. Methodists were especially interested in finding converts in the backcountry, where the residents enjoyed relaxed sexual mores, and where they were outside the purview of law or church.[110]

Jeremiah Norman described the people of Charleston in 1797 as "wicked" and generally irreligious. He found people easily distracted and "full of levity." After a "sultry" day of preaching in Charleston, he complained to his journal: "[T]he nature of my Subject, & disposition of my hearers was another affliction to me, the Subject was full of matter. but the People was as full of levity. it was with very great difficulty that I could help them in any kind of moderation in their manners. I was attacked very closely by a young Buxome Woman. to know who it was that I reproved for Laughing."[111] Norman's journal describes the futility of preaching morality among a population adverse to "any kind of moderation."

Sexual disorder in the South included cohabitation, marriage between close relatives, and openly sexual banter. These practices seemed particularly common in Norman's circuits in North and South Carolina. He wrote about "people torn to pieces by the Devil,"[112] a woman who became pregnant by her stepbrother,[113] and a Brother S. Blacke who was living with "one of the most wretched of the fair sex now in being."[114] While Norman wrote about the sexual behavior of others, he rarely reflected on his own. Norman kept his congregants' behavior at a distance and often wrote that he hoped their sinful ways would not contaminate him. In November of 1795, he wrote a characteristic entry: "My mind was much Exercised while seeing ye ways of ye ungodly. The Lord keep me from being let away by the error of the wicked. or from falling."[115]

Methodist preachers' descriptions of southern sexuality emphasized the gulf between their own morality and the behavior of their flock. Preachers like Norman engaged in a high-minded critique of the crass immoderation that they encountered on their southern circuits. Evangelicals bridged these class divides by drawing their ranks from educated and uneducated, rich and poor, black and white. Yet, once in the preaching ranks, itinerants marked themselves as a class above much of their flock. They underlined this class distinction in their discussion of the sexual behavior, deportment, and manners of their congregants. The association of sexual licentiousness and lower-class behavior was a potent one for transatlantic Methodists, whom outsiders often viewed as being lower class. Despite preachers' desire to be seen as a class above, the sexual accusations from their critics kept them rooted in their image as lower class and less educated than their Anglican and Congregationalist counterparts.

Aside from the class divide that separated moralizing preachers from their less holy-minded flock, preachers exhibited particular discomfort with women who did not conform to the polite, godly talk and dress of Mothers in Israel. Jeremiah Norman reported his shock at a conversation with a young woman near Pisgah, North Carolina, in 1794: "[I]n the evening I conversed with a young woman in preasence of the Family. I think she was the most singular that I ever saw in my life. She astonisht me with her talk." She shocked Norman by frankly confessing that she checked out "young men in the time of preaching," and that it was impossible to "Pray while the Beautifull young men" were there. The woman continued to scandalize the preacher by turning the banter toward him, asking him, "how could you be in love with and courting of a young woman and not be looking in time of meeting . . . I exerted myself to stop her but for sometime all in vain."[116] Clearly the young woman was flirting with Norman and enjoying some playful, transgressive banter with a preacher, but there was little humor in Norman's journal entry.

Like Norman, Zachariah Yewdall was a Methodist preacher who also noted frequent temptations from female members of his flock and placed the blame clearly on them. Yewdall was an itinerant on his first circuit in southern Wales in 1780, as he battled sexual temptations, often in rather inappropriate circumstances, while praying and visiting the sick. After one such visit, he wrote: "[I] had some strong temptations thro' ye Salutation of a young-woman: in this I felt much of my own weakness, Satan, at ye same time dressing up natures gilded toys, in ye most beautifull manner: my Cry to God, was Lord: keep me, save in this house, so he soon heard my Cry's so that I found ye Lord very present & presious in the evening, in speaking his Word. O! May I never be found of my guard, but may I always watch, lest I enter into temptation."[117] He repeated this association of women and the devil after a particularly good morning of preaching when "notwithstanding this, I was tempted afterwards. From a Certain young woman: which Satan dressed up as well as he was able. But glory be to God, who kept me from falling into temptation."[118] In this desire to remain separate from sexual desire, Methodist preachers risked distancing themselves from the humanity of regular converts. As well, Yewdall's entries betray a pronounced misogynistic streak, blaming women for his sexual desire and aligning femininity with satanic forces.

Despite the best efforts of many Methodist preachers to remain above the fray, and therefore above reproach in the arena of sexual transgressions, critics persisted in accusing them of adultery. In March of 1767, English preacher John Valton discovered that he had a reputation as an adulterer. He had traveled to exhort to a mixed evangelical crowd in a town on the outskirts of London, where they lacked a regular Methodist preacher. They were meeting in a private home, when a man suddenly attacked Valton, calling him "that Dog from Purfleet" and nearly throwing him in a fireplace. As he left, a mob of forty people, by his account, attacked him and ripped his clothes. Before he had a chance to escape this inhospitable town, the final blow came from an unexpected corner: the local pastor. Just after outrunning the mob, he met up with a Reverend Watters, who "flew into a passion, called me several times 'Villain' saying, 'how dare You preach, where is your Licence?' I told Him, I did not preach, 'You do You Villain, You go about poisoning the Principles of the People, ruining Families, You have ruined Mr. Edwards Family.'"[119] Watters had gotten wind of his entanglement with Mrs. Edwards, who had been his spiritual mother.

Accusations of adultery were particular to Methodists. In the case of Valton and Edwards, it appeared to critics that the Methodist family had wrecked another family, by drawing out its members, confusing a wife's allegiances, and cuckolding the husband. Valton's fraught relationship with Mrs. Edwards carried with it a multivalent challenge to the traditional ideas of family. There were certainly implied tones of sexuality to the intimacy of their relationship. Their exclusivity and the ways in which this may have impinged upon Mrs. Edwards's marriage did not go unnoticed by others, least of all, Mr. Edwards, who resented Valton's intrusion and his usurping of Edwards's religious authority. Reverend Watters felt fully justified in accusing Valton of perverting the natural order of families and corrupting good marriages. This incident prompted Valton to consider marriage as a way to clear himself of these charges of sexual impropriety and also alleviate his persistent depressions.

It is perhaps not surprising that most of the explicit mentions of sexuality in Methodist private papers surfaced in men's writings. Women wrote about love, suitability, and marriage, but they were less likely to note physical gratification or denial. It is very unlikely that such writings would have been preserved through the generations. One may presume that eighteenth-century women had the same sorts of yearnings for physical intimacy, but their writings were less likely to contain mention of explicitly sexual desires. Their sexual, ecstatic, desirous language was aimed at God and Jesus, and the occasional preacher.

Conclusions

The Methodist language of love employed sensual language to describe their most ecstatic, God-centered feelings and relationships, a language that celebrated themes of obsession and single-mindedness. This romantic language underlined their familial bonds to one another. The passionate language of evangelicals created a syntax that bound them together and a form of language that registered as disturbingly sexual to those outside the family. The passion normally reserved for couples or family members was transferred to unrelated Methodists. Many Methodists felt that close familial and romantic bonds were not unlike their love for God, and therefore those earthly bonds were not improper. While the ultimate romantic object of these sensations was not supposed to be individuals, but rather God, clearly evangelicals experienced deep intimacy with each other. Fellow Methodists were the co-authors of any single believer's conversion and helpmates throughout the convert's spiritual life, and occasionally believers expressed the ecstatic feelings of religious exaltation toward their evangelical companions. While the Methodist ideal may have celebrated the lone individual's struggle toward a religious goal, despite unfathomable degrees of pain and suffering, the truth was that a converted person never stood apart from the evangelical family. Romantic bonds cemented the Methodist family, as we saw in the cases of Sarah Perrin, Thomas Hutchinson, and Stith Mead; these writers felt themselves romantically drawn to others in the family, and this seemed like an appropriate way to express their love of God.

Evangelical women and their use of language were targets of criticism for anti-Methodists. Methodist women used romantic phrases, the ideals of passionate love, to describe their love of God. It was not about sexualizing their God but about imbuing this relationship with all of the ardor that one would find in descriptions of intimate relationships.[120] Romantic love and religious enthusiasm actually sprang from a similar well. Both enthusiasm and romantic love derived from the imagination, which people described as their heart and soul. The language of sentiment, which supported both romantic love and enthusiastic expression, was essentially an exercise in fully expressing the ideal of sympathy and feeling deeply. Without the coherent code of Methodist language, religious enthusiasm might be incoherent and disconnected. Within Methodism, the language of sexuality did not bother fellow adherents, except for fearing the appearance of impropriety. Within Methodist bands, this language was the perfect encapsulation of the sublime and the divine. This language was recognizable and understandable within the Methodist family, while it was lampooned from without.

Did the sensual language of evangelicalism perform a sort of valve for sexual expression in an acceptable religious context? Were women expressing their sexuality through these ecstatic writings? E. P. Thompson wrote that Methodist hymns were actually sexual in nature (which is a fitting criticism from a latter-day anti-Methodist), and it seems a reliable explanation for the popularity and effective control that Thompson sought to ascribe to this group. However, women's writings reveal that they used this language of sexuality themselves and that they saw this as a valid outlet for their ecstatic religious feelings. They were not controlled or seduced by Charles Wesley's hymns, but they did find resonance in the ecstatic images of Methodist discourse.

While Methodists promoted a sensual language when voicing their innermost religious feelings, they were reserved in their actual sexual practice. The portrayal of Methodists as sexually deviant dissenters was a troubling image for a group committed to sexual continence. Anti-Methodists combated this new religious family with the accusation that this was an unnatural sort of union, an incestuous family. Methodist sensibility called for them to make a strict accounting of their sensations, probing signals from many sources, to sift through what was divine and what was devilish. Although Methodists publicly denied loose sexual practice, they nonetheless spent a fair amount of time accounting for their sinfulness in their private writings. Hogarth and other anti-Methodists took this obsession with lust and sexual continence to be proof of the perversion of religious enthusiasm.

This romantic language was part of the rise of sensibility. Preachers, exhorters, and laypersons exhibited this language of sensibility, where feeling trumped all other constraints. Methodists honed their sensibilities in their letters and narratives, finding phrases that expressed their love for God and each other. The use of florid language to describe religious sensation was remarkable in the eighteenth century, but became much less so by the mid-nineteenth century. As Methodism established itself, there were further constrictions of both sensual language and female power within mainstream Wesleyan Methodism. The language of feeling lingered into the nineteenth century, transformed into a cooler language of sympathy and eventually a Victorian sentimentalism toward social causes. At the heart of Methodism remained this fiery passion toward God, but the expressions became more rote and restrained. In the nineteenth century, Methodists sought to alter the way that their ecstatic religious spaces and practices were interpreted, as they evolved into a respectable denomination with their own churches on both sides of the Atlantic.

Chapter 5

Celibacy in the Methodist Family: The Case Against Marriage

> It is sixteen years this day, since my husband went from me, and from that time I have believed I should see him no more in this world; but from that time, thou my God, hast been my husband, father, and friend. My wants have been richly supplied out of thine abundant fullness through Christ Jesus. "I need no man, who all possess, In Jesu's heart-felt love."
>
> —Sarah Crosby, diary entry, February 2, 1773

When Englishwoman Sarah Crosby wrote this entry in her journal, she was marking the anniversary of starting her new life as a celibate Mother in Israel.[1] In 1757, when her husband had deserted her, she had already been a Methodist for over six years, having been inducted into the group by John Wesley. Her husband's desertion, however, provided the impetus for a new stage in her life, in which she had a more fruitful commitment to Methodism. In 1761, four years after Mr. Crosby's exit, she went from being a sister to a mother in the connection, leading class meetings and preaching to large groups. Her story provided a direct example for other Methodists of how crucial it was to form the right sorts of social bonds. Mr. Crosby was probably a poor choice as a lifelong spiritual partner; her Methodist family was better.

The difficulty of finding a good spiritual partner raised the question of whether sexual activity, marriage, and family formation were essentially good for the soul. Methodists, like their Baptist competitors, were critical of some social activities, a position that earned them a puritanical image.

At the same time, Methodists participated in an ecstatic worship and discourse that seemed to contradict their repressive image. Nonetheless, religious ecstasy oriented believers to the shared rituals of the Methodist connection. In the same way, the practice of celibacy oriented some prominent believers toward the Methodist family, away from competing allegiances to husbands, wives, and children. Eighteenth-century Methodists often thought of themselves as following the lives of primitive Christians in their fellowship, persecution, social ways, simplicity, and spiritual ardency. Methodists revived an early Christian ideal of a fellowship composed of unmarried, celibate members.[2] In addition, eighteenth-century Methodists revived less distant debates over whether marriage was beneficial for the truly devout. During the Protestant Reformation, Protestants had insisted that Catholic priestly celibacy encouraged deviant, illicit sexuality. Protestants distinguished themselves from Catholics in their positive view of marriage. In the seventeenth century, Puritans in England and America made marriage and the family the cornerstone of the church.[3]

While Puritans had focused on the family as the central unit of worship, early Methodists focused on the individual convert. Because of the focus on individual conversion as central to Methodist faith, there was no presumption of converting families in early Methodism. This focus on individual faith, rather than family worship, prompted a radical reconsideration of the purpose of marriage and family formation within the first seventy-five years of Methodism. In the eighteenth century, various religious groups were reconsidering sex and its utility for religious individuals.[4] Shaker founder Ann Lee devised a religious order that included gender segregation and celibacy after having visions of carnal sins in 1770, while jailed in Manchester, England.[5] She took her visions to America, where she founded a community that strove to free individuals from traditional familial needs and procreation in order to devote their energies to achieving salvation.[6] As a decidedly different approach, Moravians considered sex and reproduction to be entirely consistent with religious norms, particularly when these practices were oriented toward communal goals. Eighteenth-century Methodists also prioritized the communal family and individual salvation over blood families and earthly desires, but many prominent Methodists decided that sexual abstinence was the only way to remain truly religious.

Single, unattached Methodists were held up as ideals of religiosity, especially in the eighteenth century. John Wesley was somewhat conflicted about whether marriage was a beneficial path for the truly religious. He tended to be suspicious of the value of marriage, perhaps reflecting on his own matrimonial failures. Some early Methodists felt that marriage would prompt Methodist brothers and sisters to put their private concerns for spouses and families above their collective religious goals. Celibate individuals would not have a conflict between their own families and the larger Methodist family. A celibate member was always a convert first and foremost, a child within the Methodist family.

Eighteenth-century preachers were particularly strong proponents of celibacy within their ranks, but they were not advocating a return to priestly celibacy. While the anti-Methodist press was quick to associate Methodism with Catholicism and dissent, John Wesley drew a sharp line between Catholic celibacy and Methodist sexual abstinence.[7] In pragmatic terms, it made sense for itinerant preachers to remain unmarried, since they could barely afford to keep themselves dressed and fed, much less support a family. While celibacy was not the rule for all preachers, John Wesley still advocated celibacy, formally and informally. In his letters and publications, John Wesley discouraged itinerant preachers and some female exhorters from marrying. In 1743, when Wesley first published his *Thoughts on Marriage and a Single Life*, he confirmed that it was simply easier to serve God as a single person. In 1781, Wesley told English preacher Zachariah Yewdall, "I commend you for being exceeding wary with respect to marriage. St. Paul's direction is full and clear: 'If thou mayest be free, use it rather.' 'Art thou loosed from a wife? Seek not a wife.'"[8] Wesley drew his advice from Paul's writings in 1 Corinthians 7, which centrally deal with the question of marriage. However, when Paul wrote, "But if thou mayest be made free" he referred to the state of slavery, and the preference for freedom.[9] In Wesley's writings on this section of Corinthians, Wesley equates the sense of freedom from marriage with freedom from bondage.[10] In a subsequent letter to Yewdall, he repeated this quote, "if thou mayest be free," writing that it was the duty "especially to a preacher, and to a Methodist Preacher above all" to remain celibate.[11] Other Methodist preachers on both sides of the Atlantic advocated celibacy for the itinerancy. As late as 1806, when Brother Ellis asked the North Carolina preacher Thomas Mann about whether Ellis should marry, Mann counseled that if he could help it, he should remain single, but if not, he should consult God and be sure it was God's will.[12]

Some laity and preachers embraced what we could call "temporal celibacy," practicing celibacy while they were intensely engaged in religious work, rather than having a lifelong commitment to celibacy. Methodist commitment to celibacy differed from other sorts of Christian celibacy in this respect. They did not, on an official level, advocate lifelong celibacy for Methodists, even for preachers. This differed significantly from the Catholic call to celibacy for its clerical class, as well as the Shakers call for celibacy for all members.

When John Wesley called on followers to refuse marriage for a higher religious purpose, it was a paternalistic pronouncement, a way to control his most valuable religious followers. In contrast, some members of the laity embraced celibacy as a means to significant self-determination and refutation of parental and societal pressures. For Methodist laity and preachers, the notion of "religious calling" was a potent rationale that allowed holy men and women to refuse unsuitable marriage offers, delay marriage indefinitely, or separate from unsuitable spouses. Methodists reconsidered marriage and, unlike their Baptist and Anglican counterparts in England and America, engaged in a serious and prolonged discussion on the subject during the eighteenth century. One of the central causes of this reconsideration was the reliance upon itinerant preachers, since circuit preachers were largely mobile and unmarried.[13] In addition, during the first decades of Methodism, celibacy was also a viable option for women. Remaining single made membership in the Methodist family more prominent than personal ties, and this decision foregrounded a religious calling. Ultimately, the choice to be celibate highlighted the individualism of Methodism, because it allowed individual believers to choose distinct paths for their commitment to evangelicalism.

The Case Against Marriage

Many prominent Methodists chose celibacy over marriage, distinguishing themselves from contemporaries in Anglo-American society, who largely held that marriage was a necessary step to adulthood. In contrast, Methodists agonized over the spiritual purpose of marriage, reciting in letters and journals all of their doubts about the holiness of that institution. For almost fifteen years, English preacher John Valton debated whether he should marry and questioned this decision in his journals. In 1767, he charted the pros and cons, and while he first listed his "Motives to marry," his "Objections" ran much longer:

> 1st I should love her too well and thereby rob God of my Heart. Or she me.

2nd I should car[e] for the things of the World how I should please my Wife.
3rd I fear I should not be free to leave so agreeable a companion when something required my absence.
4th I should grow soft, and slothful.
5th I am fitter for the Grave than the Marriage bed.[14]

While that last point is perhaps peculiar to Valton's gloomy outlook, the other objections would have been familiar to many evangelicals. Many of the disciplinary rules of Methodism involved denying earthly and sensual pleasures, and marriage could be the imperfect concentration of both.

Valton's diary illuminates the caution with which many Methodists approached relationships, even strong friendships. Valton had found a soul mate in a married Methodist, Sister Healey, and they met often to discuss spiritual matters. He worried that his relationship with Sister Healey sometimes crossed into an idolatrous love, and he likened her to Isaac (comparing his own difficulty to Abraham's in sacrificing Isaac for God). Valton cautioned, "if it should please the Lord to call Her! I had often told her to beware not to love me, so as not to give me up, when called for with all readiness and resignation."[15] The danger in all deep attachments, including marriage, was that believers might value their temporal relationships more than their relationship to God. Private unions, especially between the converted and unconverted, were troublesome to many Methodist preachers and laypersons alike; they were potential impediments to the unity of the Methodist family.

John Wesley discouraged particular Methodists from marrying and promoted celibacy among the leading laity and preachers, even though his own views and practices concerning marriage varied widely over his lifetime. In 1743, Wesley summed up his beliefs in *Thoughts on Marriage and a Single Life*, and these ideas remained important to Wesley throughout his lifetime; he revised and republished this work again toward the end of his life in 1785. In this tract, one finds some of the ambivalence that Wesley felt toward the institution of marriage and sexual practice more generally. He never outlawed marriage, but he made it clear that continence (true celibacy) was a profound gift to the religiously minded.[16] He grounded this argument in Paul's words: "The unmarried woman careth for the things of the Lord, that she may be held both in body and spirit but she that is married careth for the things of the world, how she may please her husband." While Wesley understood that remaining single was difficult, he argued that every truly converted Christian had the power to resist sexual temptation. " 'But who are able to keep themselves thus pure?' I answer, Every Believer in CHRIST: Every one who hath living Faith *in the Name of the only begotten Son of* GOD. . . . Whoever find *Redemption in his Blood,* in that Hour receives this Gift of GOD. Lust then vanishes away: And if they that are *born of* GOD, *keep* themselves, shall never return."[17]

In this 1743 tract, John Wesley's final consideration on the subject of celibacy was that Methodists always had to consider God above all earthly relationships. He wrote, "Blessed art Thou, if Thou continuest *as an Eunuch for the Kingdom of Heaven's Sake.* . . . Let thine Eye be always unto Him who hath declared, *Verily, verily I say unto You, there is no Man who hath left Father or Mother, or Wife or Children,—for my Name's Sake, but he shall receive an Hundred Fold, now in this present Time, and in the World to come, Eternal Life.*"[18] Methodism was a "heart religion," in that it was all-consuming, emotive and uncomplicated by elaborate theology. Simple and to the point, Methodism demanded whole-hearted commitment, admitting no rivals.

Wesley went to great pains, though, to distinguish his call for celibacy from the Catholic requirement of priestly celibacy. In 1762, Wesley expanded his view that Christian teachings supported marriage in the revised *Explanatory Notes Upon the New Testament*: "*Marriage* is *honourable in,* or for *all* Sorts of *Men,* Clergy as well as Laity: Tho' the *Romanists* teach otherwise; *and the bed undefiled*—Consistent with the highest Purity: Tho' many Spiritual Writers, so called, say it is only *licensed whoredom.*"[19] By the eighteenth century, being antimarriage was akin to proclaiming Catholicism. As a Salem Puritan minister proclaimed in 1640, "Ye Popish dogs, at marriage bark no more. Marriage, that honorable chastity, let none but [the] filthy Antichrist decry."[20] Most Protestants held that sex within marriage was a necessary good (as opposed to a necessary evil), but even then it could be dangerous if sexual desire overshadowed one's love of God.[21] Despite Wesley's disclaimer that marriage and holiness were not necessarily in opposition, he held that there were many problems inherent in marriage for devout converts.

Wesley's main contention was that married life often interrupted individual spiritual development and religious duties; this argument surfaced repeatedly in his lifetime. In a particularly harsh (and now infamous) episode, he "consoled" his sister Martha on the death of her children, who had all died of fever in 1742, by remarking, "I believe the death of your children is a great instance of the goodness of God towards you. You have often mentioned to me how much of your time they took up. Now that time is restored to you, and you have nothing to do but to serve our Lord without care[less]ness and without distraction, till you are sanctified in body, soul, and spirit."[22] This hardly seems like the words of a sympathetic brother. Yet, other preachers were equally dismissive of the demands of child care and the general duties of a family. While traveling and preaching in Maryland in 1780s, William Colbert complained of a woman who came to hear him preach, but missed the rest of the meeting to return home and take care of her children. She explained that her family duties did not allow her enough time to attend Methodist meetings. Colbert rejected this excuse; for him, the priority of one's eternal soul over earthly bonds was irrefutable.[23] Whether or not preachers were sympathetic to the demands of secular life and family, some Methodists decided that families were indeed hindrances to attaining spiritual perfection.[24]

Evangelical views of marriage and family directly reflected ideas about women and women's religiosity. Marriage obviously affected both men and women, but talk about marriage was often code for the place of women in both evangelical and secular society. In some debates over marriage, found in the *Discipline*, as well as in Wesley's writings and laity's letters, we see marriage posited against religiosity—marriage as a snare, an obstacle, and a distraction from the work of God among the fraternity of preachers. When the English preacher Zachariah Yewdall viewed a young woman as the product of Satan "dressing up natures gilded toys," one can certainly read a sanctioned hostility toward women as obstacles to men's saintliness.[25] Francis Asbury, the celibate American Methodist leader, commended preachers to "stand at all possible distance from the female sex, that you be not betrayed by them that will damage the young mind and sink the aspiring soul."[26]

In Wesley's recommendation against preachers' marrying, one could easily infer that Methodists saw women as distractions to male spirituality. However, this reassessment of marriage was equally valid for women, and Wesley also urged celibacy for leading female exhorters. More important, women adopted celibacy as a positive step in their spiritual lives. In some cases, when women freed themselves from bad marriages, Methodism provided a positive path to celibate lives. While the commendation of celibacy may have been misogynistic at its core, based on beliefs in women's essential sexuality and sinfulness, women used the call to celibacy toward positive ends in their own lives by providing the rationale to exit bad marriages or avoid them altogether.

Joan Webb, an English layperson who wrote her conversion narrative in May of 1742, described listening to John Wesley preach and realizing that her marital woes had prevented her from devoting herself to God. She wrote, "[D]id not I Love my husband better than God [?] . . . and I was fully convinced that I did not Love God." She argued in her account that marriage and spirituality warred against each other. Her husband had left her, and these problems had distracted her from pursuing her salvation.[27] Wesley had drawn a parallel between love for God and romantic love, but Webb saw that the two were actually in conflict in her life.[28] Margaret Austin, an Englishwoman who gave her account to Charles Wesley, also wrote about how marriage prevented a depth of religiosity. In 1738, she heard George Whitefield preach on how the wealthy were too invested in this world. Austin could have surmised that Whitefield had nothing to say to her; she was barely getting by, after her abusive husband had left her with two children.[29] Yet, she saw the parallel between earthly wealth and human attachments like marriage; both elements were distractions from spiritual development.[30] It was only after her husband left her that she was open to following Methodists like Whitefield and the Wesley brothers in their itinerant preaching. It was only after the collapse of her bad marriage that she was able to experience conversion.

Ungodly Unions

The accounts of Webb and Austin exemplified how obstinate, abusive husbands impeded women's spiritual development. If a Methodist married badly, the results could be dire, by some accounts. Thomas Rankin, a transatlantic preacher and leader, illustrated the dangers of marrying someone without the proper spiritual concerns. In 1768, he wrote in his memoirs that when he preached in Cornwall, he counseled a teenage girl who was "amiable for her years, both in sense, person, and piety." This teenager was contemplating marriage, but she feared that this courtship would result in her death. She had a vision that God would rather have her dead than married to this irreligious man. Rankin recounted, "She was sensible of the snare that lay before her that she several times told me she believed the Lord would prevent their marriage. She had suffered loss in her soul on this account; but the Lord in his mercy gave her repentance before she was seized by the illness that terminated in her death. I believe I shall meet her spirit in heaven. I mention the above to show the danger which pious young persons are in from forming connexions with those who do not walk in the paths that lead to glory."[31]

There are numerous examples of Methodist bands and preachers encouraging wives to leave husbands who were abusive or simply opposed to Methodism.[32] While Freeborn Garrettson was traveling to preach in upstate New York, a man confronted him with the accusation that the Methodists had broken up his family. He raved at Garrettson, "Is it right for you to part man and wife? My wife joined your church last night. We are parted, we are parted!"[33] Some women defied their husbands by attending Methodist meetings, and preachers reported these women's fear of meeting their husbands' wrath at home.[34] John Wesley wrote that spousal abuse was indefensible. In a sermon that was later printed in the *Methodist Magazine*, he expounded, "I cannot find in the bible that a husband has the authority to strike his wife on any account: even suppose she struck him first."[35] Many of the stories of marriages that violently fell apart due to the wife's conversion were part of the canon of Methodism's pernicious effects on families. These stories were circulated outside of Methodist societies as yet more evidence that Methodism worked against the stability of society and traditional patriarchal authority; within Methodist societies, these were stories that exemplified women's suffering and the evangelical will to overcome all obstacles.

Methodists had some prominent examples of marriages that went awry within the leadership and the laity. Despite John Wesley's well-publicized objections to marriage, in his own life he tried repeatedly to find a good union. Unfortunately, his two abridged courtships with Sophy Hopkey and Grace Murray were failures, as was his eventual marriage to Mary Vazeille in 1751. His first courtship, when he romanced Sophy Hopkey in Georgia in 1736, demonstrated that Wesley was uncertain about the role of marriage in a religious life. After the Hopkey romance turned to scandal, his confusion gave way to certainty that celibacy had been his plan all along, and he published his pro-celibacy *Thoughts on Marriage and a Single Life* in 1743. Nonetheless, he did not remain certain for long.

In 1749, Wesley's second brush with matrimony came when he became engaged to his nurse, housekeeper, and traveling companion Grace Murray. During the previous year, he had reconsidered his stance on celibacy, after fellow English preachers at the London Conference of Preachers convinced him that marriage did not result in a "Loss in his Soul."[36] Wesley risked severe ridicule in this second attempt at marriage. Murray was the thirty-two-year-old widow of a Scottish sea captain. She converted to Methodism in 1739 and became a band leader at the Foundery (Wesley's home base and the main Methodist chapel in London). In 1745, Wesley appointed her as his housekeeper in Newcastle. Murray and Wesley had been friends over the years, but they became intimate while she nursed him through an illness in 1748. He wrote in a memoir that he "had never before had so strong an Affection for any Person under Heaven."[37]

As Wesley looked back on this period, he wrote that he still had misgivings about whether he should get married.[38] In classic Methodist style, Wesley composed a list of pros and cons. The list was quite long, containing over thirty points. His reasons for marrying well outweighed and outnumbered his reasons for remaining celibate. Yet, his reasons for remaining single were long-standing in many cases. Despite his multiple attempts at marriage, his commitment to celibacy had deep roots. His rationale for remaining single included:

1. From the time I was Six or Seven years old, if any one spoke to me concerning marrying, I used to say, I thought I never should "Because I should never find such a Woman as my Father had."
2. When I was about Seventeen (and so till I was Six or Seven and twenty) I had no thought of marrying, "Because I could not keep a Wife."
3. I was then persuaded, "It was unlawfull for a Priest to marry," grounding that Persuasion on the (supposed) Sense of the Primitive Church.
4. Not long after, by reading some of the Mystic Writers, I was brought to think "Marriage was the less Perfect state," and that there was some Degree (at least) of "Taint upon the Mind, necessarily attending the Marriage-Bed."
5. At the same time I view'd in a strong light St. Paul's words to the Corinthians: And judg'd it "impossible for a married man to be so without carefulness, or to attend upon the Lord with so little Distraction, as a single man might do."
6. Likewise, being desirous to lay out all I could in feeding the hungry and cloathing the naked, I could not think of marrying, "because

it would bring such Expence, as would swallow up all I now gave away."

7. But my grand Objection for these twelve years past has been, "A Dispensation of the Gospel has been committed to me. And I will do nothing which directly or indirectly tends to hinder my preaching the Gospel."[39]

According to Wesley's long list of objections to marriage, there were diverse reasons to remain celibate. Some were contextual, pragmatic, or financial, but other justifications were more philosophical and theological. These doubts can be reduced to one principle: it was simpler and easier to serve God as a single man.

Wesley overturned all of these objections with a lengthy counterargument in his account of this courtship. Wesley found exceptions to the broader religious principles, but it also seems from his account that Murray was giving him good reasons to question his previous misgivings and that he felt that she in particular was an individual who would make an ideal wife. Her eminent qualities included her proven abilities as a housekeeper, a "patient, and inexpressibly tender" nurse, a good companion and friend, and a "Fellow Laborer in the Gospel."[40] In John Wesley's decision to marry Grace Murray, Wesley recognized a desire for intimacy and seemed to soften his stance that sexual relationships precluded spiritual perfection.[41] Murray had put off another suitor, John Bennet, while she traveled with Wesley in Ireland for three months, during which time Murray and Wesley became engaged, according to Wesley.[42] John Wesley's brother Charles was unhappy about this imminent union. Charles Wesley and George Whitefield apparently constructed a diversion and spirited Murray away to marry the rival suitor, John Bennet. John Wesley was not completely surprised by his brother's betrayal. He had dreamed that Grace Murray had died and had interpreted this as a sign that she was done with him.[43] Charles Wesley believed that, as Henry Rack describes, Grace Murray "was not as spiritual as she seemed, but above all, apparently, that she was too mean in status for his brother and that this would cause division and scandal."[44] Many Methodists apparently objected to this romantic development, particularly the transgression of class boundaries.[45]

Though he eventually found a wife after Murray, Wesley held a clear preference for the unmarried life. Throughout the two failed courtships, Wesley was fairly passive in his desire for marriage. His declaration of love to Murray was overly vague and conditional: "If ever I marry, I think you will be the Person."[46] Dee Andrews has called Wesley's life one of "virtual celibacy," and even the woman who ultimately became his wife, Mary Vazeille, might have agreed.[47] John Wesley's marriage to Mary Vazeille in 1751 did nothing to assuage scandalmongers, since it was a notoriously troubled marriage.

Mary Vazeille might have seemed like a good match, because she was a wealthy widow, frugal, religiously minded, and held the same class and social standing as Wesley. While they did share some happy early years, their marriage became infamously unhappy and ended in separation. Wesley repeatedly stated that marriage had not hindered his traveling and preaching one iota, but Vazeille rebelled against his religious duties. Wesley wrote during his marriage, "I cannot understand how a Methodist preacher can answer it to God to preach one sermon or travel one day less in a married than in a single state. In this respect surely 'it remaineth that they who have wives be as though they had none.'"[48] Perhaps Vazeille believed he was acting too much the single man. She suspected that his relationships with prominent exhorters and female laity included romantic or sexual desires, and she repeatedly embarrassed Methodists with these suspicions, which mirrored the accusations of anti-Methodists. While John Wesley had believed that his marriage would quiet critics who accused Methodists of being philanderers, his wife ironically added fuel to the fire.

What little we have of Mary Vazeille Wesley's autobiographical voice are a few notes on a small page, one obviously torn from a book and likely scribbled impulsively, perhaps while reading or on a carriage ride. Mary wrote on November 23, 1765, that she had left Bristol and knew she was expected at Sacrament taking, a service, for some time. "But as this was don only to Make people think My Husband and I whare united, when there was No Such thing, I was Convinced this was Trifling with God and My own Soul, so I received it but 3 times sin[ce]." She wrote again on December 11 and 12, "Mr. W is running after Strange Women. He Did Not Stay to Meet the Interscion, but went away with Betty Decine To Dine at the Other End of town, but was soon to get into a coach together the 13th at 11 oclock He came home I being in great grief seeing that he had no regard to Truth Nor His Caractor I cod Not help Speaking to him in a Loving Mannor to desist from running after Strange Women for your Caractor is at Stake this he resented Hily."[49]

Mary Vazeille Wesley's marriage to John Wesley likely fell apart for a number of reasons. From her side, she seemed to feel the burden of making appearances, particularly maintaining the image of a happy wife to a religious leader. Mary Wesley resented the time he spent with other women, not only at public meetings and worship, but also in private meetings in other women's homes. Betty Designe was a well-known Methodist, whose family had strong Methodist ties, but this would not have comforted Mary Wesley. John Wesley's self-righteous claim that he thought very little of any man who altered his religious duties after marriage must have irked Mary Wesley, who saw these duties as pretenses for spending time away from her with other "Strange women" whom John could not "desist from running after." She intentionally baited him by implying that this was ruining his reputation. Ironically, thanks to her vocal dissatisfaction, their marriage only undermined his status as a mature leader of a growing denomination.

In their final episode of marital discord, Mrs. Wesley had found some letters written by Methodist women to her husband, perhaps like those of Sarah Perrin, which had crossed some lines of affection, and she accused him of infidelity. His correspondences with women were warm, personal, and contained many ecstatic declarations on the women's side. As described above, they denoted an attachment to Wesley, even while they conformed to a larger Methodist vernacular in describing their relationships to Methodist preachers in intimate language. Mary Vazeille Wesley may have had cause for complaint in feeling insignificant compared to the myriad claims to Wesley's time and attention, regardless of whether Wesley was indeed "running after" other women to have extramarital affairs.[50] In the end, Wesley's marital record demonstrated to other preachers that marriage did not suit those who were religiously devoted. Their marriage also provided a powerful cautionary tale to bolster Wesley's own position on the subject of marriage: it was necessary to enter into a union with the utmost caution and to find a mate who was equally devoted to the Methodist mission.

Sarah Ryan's Case Against Marriage

Although Mary Wesley was well known in English Methodist circles in the 1750s, she has been somewhat neglected by church historians, who have been perhaps embarrassed by this rather ugly wrinkle in John Wesley's personal life. She was, after all, quite good at embarrassing her Methodist contemporaries. Not only did she give Methodist sexual mores a bad name by accusing John Wesley of infidelity, she set about to denigrate the society as a whole by exposing one of London Methodists' prominent female preachers, Sarah Ryan (1724–68). Ryan had gained prestige as an exhorter and leading female Methodist in the tight Wesleyan London circle. Mary Wesley and Sarah Ryan had shared a "great intimacy," until Mary Wesley took the liberty of pasting scandalous posters "all over" London to advertise that this "handmaiden to the Methodists" was in fact one of the worst sorts of sinners—a reprobate who brazenly presumed sanctity. Mary Wesley broke into a conference of about sixty to seventy preachers and exposed Sarah Ryan as a polygamist. She dramatically shouted, "See that Whore, who is Serving You! She hath three Husbands now alive!"[51]

This shocking publicity spurred Ryan to record her autobiography, which she dictated to Mary Bosanquet Fletcher. In her narrative, she provides a rare depth of detail about marriage and sexuality. Ryan's narrative also illustrates the complexity of Methodist temporal celibacy; her route to the state of religious celibacy was through a string of suspect marriages, including multiple counts of extramarital sex. Her account framed her past indiscretions in a sympathetic light: she was religious at the core, but misled by other impulses. Ryan painted herself as a martyr and a victim of bad marriages. Methodism provided the perfect antidote to waywardness and allowed her to abandon her third husband with a clear conscience.

As in other Methodist accounts, Ryan described herself as a religious child who had visions of God at an early age. Nonetheless, by her teenage years she enjoyed the attentions of men and "so sinned away both my Peace and Power—by becoming extravagantly fond of Dress and admiration."[52] She married a cork cutter who had a good income and gave her a lovely wedding; her friends were impressed, but Ryan was still uneasy.[53] In the end, her misgivings were well founded, as this was not a marriage made in heaven. While her husband was away on one of his frequent trips, one of his friends began to romance Ryan, saying she was a "Ruined Woman already."[54] In fact, her husband was already married, and he had tricked other women into believing that he had a sizable estate. Ryan considered the marriage invalid, but it is unclear if she legally annulled her first marriage.

Soon after this marriage dissolved, she met Mr. Ryan, a charming well-spoken Irishman. He was often away on business trips to Holland, and, in his absence, Sarah Ryan met another man, Solomon Benreken, a Jewish Italian cook for the East India Company. She alternated between these two lovers, depending on who was at port. She became engaged to Benreken, "who loved [her] Exceedingly."⁵⁵ Friends and family agreed that he was the right mate for Sarah. In many ways, Sarah considered herself married to Benreken, despite the lack of a legal marriage, and undoubtedly engaged in sexual activity with him.⁵⁶ Yet, when Mr. Ryan returned, "the moment I saw him it was as if Satan entered into me—and it seemed as if I could give me Life to have him, rather than the other."⁵⁷ She maintained in the autobiography that she desired a proper marriage to Benreken, but Ryan's hold over her was "diabolical."⁵⁸

Sarah rhetorically questioned herself in the narrative, "who is my Husband—if I knew, I would forsake all others and Cleave to him,"⁵⁹ but there were too many to reckon. In the end, "diabolical" forces overwhelmed her. One night, the devil duped her into having sex with Ryan; he called her to his sickbed and made Sarah feel responsible for his illness. She recounted that night rather dramatically, in terms that would not have surprised contemporary romantic novel readers: "He was bent on my Ruin—and affection joined with fear [crossed out by Bosanquet and written as "force"]—made me that night wholly his own!" After this point, she felt she had no choice but to marry him, even though he had abused her, given her a sexually transmitted disease, and told her mother: "Her[e] Madam take your daughter for I have had all of her I want!"⁶⁰

Her journey to Methodism began during this final unhappy marriage. Ryan had continued to abuse her and lived off her wages as a laundress and then a servant. After she began suffering from the sexually transmitted disease, she moved to an infirmary.⁶¹ There she met many young women like herself, teenagers who had had illicit affairs and were now suffering from the aftereffects. They had all become ill after men deserted them and consequently found themselves "in the ward with the Bad women."⁶² In this syphilitic ward, her evangelical life was born, and she exhorted the other young women to reform their ways. She and a fellow "Bad woman" decided to go hear John Wesley preach and "something said in my heart—This is the Truth—This is the Truth! I shall live and Die by It.... My soul was melted down before him [Jesus]—I longed to be joined to this People."⁶³ Wesley himself accepted her into Methodist society.

Yet, Sarah Ryan was still married, and her husband violently opposed her membership in this group. She suffered his abuse as a martyr: "Mr. Ryan came home again—and my sufferings were great—but Resistance was over—the Iron sinew in my Neck was broke—and I read my Sin in every Punishment, and Adored God for his Justice as well as his Mercy! quietly taking the most Barbarous Treatment!"[64] Sarah Ryan used the imagery "the Iron sinew in my Neck" to describe her pride, her iron willfulness, which was in direct contrast to the selflessness of "melting" in Methodist faith. Her continued attachment to her husband was a token of the pride she hoped to melt down. "[T]he hope of one day being happy in his affections stood as an Idol between God and my Soul—Indeed here was the gret hurt it did me—it employed my thoughts, and kept my mind from uniting Itself to GOD."[65] In 1754, she finally left her husband, and the rest of the account quickly sketched the details of becoming fully committed to Methodism and working as Wesley's housekeeper in London.

Instead of describing her exemplary actions as a Methodist saint, Ryan's narrative dwells on her struggles toward religious life, through the serial tangles of snares that cropped up in her early life. This emphasis makes sense when one considers the impetus for this narrative—defending her past polyandry from Mary Wesley's attacks. More than that, Methodist narratives tended to exemplify and glorify the insurmountable nature of obstacles to the good path. Her multiple marriages caused her to throw her hands up and declare that she had no idea who her real husband was and, even more profoundly, what to call herself. She was not clear, among her husbands, whose last name she should claim. Finding Methodism and adhering to the strictures of this religion were antidotes to this lack of self-definition. Sarah Ryan's quest to find herself in the Methodist framework was a complicated venture. As Phyllis Mack points out, the sense of religious self would seem contradictory to secular notions of agency. Mack argues that in the religious sense of agency "autonomy is less important than self-transcendence and in which the energy to act in the world is generated and sustained by a prior act of personal surrender."[66] Ryan had to surrender her attachments to her marriage, her pleasure in being attractive, and the snares of her multiple relationships with men to find her true power and religious identity.

The narrative of losing one's self and finding it again mirrored romantic themes in eighteenth-century secular literature. Ryan had an essentially good nature as a child and then lost her way rather spectacularly. In presenting herself as blameless and emphasizing the martyred aspects of her earlier life, she echoed a generic trend in novels that portrayed young women as honest, if misled, in their impulses. Polygamy and sexual duplicity in general still tapped into powerful currents in eighteenth-century society; people feared dishonesty and misrepresentation.[67] In 1748, Samuel

Richardson's *Clarissa* dealt with the themes of parental control over marriage choices and sexual duplicity. The character of the rake represented the standard form for sexual duplicity in novels that were popular on both sides of the Atlantic.[68] Women had to navigate the perilous duty of distinguishing rakes from honorable men, even when the manners of rakes and good men were identical. Novels like *Clarissa* depicted parents who were willing to forgo their daughter's happiness if the prospective husband was rich. Cathy Davidson argues that the theme of women vulnerable to both greedy parents and sexually avaricious men was important to the Revolutionary era, when women were legally and economically dependent upon their fathers and husbands.[69]

Daniel Defoe's infamous protagonist Moll Flanders had many more strikes of adultery against her than Sarah Ryan, and in gothic novels, false identity and suspect marriages were popular themes.[70] Polygamy functioned in novels as a metaphor for the barometer of the moral state of the individual, and also as a warning of instability in society more broadly. Where polygamy was possible, a slipperiness of identity was not far behind. This sort of transgression signaled a failure of the stable self, where accountability and rational truth floundered. This was particularly true of polyandrous women, who were simultaneously overturning monogamy and good women's natural inclination toward chastity.

While polygamy was a common theme in novels, it was in fact becoming less common in reality. English and American legislation necessitated the publishing of marriage banns in the late seventeenth century.[71] Wesley's attempt to force Georgia colonists to adhere to the marriage laws may have been high-handed, but greater adherence to marriage laws was becoming normative throughout the Anglo-American world. Stringent licensing laws, such as the Marriage Act of 1753, attempted to ensure greater awareness and lawfulness in marriage. While these laws curtailed irregular marriages among most classes, working-class men and women like Sarah Ryan retained freedom in marriage and were more likely to marry and separate from their husbands outside of the church and law.[72]

Ryan's autobiography made the case that a bad marriage was likely to draw an unsuspecting woman into sexual sin and the loss of her true self. Mr. Ryan doubles as evangelicalism's devil and romanticism's rake in Sarah Ryan's self-narrative. Luckily for Sarah Ryan, unlike the popular tragic heroines such as Richardson's Clarissa and Susanna Rowson's Charlotte Temple, she was not left pregnant or dead, but redeemed. The source of her redemption was not the love of a good man, as Richardson's *Clarissa* suggested, but the love of God. She had a vision in 1757, three years after leaving her third and final husband, that she was a teenage bride who was ready for her bridegroom Jesus "all white and beautiful." She concluded that she found everything in him, "A God, a Saviour, a Friend, a Father, Brother Husband; and Oh! My all in all!"[73] This ecstatic statement echoed the feeling of other female celibates, particularly Sarah Crosby, who had stated after the dissolution of her own marriage, "I need no man, who all possess, In Jesu's heart-felt love."[74]

The Case for Celibacy

Rather than risk an unsuitable marriage with someone who lacked religiosity, some eighteenth-century Methodist women and men chose to remain single. Women could choose to delay marriage or avoid it altogether if they wanted to exhort or devote themselves to Methodist fellowship, and they used their spiritual calling to combat family pressures to marry. Prominent Methodists practiced temporal celibacy when they were most active in the movement. Women from all classes could remain single in England and to a lesser degree in America, by working in various Methodist households as household managers, servants, and secretaries alongside their roles as Methodist exhorters.

Methodist literature lauded members of the Methodist family who died unmarried and celibate. For example, Mary Bosanquet Fletcher immortalized her adopted daughter, Sarah Lawrence (1759–1800), whom she described as an eternal child and obedient to a fault. Lawrence lived out her years under Fletcher's roof and became the leader of children's meetings at Madeley, Fletcher's estate.[75] Her children's meetings were one of the few examples of Methodist religious organization aimed at children, which is fitting given her image as an eternal child. After Englishwoman Sarah Crosby's husband had deserted her when she was only twenty-seven, she lived most of her life celibate, traveling, preaching, inspiring, and organizing Methodists.[76] Sarah Crosby drew a circle of unmarried, dedicated women around her, including Mary Bosanquet (who was celibate for most of her life) and Sarah Ryan. Ann Cutler, who was also known as the "Praying Nanny," was celebrated for her intense personal piety, praying upwards of a dozen times a day.[77] She exhorted in the Yorkshire and Lancashire region, and, after she died in 1795, William Bramwell praised her as "simple and artless."[78] All of the women in these connections were Mothers in Israel, women who devoted their whole lives to the cause of spreading evangelical fervor, inculcating spiritual development in others, and organizing Methodist societies. They were preachers, exhorters, travelers, and tireless workers for the Methodist cause in ways that their married sisters would have found very difficult, if not impossible.

Male itinerants on both sides of the Atlantic provide the most common examples of this phenomenon of temporal celibacy. Itinerant preaching was a calling for young men who could remain unattached for economic, practical, and spiritual reasons. Male itinerants were explicitly encouraged to remain unmarried; Wesley made it clear to many English preachers that celibacy was a prerequisite to retaining one's circuit. Historian Nathan Hatch has called American Methodist itinerants a "stern fraternity," arguing that the trend toward celibacy was even stronger among Americans than the English.[79] For instance, there was the overwhelmingly unmarried group who attended the "Bachelor Conference," Virginia's Annual Conference in 1809, where only three of the eighty-four preachers present were married.[80] Hatch notes that about 25 percent of Methodist preachers in England were unmarried, compared to 75 percent of American itinerants during the same period.[81]

The difficulty of comparing English and American rates of celibacy is highlighted when we study only itinerants and when we consider only a particular time period. Hatch's comparison includes only "functioning itinerants," which presumably excludes localized preachers. Localized preachers were those who gave up their circuits, usually for the purpose of establishing a family and a home. Annual Conferences in England were more likely to include married ministers by the beginning of the nineteenth century, yet throughout the eighteenth century, unmarried preachers were more common than married preachers in England. In America, unmarried preachers continued to be the leaders of the conferences well into the nineteenth century. However, because of the pattern of temporal celibacy, understanding these comparisons can be difficult. When one looks at a snapshot of the type of itinerants functioning at the peak of their traveling and preaching, one is more likely to find a celibate preacher. When one looks at the same preacher throughout his lifetime, one is more likely to find a period of celibacy and a period of marriage and localization, in both England and America. It was a common pattern to itinerate for five to fifteen years, then marry and become a local preacher, though some also continued to travel. About two-thirds of American preachers in the late eighteenth and early nineteenth century became married after some time on their circuits.[82]

The stakes were high. By choosing to locate, preachers lost their power within the Annual Conference, as many Methodist preachers discovered through the late eighteenth and early nineteenth centuries. Of the 1,616 preachers who joined the American Methodist connection before 1814, just over half had located.[83] Preachers who located or left the itinerancy were at risk of losing the respect and closeness of this fraternity of religious brothers. Nathan Hatch surmises that young itinerants were often "contemptuous of their elder colleagues who had been forced to locate." In this case, "elder" meant over thirty years of age, when itinerants were likely to feel the wear and tear of circuit preaching, the urge to settle down, or the desire to marry.[84] Hatch writes, "Asbury's system simply did not allow halfhearted participation. If a preacher chose to 'locate' for reasons of marriage or convenience or was forced to do so for reasons of health, he forfeited the right to full membership in the Methodist Connection."[85] American preacher William Colbert (ironically, on the eve of his own decision to marry) chastised a young preacher, Samuel Budd, for failing his duties and marrying. In 1804, Colbert was on his Maryland circuit, preaching with Budd who was still a teenager but "apparently very zealous and had been useful." Colbert talked about Budd's decision to marry as a betrayal of the fellowship of single itinerant preachers around him "unto whom he appeared to be united in heart." How then could he marry Liza Ross, a young woman who had only joined the Methodists after Budd began preaching in her neighborhood? Colbert blamed Ross for taking Budd away from his business, after a short courtship, which lacked the requisite "righteousness" in purpose. Colbert pronounced with indignity, "I look upon such men to be a disgrace unto the ministry, and I should not wonder if the curst of God was to follow such men as would leave the work of God for the sake of a woman."[86]

Methodist preachers had additional incentives to remain celibate, because their lifestyle and economic means made them ill-suited for marriage. Wesley and other preachers argued it was simply too difficult to maintain a family on a preacher's salary, and conflicts of priorities were inevitable. American Methodist leaders preferred young men who could do the hard work of connecting widely separated American communities on horseback. Freeborn Garrettson, for instance, claimed he traveled over

100,000 miles between 1776 and 1793, before he married Catherine Livingston.[87]

American Methodist bishop Francis Asbury, who rarely agreed with Wesley on anything, also denigrated marriage for Methodist preachers, while maintaining that it could be good for regular laypeople. Asbury's hard line on the celibacy of preachers was mirrored in his own practice. As historian John Wigger's work on Asbury has revealed, Asbury was a tireless traveler and allowed himself few luxuries, preferring cheap horses and saddles. Wigger found that for much of Asbury's career he visited almost every state annually and traveled more than 130,000 miles on horseback over the course of his life. Married life would not have allowed such constant itinerancy.[88] Asbury was fairly exceptional in his lifelong commitment to celibate itinerancy. But like his female counterparts in England, he saw celibacy as the only answer to continuing his work as an evangelical and he found greater satisfaction in the Methodist family. As Wigger writes, "The church was his family, and he viewed its women as mothers, sisters, and near cousins, but not potential romantic partners."[89]

When American bishop Thomas Coke married in 1805, he was fifty-seven and he implored American preachers to let him remain bishop even while traveling less for the sake of his "delicate" wife, but they refused. The primary reason was the disaffection between Coke and American preachers, but there was also strong opposition to the idea of a married preacher being bishop.[90] In response to Coke's marriage, Asbury wrote, "Marriage is honourable in all—but to me it is a ceremony awful as death." Asbury justified this rather dramatic statement by surmising, "we have lost the traveling labors of two hundred of the best men in America, or the world, by marriage and subsequent location."[91] The preachers were also opposed to Coke's remaining in his position after marriage. In 1806, every preachers' conference met and came to the same conclusion, that Coke was no longer a leader of American Methodists. The Baltimore conference accused Coke of making competing "engagements without our knowledge or consent," presumably by remaining in England with his wife. The conference continued, "It is not our wish to debar any of our Bishops or Preachers from entering into matrimonial or other engagements if they think it right; but if they do, and thereby disable themselves from serving us in the respective relations," then the preachers felt entitled to replace their bishop. In 1808, the General Conference of Methodist preachers announced that Coke had officially resigned the episcopacy.[92]

In contrast to Coke, Jeremiah Minter was a preacher whose life seemed a direct answer to Asbury's call for celibacy. Minter had come from an elite Virginia family, and when he converted to Methodism, he found that the Methodist family rejected the mores he had grown up with in the South. He first entered Methodism because he liked the prescribed strictness and self-denial, particularly in abstaining from alcohol.[93] He had to give up dueling and attending dances, turning his back on many of his pastimes and friends.[94] He became a preacher in 1787, traveling on various circuits in Virginia.[95] After three years of preaching, he decided to remain celibate and never marry. He had been facing temptations in his single life, and he thought about how to end his struggles and commit himself to God. His conclusion was to undergo castration in 1791. His radical solution for sexual temptation meant he could "serve Christ's kingdom in this world without the allurements and entanglements of marriage, and lay up my treasures in the future and Eternal kingdom of Heaven, in doing spiritual good to immortal souls . . . being more entirely devoted to a holy, and heavenly minded life."[96] He became, as he described it, "an eunuch for the kingdom of heaven's sake."[97] These words echoed the exact phrase that John Wesley had used to extol the virtues of celibacy in his 1743 *Thoughts on Marriage and a Single Life*.

As far as we know, no American Methodists followed Minter's example; there was no wave of preacher castrations in the late eighteenth century. In fact, Methodist leadership discouraged anyone from thinking of Minter as a model Methodist. Methodist leaders barred Minter from preaching in 1791. In the end, Minter felt like an outcast from Methodism; he felt betrayed by the group that seemed to lead him to this extreme act.[98] While Frances Asbury felt some sympathy for Minter, he sought to avoid having Methodism associated with this extreme behavior. Asbury and other Methodists feared their critics would conclude that Methodists were so hypersexual that they had to resort to castration in order to keep their bodies pure.[99]

Minter's story underlines the fact that Methodists did not have an easy time committing themselves to celibacy. There were certain risks and obstacles in remaining celibate, primarily the risk of committing a sexual sin. Marriage for all Protestants was a religiously sanctioned outlet for sexuality, while remaining celibate meant all sexual actions and desires carried the stigma of sin. Some celibate Methodists lived in constant fear of sexual temptations toward sin. English preacher John Valton wrote in his journal that he feared that he would be fostering sinful desires and even adultery if he did not marry. He felt tempted by the opposite sex, while he remained unmarried. "I carried it before the Lord, and begged He would shew me, if He had not delivered me from Sin; and whether it was expedient that I should marry."[100] While celibacy was ideal, Wesley agreed that it was difficult to maintain for one's entire life. He wrote, "A clear conviction of the superior advantages of a single life certainly implies a call from God to abide therein; supposing a person has received that gift from God. But we know, all cannot receive this saying: And I think none ought to make any vows concerning it; because, although we know what we are, and what we can do now, yet we do not know what we shall be."[101] Wesley seemed understanding in this passage, allowing for human desire and natural flux. Yet, he was inflexible when he considered those who ignored their "gift from God" and wantonly (as he saw it) entered into marriages.

When Chappell Bonner wrote to a fellow Methodist in 1810, he reported of his local Methodist preacher in Kentucky: "Mr. Sandford is going to be Married Which is very strange to me, as I thought he thought of nothing but preaching, however he is nothing but a man is going the way of all men."[102] Bonner's dismissal of Sandford is clear in his phrase "nothing but a man." This was a surprise to him, because, after all, preachers were not supposed to reveal these sorts of base desires; preachers were above being men. Celibacy was in fact so widely supported among Methodists—and itinerants in particular—that in 1816 an English preacher felt it necessary to defend marriage in his sermon in Stafford. He demonstrated its biblical and divine basis. "Marriage is honorable in all men," he quoted from the Bible. He continued, "All men of all ranks may enter into this state, without any discredit to themselves or to their character."[103]

Conclusions

When Luke Tyerman, a prominent nineteenth-century biographer of Wesley, came across Wesley's *Thoughts on a Single Life*, he wrote, "This is a queer tract; and the less said about it the better. A man holding such sentiments had no right to have a Wife; and yet Wesley declares; 'My present thoughts upon a single life are just the same they have been these thirty years, and the same they must be, unless I give up my Bible.' "[104] The serious consideration and practice of celibacy by Wesley and other prominent Methodists was clearly disturbing to Tyerman as an early Methodist historian. Yet, celibacy was as serious to Wesley as the Bible, and it was important to other Methodists as well. The practice of celibacy was strongest on both sides of the Atlantic during the eighteenth century, but it also remained a significant trend through the first decades of the nineteenth century, almost a century after Methodism was founded.

What purpose did celibacy serve for eighteenth-century evangelicals? The answer was different for men and women. For some women, Methodism was a helpful escape from the trap of bad marriages. Bad marriages in women's accounts shared some key similarities: husbands were abusive and they actively prevented or distracted wives from participating in religious meetings. In some cases, women were in social and economic limbo, after the desertion of a husband or lover. There were few accounts that illustrate the opposite idea, men trapped in bad marriages to spiritually inferior or abusive spouses, though John Wesley's marriage to Mary Vazeille provides a high-profile, rare exception. In this way, women seemed to be more vulnerable to the circumstances of secular distractions, or they required more nurturing of their religious lives. Economically trapped by English laws in the eighteenth century that denied married women's ability to own property, women had real cause to feel imprisoned by bad marriages. Evangelical work gave some women the option to continue their lives as single women, unattached to particular men, but thoroughly embedded in the Methodist family.

Celibate sisters were more likely to become Mothers in Israel than their married counterparts. Most examples of women who were seen as spiritual leaders, independent of men, were women who had practiced temporal celibacy. The higher number of Mothers in Israel found within English societies, compared to American groups, has a direct correlation to the higher incidence of celibate Methodist women in England than America. Another factor associated with this difference is that there was a stronger employment network within English Methodist societies, where women could be housekeepers and religious organizers associated with Methodist centers like the Foundery in London or Bosanquet Fletcher's homes in Leytonstone and Madeley. The possibility for women's independent religious authority posed an interesting outlet for spiritually gifted women in English Methodism. It is an example of the ways in which eighteenth-century Methodism challenged traditional modes of both authority and allegiance.

How much was celibacy a truly radical challenge to Anglo-American society? Regarding preachers, some have argued that celibacy was simply the handmaiden of necessity. Methodist historian John Wigger argues that the first generation of Methodist itinerants was celibate due to the circumstances and demands of the circuits, not for any considered religious reasons. According to Wigger, eighteenth-century Methodists were more zealous than their mid-nineteenth-century counterparts and were therefore "willing, at least for a time, to sacrifice all in their quest to evangelize the nation."[105] However, Wigger contends that this did not mount a real challenge to the contemporary social order. He wrote, "The celibacy of the itinerants was never an overt attempt to redefine sexual relations and the family, but rather a matter of pragmatic expediency during the movement's most volatile, formative years. When the immediate need for celibacy faded, so too did the practice among Methodist preachers."[106]

Methodist celibacy served an undeniable pragmatic purpose for unattached itinerant preachers and exhorters. It was much easier for circuit riders to remain celibate than to marry; the most important obstacle to marriage for any itinerant was the absolute poverty wages paid to preachers. Yet, there is some evidence that this movement made an overt attempt to redefine sexual relations and the family. For many preachers, the more profound reason for not marrying was the radical opposition to marriage mounted by Methodist leaders, preachers, and laity.

Methodists' considerations of celibacy were significant because this trend underlined the willingness of Methodists to put their individual desires aside to serve the religious family and to prioritize their religious membership over personal comforts or starting a family. On the whole, celibacy confirmed the ability of Methodists to make their own decisions and to put themselves at odds with the predominant culture and parental pressures to marry and have children.

Chapter 6

"The Whole World Is Composed of Families"

Eighteenth-century popular literature characterized Methodists as being home wreckers or antifamily, at least in the conventional sense.[1] One reason for this association was the way that converts left behind their families' traditions and committed themselves to a new religious family. When it came to the decision of marriage, converts tended to further diminish parental authority by relying upon their own interpretations of divine authority and seeking advice from others in the Methodist family. Rather than give primacy to the nuclear family unit, early Methodists more commonly counseled individuals to resist pressures from oppositional parents or friends.

Evangelicals questioned the purpose of marriage and family formation in the context of designing their ideal socioreligious order. Despite the numerous Methodist arguments against marriage, many eighteenth-century evangelicals married and made their own families. Even as individual families became more prevalent within the larger Methodist family, late eighteenth-century Methodists continued to describe marriage as a deliberative quandary. It was not easy for many prominent Methodists to make this decision, since many saw it as compromising their religious goals. Nevertheless, some Methodists mounted a counterargument to the holy calling of celibacy by asserting that marriage brought them to higher levels of religiosity. By the end of the eighteenth century, there was a growing practical necessity for thinking further about evangelical families as a whole. While early Methodism had been focused on the individual convert, the challenge for maturing Methodist societies was how to mesh individual Methodist families into the wider Methodist connection.

Throughout the eighteenth century, Anglican and Presbyterian ministers promoted family prayer as a practice in various pamphlets and books.

These works decried a declension in family-centered worship, beginning in the 1730s through the 1760s, during the rise of evangelical revivalism in England and America.[2] Many of these works called upon family patriarchs to bring order to disordered, religiously splintered, or disaffected households. In the evangelical context, though, the disaffected family, who only nominally belonged to a traditional church, was exactly the opening that evangelicals hoped to breach, drawing individuals away from their traditional religious practices.

As a contrast to the Anglican literature on family worship in the eighteenth century, no eighteenth-century pamphlets were directed at Methodist families, instructing fathers, mothers, and children on proper relationships and religious practice. Instead, Methodists gave the responsibility of addressing family worship to the preachers. In the late eighteenth century, preachers were at the forefront of the movement to acknowledge the centrality of families to Methodist growth. Preachers repeatedly described leading family prayers when staying in American and British Methodist households on their circuits. In 1780, American Methodist leaders instructed preachers to make a concerted effort to use their position as lodgers within evangelical families as an opportunity to increase family spirituality by speaking to individual family members and praying with them. In 1784, the American Methodist *Discipline* marked American Methodism's first foray into converting whole families instead of individual souls by making "family religion" a priority. In 1798, the Methodist *Discipline* called for preachers to pay particular attention to families: "[t]he whole world is composed of families. A traveling preacher may bring as many souls to glory by his fidelity in the families which he visits, as by his public preaching."[3] Family prayers were intimate forms of worship that took place at the close of day, gathering the whole family, including servants, in order to read the Bible and pray together. In the Methodist family, when preachers stayed in households on their circuit, preachers led the family prayer in the place of the fathers, and in the eighteenth century, these preachers were oftentimes unmarried.

Methodists also began to pay closer attention to the inculcation of children into Methodist practice and belief. Children had always been a part of the Methodist mission, through the familial institutions of orphanages and schools, particularly Wesley's Kingswood School in Bristol, founded in 1748. In the late eighteenth century, preachers began to focus more on children who were born into Methodist families. In 1763, Charles Wesley turned his poetic skills toward a hymnbook composed for children. Though, the themes were clearly still quite adult, including a hymn titled "Of Hell," which warned:

> Dark and bottomless the pit
> Which on them its mouth shall close:
> Never shall they 'scape from it:
> There they shall in endless woes
> Weep, and wait, and gnash their teeth,
> Die an everlasting death.[4]

In 1779, the minutes of the American Methodist preachers' conference at Fluvanna, Virginia, included a short reference to the idea of families. It asked, "What shall be done with the children?" The answer was for preachers to "[m]eet them once a fortnight and examine the parents with regard to their conduct toward them."[5] There was nothing about the design of any sustained instruction, and, indeed, eighteenth-century preachers' journals contain scant reference to instructing children.[6] The English Methodist *Discipline* included more detailed ideas about children, suggesting that preachers meet with children's classes in their circuit, whenever there was sufficient number. By the nineteenth century, there was a standard plan to catechize children weekly, but the concept of Sunday school was not included in the *Discipline* until 1828. Methodist Sunday schools were not fully established until the 1840s.[7] In America, the *Discipline* similarly enlarged this theme year after year, modeling itself after the English Methodist plan for increased involvement with evangelizing children.[8]

Domestic religious life changed remarkably over the course of the eighteenth century. For the first half of the eighteenth century, ministers who sounded the call for family religion sought to redress the failure of religious patriarchy on the family level by reinstituting the father as religious paterfamilias.[9] In contrast, by the close of the eighteenth century, the call for conversion was not aimed specifically at fathers, but at families. Evangelical groups mirrored the shifts made in the standing churches by shifting from a focus on the individual to family religious practices in the late eighteenth and early nineteenth centuries. Post-Revolutionary American Baptists settled into their domestic routine, disciplining disorderly men and women away from their expressive roots toward a more placid domestic religious practice.[10] By the beginning of the nineteenth century, English and American Methodists began to reflect the wider societal attention to the family as central to religious life.

John B. Matthias described his marriage to a fellow Methodist in 1790, as a boon to his religious life. He wrote in his memoirs, "I now was in my twenty forth year, and thought proper to alter my situation for I thought I could serve God better in a married state, then a singel one, and the Lord knows that I had no other motife in getting maried then the glorey of god and his cause, accordingly I mad my [advances] to one sarah Jurvis a member of the mathotist chursh . . . and at our wading too of the gests ware powerfullay awackent, and be fore thay whent home I had the plaser of praing for them, that the Lord might convert thar souls."[11] This description underscored the solemnity, gravity, and holiness of Methodist weddings. In Matthias's account, evangelical weddings could double as revivals.

Matthias characteristically sought to portray himself as an earnest Methodist. He had begun his adult life in Philadelphia as a carpenter, and when he joined the preaching ranks in 1793, he was already married. While Matthias portrayed the wedding ceremony as a powerful tool for conversion, he was also clearly defensive about his status as a married preacher. Matthias described the courtship in serious terms, reiterating that his first priority was his religious purpose. His defensive posture stemmed from the fact that celibacy was still prevalent among circuit preachers in the 1790s, and the American preachers' conference particularly expected its leaders to be celibate.[12] Getting married, in Matthias's account, was a serious decision and demanded nothing less than understanding God's intentions for his life.

As Methodists argued, ultimately, potential spouses, parents, and preachers did not determine who made a good match, God did. If God was the ultimate authority, who was capable of interpreting God's will? English Methodist Sarah Crosby advised a fellow Methodist that God was the supreme deliberator in the case of marriage. Crosby wrote, "One thing that you want my dear is to be Loved from the most refined desire of any Creatures loving or preferring you: So will you find [thine] inward rest. It is the Lord alone that can unite hearts. If you desire union with any one, pray the Lord to give it, if he See it will be for good, &, if he does not, rest contented."[13] God was the final adjudicator. Yet, while Methodists' decisions rested on God's approval, their own religiosity empowered them to interpret God's will. The subject of marriage raised issues of authority, both internal and external, both heavenly and earthly.

Many historians have concluded that the eighteenth century saw a shift toward couples' making more independent decisions regarding marriage partners. As individual choice became more prevalent, the standard narrative asserts that love replaced economic motives for marriage. Separate studies by Daniel Scott Smith, Nancy Cott, and Carl Degler confirmed that late eighteenth-century America experienced a period of transition toward the ideal of love as the basis for marriage. A parallel movement occurred in English society in the eighteenth century.[14] Up to 75 percent of English marriages were based on love matches by 1780.[15] On both sides of the Atlantic, historians have contended that the degree of parental involvement waned as individualism and love matches rose. Yet, this shift was not stark; eighteenth-century romantic matches did not suddenly push aside the mode of parental or pecuniary concerns in marital choices.[16]

Some histories of the family have stressed religious authority as coincident with parental authority, but Methodists complicate this easy association in many ways. Lawrence Stone argues that secular English society asserted romantic views of love, while theological arguments refuted love as the basis for marriage in the late eighteenth century. The tide could not be turned, though; in Stone's narrative, romanticism triumphed over these religious strictures.[17] Yet Stone also presents evidence that religious groups may well have helped to assert a shift toward individual marital choices. Seventeenth-century Puritans had emphasized that marriage was a covenant of love. In the eighteenth century, dissenting religious groups like the Methodists led the way in asserting the right to select marriage partners.[18] By analyzing the advent of sensibility and the key Methodist contributions to romantic expression in the form of ecstatic language, bodily sensation, and experiential religion, it becomes difficult to separate the rise of romanticism from its religious roots in evangelicalism.

Marriage, like celibacy and conversion, was an individual choice, and another element that decoupled parental authority from serious life decisions for eighteenth-century Methodists. For Methodists, marital choice required deep consideration on the part of prospective partners. The unconsidered marriage was not worth having. If a convert entered into the union having consulted God, weighing the benefits of the marriage and all of the religious implications, then this was a good marriage. Methodists emphasized that good marriages required deep thinking by the prospective partners and that finding a good match was difficult. All of this deliberating on the subject made evangelicals central participants in the movement toward allowing young adults to have the predominant say in choosing marital partners. Yet, Methodists did so by portraying themselves not as individualists above all but as cautious consultants of divine authority.

Many of the models of Methodist marriage during the group's early years, 1738–1815, were of evangelical men and women who married each other, stressing that God had ordained their unions. The aggressively individualist tone of early Methodism gradually gave way to a more domesticated one by the early nineteenth century. Many early Methodist accounts demonstrated the difficulty of balancing religious duties and family duties. Yet some accounts revealed that family life enhanced spiritual development. Those who made the decision to marry often provided fairly developed arguments about the holiness of marriage, which balanced the eighteenth-century discourse on celibacy. If marriage could do great harm, it could also deliver a great boon in the right circumstances. Methodist marriages were distinct in that temporal celibacy produced a tendency toward later marriages. For instance, in Mary Bosanquet's life, celibacy was the rule, and marriage was the exception. With Mary Bosanquet and John Fletcher, the decision to delay marriage meant that there were no offspring from their eventual union, and Fletcher's death in 1785 ended their marriage after just four years.

Not all leading Methodists were childless, of course, and in the case of some prominent exhorters and itinerants, the choice to start a family mounted particular challenges to their religious lives. Freeborn Garrettson and Catherine Livingston married in 1793 and immediately had a daughter. Having only one offspring ensured that Catherine could continue her work as an exhorter and organizer, and that Freeborn could continue to preach. In contrast, American Methodists Edward and Sarah Dromgoole had several children after marrying in 1777, and this large family prompted Edward's decision to give up the life of a circuit preacher. In general, having any offspring was a considerable challenge to any preacher's ability to continue itinerating.

Marital Choices and Authority

Many Methodists maintained that the key element to a happy marriage was matching religious temperaments, preferably from those within the Methodist family. In the eighteenth-century Methodist *Discipline*, the rules for marriage were clearly stated: members could face expulsion if they married an "unawakened person." Like Baptists, Methodists explicitly urged believers to marry within the group, echoing the biblical caution: "Be not unequally yoked with unbelievers." In the *Discipline* and in American preachers' conferences, preachers were told to discourage marriage between Methodists and non-Methodists. The *Discipline* stated that laypersons should "take no step in so weighty a matter without advising the most serious of the brethren."[19] On both sides of the Atlantic, laity felt compelled to gather advice from their preachers when deciding whom and when to marry. On the English side, John Wesley was the central voice of authority on spousal choice during his lifetime, particularly controlling preachers' choices. These layers of authority mitigated the individual determination in many cases; individuals waited for divine approval, John Wesley's personal blessing, and/or the approval of other preachers.

Wesley wholly approved of Mary Bosanquet's marriage to John Fletcher in 1781, and he wrote extensively about their match in *A Short Account of the Life and Death of the Rev. John Fletcher*. Bosanquet's marriage to John Fletcher was one of the most renowned evangelical unions of a Father and Mother in Israel. Yet it was an odd pattern to follow, with a remarkably protracted twenty-year friendship and courtship before a late middle-aged marriage, which lasted only four years. Wesley commented in his account of Fletcher's life that he gave almost immediate blessing to this engagement, but he still felt compelled to preface the account with an apology for the fact that a prized preacher was forsaking celibacy. He wrote, "[M]any were surprised that so eminent a Christian as Mr. Fletcher should take this step. And they could hardly help think that he had lost some degree of his excellent piety."[20] Yet, Wesley felt that this was a good match. He wrote to Hester Roe in December of 1781, "I should not have been willing that Miss Bosanquet should have been joined to any other person than Mr. Fletcher; but I trust she may be as useful with him as she was before."[21] The primary consideration was that they both had religious freedom, the ability to serve in the Methodist family after marriage. In Wesley's biography of John Fletcher, he lavished considerable praise on the holiness of the wedding ceremony and the manner they entered into their marriage.

The Fletcher-Bosanquet courtship gave other laypersons a model for waiting for divine approval for their decisions. For over two decades, Bosanquet delayed and debated the question of marriage. When she was eighteen, she had committed herself to a single life, "for my present Light is to abide as I am."[22] After she incurred large debts while running an orphanage, she thought of marriage as a way out of her dire financial situation. Yet, she had a vision that she should delay marriage. In October of 1777, Bosanquet recorded a meaningful dream in her journal: "A man came to me and brought a young child Saying it is the will of God you should take and *Suckle this Child*—I took in my arms saying I will *feed it*. No replyed he *'you must give it Suck'* 'that (answered I) is impossible but in obedience I will try'—on which I put it to my Breast and but it gave me so much pain—I drew it Back and Said to the man in much distress Do take and feed it till my milk Comes then all will be well. I thought I do So in obedience and immediately two Streams of Milk began to flow from me—on which with astonishment I cryd out 'Bring me all the Children of the world for I have milk enough for them all.'"[23] Bosanquet wrote that this dream was perfectly transparent to her. God desired that she should continue her work as an organizer and preacher. Particularly, she believed the dream signified that she should subsist on her current funding for the orphanage, and her economic woes would soon pass. Breast milk became to Bosanquet the perfect metaphor for female self-sufficiency in the face of increasing pressure to marry. The ultimate irony in this imagery was probably not lost on her. She acted as "mother" to her adopted family, but she never nursed her own children.

Methodists pointedly discounted economic considerations as reasons for marrying. Spiritual concerns were paramount, their narratives stressed, but where economics were also an issue, financial windfalls confirmed divine approval of the marriage. In June of 1781, only four years after she disavowed marriage, letters from John Fletcher caused Bosanquet to reconsider her destiny regarding marriage. She continued to have financial difficulties, which she worried would prevent her marriage to Fletcher. She wrote that a letter from him had "[c]aused my mind various agitations—1. A fear least I should mistake my way, and a step out of Gods order . . . 2nd I cannot see how it can be unless my affairs are settled first 3rd Should he not be happy with me: how miserable Shall I be and I don't seem Either to have *grace* enough or *Since* enough to be suited to such a one as him. Lord shew me what to do—and do thy will upon me."[24] John Fletcher was a well-known spiritual luminary among early Methodists and was lionized as the spiritual father of Methodism for providing some of the more graceful writings on Methodist religiosity, which were widely read by early English and American Methodists. Bosanquet was an independent and powerful presence in Methodist networks. Would marriage compromise her ability to be a leader? The financial issues were part and parcel of these apprehensions, since she needed money to maintain her orphanage, the Madeley chapel, and Methodist meeting places. Her financial insolvency was the final obstacle, which she begged God to remove if God approved of her marrying Fletcher.[25]

Decision making among ardent Methodists was never perfectly clear, because they framed these crucial life choices in passive language. They waited for divine interventions, signs, dreams, and visions to point the way. In this case, Bosanquet had wonderfully vivid dreams, and she relied on her friend Ann Clapham's vision to provide assurance that marriage was the right step. The decision was complex and dependent upon a third party's interior authority, and Clapham's sense of divine will. Clapham had a vision "in her mind's eye" that Bosanquet and Fletcher were indeed divided by money, but foresaw that Bosanquet's younger brother would provide the necessary assistance. This became the crucial sign in Bosanquet's narrative, when she could quiet all the questioning in her mind. Clapham's vision was confirmed by an unexpected settlement from Bosanquet's brother, which gave Bosanquet the sign that God sanctioned this union. Thus, she and Fletcher were married in November of 1781, when Bosanquet was forty-two years old and Fletcher was fifty-two.[26]

Dreams and visions were particularly powerful portals to divine will in Methodism. Evangelicals made no real distinction between visions and dreams, since both straddled the states of consciousness and both were susceptible to divine influence. Dreams were commonly seen as communications from God—the consequences of certain religious paths unfolded through imagery, metaphor, and direct example. In Methodist accounts of marriage, dreams became irrefutable instruments of conviction.

Like Mary Bosanquet, Hester Roe also interpreted dreams and signs in order to ascertain whether God approved her marriage prospects. Her sexual coming-of-age coincided with her discovery of Methodism, and she had withdrawn from the usual social activities that would lead to marriage by avoiding mixed company and shredding her finer clothes. She delayed marriage for a number of years. Even when her cousins Charles, Joseph, and Robert Roe initiated courtships in competitive bids for her affection, she resisted their advances for more than two years. She appealed to God after repeated petitions from Charles, "O Save me from every Snare—keep me Steadfast, firm and disengaged and free—Seeking All my Bliss in thee."[27]

In Roe's case, John Wesley had taken a paternal interest in her marital prospects and supported her decision to remain single. During a particularly fraught period with her cousins, she wrote about a visit from Wesley to her parish: "[H]e behaved with fatherly affection—I had never more solid comfort in his Company, never found it more profitable."[28] Wesley helped to disentangle the suitors and presumably delivered paternal talks to the cousins as well. Roe was quite happy to remain single after seeing married Methodist sisters, whose religious ardor seemed to dull after marriage. She wrote to God, "Thy loveliness my Soul hath prepossessed and left not room for any other Guest."[29]

Hester Roe did eventually consider admitting a "Guest" after befriending a couple, a Methodist minister named James Rogers and his wife Sarah. Roe became godmother to the Rogerses' last child, and she nursed Sarah Rogers, who had contracted a fatal case of tuberculosis. During her time at Sarah's bedside, Sarah asked whether she had thought of becoming James's wife after she died. Sarah stated that this idea was "the will of God and that he will bring it to pass."[30] Hester quickly determined that divine will would be tested through her parents, that is, her mother and John Wesley. This seemed highly unlikely given her mother's opposition to all things Methodist and Wesley's opposition to most marriages. If both of them agreed with this prospect, it would definitely reveal divine approbation.

Amazingly, Mrs. Roe's support came quickly after she foresaw her daughter's marriage in a dream. This dream preceded her mother's knowledge of any actual marriage plans, so her mother was providentially convinced through this dream. This was a good sign indeed, as Hester wrote, "Who but the Lord could thus have taken Away her deep prejudice and thus prepared her mind for an event which I should have expected to fill her with Grief and with resentment?"[31]

Good English Methodists like Hester Roe, among others, sought Wesley's sanction before marrying, and he was more likely to bless marriages between religious equals. Roe recounted in her journals that when the minister James Rogers proposed marriage in 1784, she waited for Wesley to visit and give his blessing. Finally, Wesley told her, "I never saw it right Hetty that you should Marry till now. As to Mr Smith [an earlier suitor] he asked if I thought he would do well to Marry *you*, and I answered yes—for I thought so—but I never thought you to have done well to Marry *him*.—but I know James Rogers is all you take him to be and I believe you will be more useful than ever if you Marry him."[32] Wesley even went so far as to set the date of their wedding, since he wanted Rogers to be stationed in

Dublin as soon as possible and sternly ordered Roe not to "hinder the Work of God" by delaying the wedding. Yet, Wesley was not only apprehensive about the marriage's effect on preaching schedules. His advice to Roe expressed a genuine concern that married women should continue their religious growth and their involvement in the larger Methodist family. Wesley would display fatherly regard, usually through letters, when he talked with Methodist women about marrying. Though Wesley was not supportive of preachers marrying, he often relented when the bride was also a devoted Methodist.

While dreams, visions, Wesley, parents, and evangelical friends centrally figured into ascertaining the rightfulness of these marriages in both Hester Roe's and Mary Bosanquet's narratives, there is little mention of discussions with the prospective grooms. Mr. Rogers was curiously absent from the decision making, as were Hester's deliberations on marrying him in particular. In writing her narrative of this final courtship, Hester recorded conversations with her mother, Wesley, her bands, her cousins, even Rogers's wife, but it would seem that Rogers himself never figures into her decision to marry! Omitting James Rogers from the narrative might have helped Hester Roe emphasize that this marriage was divinely ordained, despite the impropriety of their quick marriage after Mrs. Rogers's death. Their marriage had stirred some controversy for this reason. Thus, Roe carefully portrayed herself as following God's will in order to assuage any criticisms of her marriage as opportunistic or ill-timed.[33] The omission of the suitor, along with his desires and pleas of love, made the courtship seem devoid of any earthly passions in her narrative. It also might strike the modern reader as not just passionless, but also passive. Methodists waited for visions, God's will, others' approval, but never mentioned their own desires.

Roe's need for parental approval before marrying would have sat well with some of her eighteenth-century contemporaries. The rules governing spousal selection in this period were shifting, and parental approval was still central to the success of a match. Parents were instrumental in determining the suitability of the match, in terms of economic and social standings of the partners. Of course romantic love was rising as a central theme of marital happiness, but the economic standing of the prospective spouse was clearly consequential in the ultimate fitness of the match.[34] In the American South, where Methodist societies were espousing the idea of individual conscience guiding both religious and marital decisions, Methodists commonly ran into staunch opposition. Christine Heyrman suggests this was because the American South clung to more traditional ideas about parental authority.[35]

In Methodist practice, there seemed to be a conscious bridging of the two models of love-based marriages and parental authority in matchmaking, and this echoed the broader sense of balance regarding marital choice in eighteenth-century Anglo-American society.[36] On the one hand, Wesley had dissolved the tradition of giving away the bride in the marriage ceremony. Yet, despite this revision of the traditional Anglican ceremony, Wesley insisted that Methodists seek parental approval before marrying. He wrote, "See how necessary it is that children should take their parents consent with them in marriage; and how *unjust* they are to their parents, as well as *undutiful*, if they marry without it; for they *rob them* of their right to them, and interest in them, and alienate it to another fraudulently and unnaturally."[37]

Wesley emphasized the filial duty to keep parents central in one's life choices. In 1768, he encouraged one woman to marry her choice but added that her parents had to agree: "without this there is seldom a blessing."[38] When preacher Elijah Bush asked if he should marry without his parents' approval, Wesley replied, "I was much concerned yesterday when I heard you were likely to marry a woman against the consent of your parents. I have never in an observation of fifty years known such a marriage attended with a blessing. I know not how it should be, since it is flatly contrary to the fifth commandment. I told my own mother, when pressing me to marry, 'I dare not allow you a positive voice herein; I dare not marry a person because you bid me. But I must allow you a negative voice: I will marry no person you forbid. I know it would be a sin against God.' Take care what you do."[39] In this letter Wesley found a middle ground between complete filial duty and free choice. It was up to the children to select their own mate, but their parents should still hold veto power. As John Wesley had advised another preacher who was disappointed by his fiancée's parents ultimately voting the match down, "I hope you are able to say, 'Lord, not as I will, but as Thou wilt' . . . I hope you will think of it nor more, but will be now more unreservedly devoted to God than ever!"[40] Wesley's position was not merely a confirmation of parental powers in spousal selection, but a confirmation that parental obstruction could be a sign of God's ultimate will in the matter.

Methodist narratives and Wesley's writings introduced a new primary consideration for marriage, the spiritual match. Matching religious ideals was the most important factor and should reign over any other consideration. Wesley believed that parents forfeited any say in their children's marriages when parents tried to promote a match for financial gain rather than spiritual benefit. Wesley wrote in his sermon "On Family Religion," "[I]f you are wise, you will not seek riches for your children by their marriage. See that your eye be single in this also: Aim simply at the glory of God, and the real happiness of your children, both in time and eternity. It is a melancholy thing to see how Christian parents rejoice in selling their son or their daughter to a wealthy Heathen!"[41]

Wesley and leading Methodists affirmed this commitment to the importance of religious matches in Methodist preachers' conferences in England and in the American *Discipline* in 1789. The official line was still cautious. Generally, a woman should not marry without the consent of her parents. However, there were exceptions: if "[a] woman be under a necessity of marrying" or if "[h]er parents absolutely refuse to let her marry any Christian; then she may, nay, ought to, marry without their consent. Yet, even then, a Methodist Preacher ought not to marry her."[42] In many individual cases, Methodists overturned family opposition to marriages or tempered parental power. In 1799, South Carolinian Methodists expelled a couple from their society, because they had interfered with their child's spousal choice for illegitimate, probably economic, reasons.[43]

Family resistance was the central obstacle to the courtship between Freeborn Garrettson and Catherine Livingston. They met in 1789, but they had a protracted courtship because Catherine's mother was opposed and they needed to sway her. Their decision to marry was as tortured as many other godly unions in which the decision to marry was left to divine providence. However, Catherine Livingston was convinced that this was the right choice and would win in the end. Like Bosanquet and Roe, her spousal selection was backed by divine providence in the form of dreams. Livingston dreamed in May of 1789, "I was with Mr Garrittson in a scene of confusion and hurry, but were at length seated in a room, which a maid servant was washing. We had a long and interesting conversation. All that I remember is this. I told him he had great obstacles to encounter, and I doubted wether there was one in the family that would not oppose his pretentions. I thought he looked in my Face and smiled, which look expressed tho he said nothing. 'He that is for us is greater than all that are against us.'"[44]

As the movement progressed, religious authorities within the group, leaders like Wesley, Asbury, and other preachers, had less to say about whom the laity married. Laypersons were less likely to feel compelled to marry within the Methodist fold, though leaders recommended this throughout the eighteenth century. In 1804 the Methodist *Discipline* recommended endogamous marriages but did not advise expulsion in cases of Methodists marrying outside the group.[45] In general, this confirmed the largely ecumenical movement of nineteenth-century Methodists, especially American Methodists. In the 1800s, revivals and camp meetings attracted evangelicals of every variety, and this would seem to confirm that the Lord was "no respecter of persons," and so neither was the heart.

Charles Wesley's Case for Marriage

Although John Wesley had mixed feelings about the benefits of marriage, other leading Methodists were more positive on the subject. Charles Wesley advocated marriage, maintained positive and compassionate correspondence to married Methodists, and used his partnership with Sarah Gwynne Wesley as an exemplar of the benefits of married life.[46] As John Johnson wrote to Charles, "By the Happiness I have with my own Partner; I often, say, I know two Happy marriages at least; yours is one and my own is another, for this I desire to Praise the Lord also."[47] Charles exclaimed in his journals that his wedding "was a most solemn season of love! Never had I more of the divine presence at the sacrament."[48] His statement revealed his belief that God sanctified his marriage but also that marrying was an inherently religious action.

While John Wesley was a spiritual father figure for many Methodists, his brother Charles Wesley provided a warmer, more sympathetic father figure to married Methodists in particular. In the early years of Methodism, Charles Wesley had established his ability to gather and organize the spiritual accounts of Methodism's first converts, providing a sympathetic, fatherly ear that allowed converts to openly share their spiritual successes and shortcomings.[49] Through the 1740s, Charles was as important as John in the early leadership of English Methodist societies.[50] In Henry Rack's biography of John Wesley, he notes that John and Charles significantly differed in "one important and perhaps fateful respect"—in their attitude toward marriage and their choice of marriage partners. Biographer Frederick Gill remarks as well, "In nothing did the brothers differ more than in their approach to marriage. John sailed recklessly into it (after several near shipwrecks), but Charles came to it naturally. John was secretive, where Charles was open. John married a vixen, but Charles had the sense to choose a good wife."[51] In denigrating John Wesley's spousal choice, Gill was not alone. Many historians have blamed Mary Vazeille Wesley as the "vixen" for making this marriage a shipwreck.[52] However, it was a combination of Mary Vazeille and John Wesley's temperaments that resulted in such a different outcome from Charles Wesley's more peaceful marriage.

Charles did not have the same wrestling with human nature as John; Charles left behind no parallel, extended expositions on his doubts about marriage or whether holiness precluded sexuality.[53] While John Wesley's well-known affairs with Sophy Hopkey and Grace Murray both ended disastrously, Charles only had one serious courtship, which resulted in a successful marriage. He met Sarah Gwynne while preaching in Wales in August of 1747. Her father was a prominent Welsh evangelical, so there was no objection to the match on religious grounds.[54] During their largely epistolary courtship, Charles wrote a poem:

Two are better far than one
For counsel or for fight
How can one be warm alone
Or serve his God aright?[55]

Charles Wesley, in contrast to his brother, believed sociability definitively enhanced individual religiosity. When he asked, "how can one be warm alone," he equated physical warmth and coupling with the religious warmth of evangelical bonds. Methodists were warm with religious fervor when they were on the right path, and those who married well, like Charles and Sarah Wesley, were never cold. Sarah Wesley aided her husband's ongoing religious development. In his letters, Charles Wesley, ever the poet, used romantic terms that made marital love central to his religious life. He wrote that his imminent union with Gwynne was a divine gift. In January of 1749, he wrote, "Hope & I had long since shook hands & parted; & all my Expectation was to go softly all my Days, & be saved at last as by Fire. Providence (for I can ascribe it to Nothing else) has strangely *brought* me, the Best Gift Heaven cd bestow on Man in Paradise."[56]

Like other Methodists, Charles Wesley sought his brother's approval before marriage. Soon after leaving Wales in April 1748, he began a long tour of preaching in Ireland, where he revealed his romantic plans to John

Wesley. Charles noted that John "neither opposed, nor much encouraged" his interest in Sarah Gwynne, but eventually agreed that Gwynne was a good match for Charles.[57] John was frequently called upon to serve as a mediator in the settlement of the marriage, and Charles referred to his support in letters to Sarah Gwynne during their courtship. John Wesley's support of the marriage ended up being instrumental to the successful negotiation of the marriage settlement, which relied on the proceeds from some Methodist publications to ensure Sarah's financial security.[58]

Their wedding had been indefinitely stalled due to Mrs. Gwynne's steep demands for a good marriage settlement for her daughter, but Charles Wesley seemed unflappable. Wesley felt that the Gwynnes' approval of the marriage, on any terms, was nothing short of a divine miracle. Wesley wrote, "Your dearest [mother's] *consent so far* is plainly miraculous."[59] Wesley saw the eventual resolution of parental opposition to the marriage as providential, an indication of how God supported and desired their marriage. He wrote in retrospect to Sarah, "In reading over the Passages of *our* History, you cannot think what Love I feel towards every one of *our* Family. Yr Mother, Sister, Father, Cousin's Nurse so as to deserve my Esteem & Love during Life. I look back with Delight on every step, every Circumstance in that whole Design of Providential *Love*."[60] Wesley interpreted the approval of others, particularly the Gwynnes, as the crucial sign that this union was blessed by God.

Their wedding day was clearly a religious occasion. On April 8, 1749, Charles Wesley, Sarah Gwynne, and John Wesley arose at 4 a.m. to sing and pray together. At 8 a.m., Sarah and Charles walked to the church together. Charles Wesley wrote, "We were cheerful without mirth, serious without sadness." But a passerby noted derisively that "[i]t looked more like a funeral than a wedding."[61] A small group of friends and family were present. The approval of family was evident; Marmaduke Gwynne gave his daughter away and John Wesley married them. Charles noted, "My brother seemed the happiest person among us."[62] While the wedding day was solemn, they both had a sense of humor and triumph at getting to this moment. The couple remembered the obstacles they had faced before the wedding, as they approached the door of the church. "I thought of a prophecy of a jealous friend, 'that if we were even at the church-door to be married, she was sure, by revelation, that we could get no farther.' We both smiled at the remembrance. We got farther."[63] After a hymn and prayer, they all walked back to the house for more prayer.

Charles Wesley had found a soul match, and as a prominent Methodist, he modeled the idea that marriages were based in love. His description of their marriage was that it was providential and divine, but also romantic. Charles and Sarah Wesley had overcome opposition from every corner: wealthy parents, influential brother, and even jealous friends. Providence worked in a romantic fashion, by surmounting the seemingly insurmountable obstacles to a happy union.

Charles Wesley argued that his wife strengthened his ministry.[64] Two weeks following their wedding, Charles left Sarah to do his "Master's work."[65] Wesley continued as an itinerant minister for the first seven years of their marriage, but even during separations, he was involved in the domestic life of his family. Sarah Wesley was eminently supportive of her husband's work, regardless of his lengthy absences. Still, it must have been difficult in times of particular distress, when children were being born or were sick and dying, for Wesley to be away. These were times that tested the itinerant demands of Methodist preachers and ministers. Wesley did not turn a blind eye to practical, domestic routines; he seemed to share them fully with his wife, even when separated.[66] His involvement in their family life is clear, not only in times of distress but also during the more mundane day-to-day involvements; he gave Sarah advice on child rearing and health care. Their epistolary exchange reveals the fact that they were able to remain partners, even when they were required to be apart from each other.[67]

In 1756, Wesley made the decision to withdraw from itinerancy.[68] Yet, he remained active in his ministry throughout their marriage, particularly in London and in areas surrounding his home in Bristol. Charles Wesley's abandonment of itinerancy and his difficulty organizing preachers were indicative of his waning leadership, which has often led to his being discounted in comparison to his brother John. However, one should not minimize his continuous, significant contributions to organizing and mobilizing the laity. Charles was the human side of the Wesley brothers, and his marriage and commitment to bolstering relationships within the Methodist family counterbalanced John's chilly assessment of earthly commitments.[69] Wesley conducted tremendous correspondence with laypeople, and letters were a form of itinerancy in early Methodism. Letters did their own work to knit disparate Methodist societies together, and for the laity they were often lifelines and supports between the periodic visits of itinerant ministers. Additionally, Charles was always accessible and centrally located, whether in Bristol or London, to counsel Methodist laity in person.

Marriage did not seem to be the decisive factor in limiting Charles's impact on early Methodist leadership. In fact, his marriage strengthened his ministry, as he used his experiences with domestic life to deepen his relationships with laity.[70] He was frequently sensitive and understanding on issues involving children. John Collinson wrote to Wesley on September 11, 1772, "You can weep with those that weep. But I am too much affected to detain you with Ceremony. My Children are dead."[71] Collinson wrote about the spiritual fate of the two children he had lost to smallpox and whooping cough, and he shared this news with a sympathetic Methodist leader (undoubtedly more compassionate than his brother, who had "comforted" his sister on the loss of children in a spectacularly unfeeling manner). Charles Wesley's own experience with the loss of children gave him insight to the sufferings of fellow Methodists who struggled with similar tragedies. As most married Methodist preachers would have to concede, marriage almost certainly changed their commitment to itinerancy, particularly when children were involved. If it was one of John's faults that he tried to stay above the common humanity of his followers, Charles embodied evangelical humanity, exemplified through his love and his marriage. Even though Wesley had somewhat more limited goals and could range less far than John Wesley or other itinerants, his union to Sarah Gwynne was remarkably stabilizing. Charles Wesley's romantic life and his spirituality were not divorced from or at war with each other.[72]

Marriage and the Methodist Preacher

Itinerants found obstacles to marriage in both their arduous lifestyles and the Methodist leadership. In many cases, itinerants were forced to give up their circuit or resigned after marrying. After fourteen years of itinerancy, English preacher John Valton consulted John Wesley regarding his impending engagement to Sally Rance in 1781. Wesley voiced opposition to this marriage and told him he would have to recover his health and (paradoxically) travel one thousand miles before marrying. Valton did not marry Rance (and may well have traveled one thousand miles in the intervening years), but instead waited and married widow Judith Purnel in late 1787. In this last engagement, he made no mention of consulting Wesley before his marriage. Valton knew this would irk Wesley and hoped Wesley would "pardon for my unfaithfulness to Him as a son and Servant in the Gospel."[73] Despite his submissive language, reinscribing himself as son and servant, he did not tell Wesley that he regretted the marriage, emphatically stating in his journal that this marriage benefited him spiritually and never prevented his preaching. Yet, soon after his wedding, Wesley removed him as circuit assistant.[74]

After the well-respected southern preacher Edward Dromgoole married in 1777, following only five years on the circuit, English preacher Robert Lindsay wondered if this spelled the premature end of his itinerancy. Lindsay wrote, "Present my kind respects to your Companion; tho Unknown to me, I love her for your [sake]. Have you any Children? Or is there any provision made for Married Preachers with you? Does your Wife travel from C[ircuit]! to C[ircuit]! with you? Or are you hardy enough to be *Only a Localist*?"[75] While Dromgoole did continue the itinerancy for many years after his marriage, this was a tough balancing act. Lindsay's questions implied the difficulty of giving up the itinerant life and losing the satisfaction of preaching. At the same time, the economic and family considerations for married preachers were challenging.

Ironically, Lindsay would have his own conflict between seeking preachers' approval and starting a family, when he married a year later. In 1784, Lindsay fell in love with a woman and married her against her family's wishes. He wrote to Dromgoole, clearly hoping to secure his influence:

> This union is more honourable than I ever expected to be favoured with in this world, and I assure you that a fortune of 40 pounds per annum is the one of her least Accomplishments. But—O pity me! In securing the possession of my dear companion, I have step'd aside from the Ministers of Conference. . . . Here I stand exposed to any penalty my Brethren shall think fit to inflict upon me. . . . Each of us Ventured much, but I hope to find more lenity from my Brethren than she ever likely to find from her friends. . . . I imagine abundance of bitter invectives will be sent against me, by my Wife's friends, many of whom love the Methodists almost as much as they love the Devil. From the preachers I expect honour and respect, as I trust my choice will never put them to shame, tho' I suppose some of them will affect to blame the mode I pursued.[76]

Itinerant preachers faced pressures from both sides of the aisle: from family and friends, particularly if the bride was not a seasoned convert, and from many of their preaching brothers, who saw marriage as a betrayal of the brotherhood.

For some itinerant preachers, the choices seemed very dramatic, but for others there was a sense of flexibility within the Methodist brotherhood. John Matthias was already married when he was appointed an itinerant preacher in 1793. He had been on a circuit in upstate New York for only two years before he left the itinerancy to settle down near his wife's family in New York City. There he worked as a ship joiner for a dozen years, before he went back to preaching. While he was in New York, his family suffered through serious illnesses, and Matthias lost his mother-in-law to yellow fever. His Methodist family remained a stalwart support system, despite his leaving the circuit. He wrote about how they helped him through the death and illnesses: "the Lord provided me menny great freands and thay healpt me so that my head was held above the water for my methodist Brethern and sisters adminesterd to me and suplied my wants o I shall never forget them."[77]

One way to measure the official approval of married preachers is to evaluate the economic support given to preachers' wives. Methodist Conferences in America and England slowly decided to give married Methodist preachers support by granting stipends for preachers' wives. Starting in England in 1775, there were allotments for preacher's wives, who had the same salary as their husbands. British Methodists paid annual salaries of twelve pounds to wives, with an extra pound for each child in the household. In England, even this paltry allowance apparently led to a shortage of funds by 1780, when John Wesley declared that they would admit no more married preachers, "unless in defect of single preachers."[78] In 1780, the American Methodist Conference decided to adopt a plan that was very similar that of the English, paying preachers' wives and preachers equally, but the support was left to local circuits and it was often irregularly meted out.[79] In the American connection, Methodists were barely able to provide for preachers' families and suffered from an overall lack of funds. From some reports, it is unclear that wives were routinely paid these salaries, and some districts had more generous plans for preachers' wives than others. William Burke had become a preacher in Ohio before he married in 1796. He received an annual salary of sixty-four dollars, but he had no allotment for his wife. Other preachers pressured him to give up his circuit, but Burke continued to preach his circuit until he was charged with treating an elder "with contempt" in 1813.[80] The issue many preachers faced was adequate family support, which would not be found in their meager salaries, even if doubled. In some cases, the preachers' wives resorted to moving in with their parents.[81] In other cases, preachers relied upon the fastidious, economical habits of their wives, the godly ways in which they stretched the dollar and pound to live within the means provided by the Methodist societies. More commonly, American preachers located, settling in fixed places with their families, thereby discontinuing their circuits.[82]

Aside from economic concerns, another obstacle for itinerating married preachers was the strain of emotionally supporting their wives and children from a distance, while they were preaching on their circuits. In 1798, Richard Sneath was appointed to a New Jersey circuit that was not too far from his home, a farm outside Philadelphia. He was a farmer, father, husband, and preacher. He loved preaching, but was less sure of farming as a profession. When he returned from the conference with news of his appointment, his wife was "in a fury" to hear that he had agreed to keep on preaching, because, despite the nearness of the circuit, he was gone from home for months at a time.[83] Later in 1798, when he had returned home and severely injured himself by slicing his foot with an ax, he could think of nothing but getting back to his circuit following this involuntary furlough.[84] After he left for his circuit that November, he did not return home until the next April. That summer he and his wife experienced "turbulance" and "ill humor." It is difficult not to see the cause of her "ill humor"; they had several children, and the household generally ran without his presence for most of the year.[85] When he returned one day in February 1800 to find that his daughter had given birth to an illegitimate son in his absence, he commented, "what a distress to parents to see there children take bad ways." Still, he seemed to have little to do with their ways, good or bad, and he was back on the circuit within two weeks.[86]

Like Sneath, southern preacher Edward Dromgoole experienced difficulties with maintaining balance between his home and his circuit. Unlike Sneath, he seemed more affected by the time away from his home and ultimately made the decision to give up the itinerant life and locate for the sake of his family. Edward Dromgoole and Rebecca Walton Dromgoole had eight children, but only five survived into adulthood. In 1784, he was on his Virginia circuit when two of his children became very ill, and his first son died. His wife had sent for him, but he came home to find "dear little Neddy" in a coffin and two more children near death as well. He wrote loving tributes to his son and chronicled how deeply this death affected the family. "My wife sustained the burthen, the double burthen without an helper. I came home before the Grave had closed him quite out of my sight. . . . When I walk about the house and Plantation every thing and place renews my Grief. I miss his company and sweet expressions, which was more pleasing to me than all the melody in the world. Wherever I turn I see something to put me in mind of my sweet Child; so that my trouble sleeps not. Night and day he is in my mind."[87] Dromgoole described the pain of being an itinerant, so far removed from home in crucial times like these. Three weeks after Neddy's death, his youngest child died and still another fell sick.

Like other Methodists, losing his children challenged Dromgoole's faith in God; he felt real anger at these losses.[88] As well, Dromgoole questioned the wisdom of his decision to form a family, realizing that it had opened a source of true suffering and conflict with his religious duties.[89] He thought this was a quandary particular to the married preacher's life. He wrote:

> After repeated trials it appears to me that it is out of my power to travel in a circuit[.] I never desired to do it more than of late[.] I am sensible of many Obligations I lie under both to the Preachers and People which is a strong motive to make one Ride together with a conviction of it being my Duty to preach the gospel. I find the most peace of mind when I am engaged to save Souls. But I know the calls of a Family are so great and frequent that I am often prevented and People disappointed, etc. I know not how married Preachers are to continue in the work. For if they have a fixed place they cannot go and stay, they cannot be always in the Circuits near home, nor can Men who have small Children be moving from place to place. Our Brethren who are childless may do better, May the Preachers consider this before they are entangled.[90]

Dromgoole did decide to resign as a circuit preacher officially in 1786, but he never stopped preaching altogether. His house became a central stopping place for traveling preachers and other Methodists in Virginia and North Carolina. He continued to gather conversion narratives and was considered one of the most important Methodists in Virginia until his death in 1835.[91]

Other preachers argued that marriage ameliorated the hardships of preaching. English preacher John Valton emphasized again and again in his journal that his wife was supportive of his preaching, and her tireless scrimping helped them survive on a meager allowance.[92] Thomas Lyell, who began preaching in 1790 in Virginia and North Carolina, married in 1805. He described his wife in his autobiography: "Sixteen Years I passed with this estimable woman—happier it does not often fall to the lot of Man to Enjoy[.] [H]er Steady and [constant desire seemed] to be to make al[l] around her happy and by every means in the power to promote my usefulness and respectability as a minister in the Parrish."[93] Lyell insisted that marriage and itinerancy were not contradictory, and he castigated other itinerants for not saving enough money and complaining about the paucity of their allowances.[94] Considering that Asbury had openly preferred appointing unmarried preachers for financial reasons, Lyell surely wanted married preachers to overcome this prejudice by being happy with their economic lot.

The argument for marriage was that it brought individuals into a higher level of religiosity; the tortured indecision and backsliding seemed to wane after marriage, allowing converts to attain a more stable religious state. In many cases, prominent Methodists, who had delayed marriage and had fewer children, were able to maintain their religious activity. When preachers had larger families, they were often forced to make a choice between their circuit and their family. Individual Methodist families were still knit together, as much as individuals, into the broader network. Methodist families were responsible for succoring Methodist preachers who stayed with them on their circuits, and families were further responsible for the growth of the Methodist family as a whole.

"The Family Above and Below"

The Methodist family of this world stayed connected to Methodists who had died and gone on to the next one. Methodists who had a "happy death," a death without regret and marked by the joy of anticipating salvation, could expect to enjoy Methodist fellowship in eternity. Also following death, they could expect to be in communication with their living family and friends. When spouses and close friends saw their dead partners in their dreams and visions, they provided proof of an ultimate meaning behind the mortal illnesses eighteenth-century English and American men and women experienced. Through the power of Methodist spirituality, converts were able to reach, feel, and talk to their dead relatives and friends, providing an endless circle, an infinite "communion of saints." When Mary Bosanquet lost her adopted daughter, Sarah Lawrence, she was comforted by a vision she had of her "Little Girl" in the next world. Bosanquet dreamed of crossing a river and seeing a community of believers in heaven. "[T]hen I saw two Young Women who died in the Lord sometime since and Betty Humpaces with my Little Girl and Mr. Fletcher They were in the most Lovely White I ever Saw and Mr. Fletcher held up his hands and Looked most heavenly. My Little Girl said with a Sweet voice My mummy is coming my mummy is coming. . . . O how many ways hath the Lord to comfort his children and to Let us know the family above and below are but one."[95]

Evangelical views of death extended both early modern folkloric beliefs in death as a supernatural event and puritanical beliefs in death as a sign of God's providence. As the eighteenth century progressed, English society began to discount the importance of death as a religious rite of passage; insurance practices and new secular approaches replaced God's will as the primary signification of death, a triumph of probability over providence.[96] Yet, evangelical views of death were not entirely backward looking. Methodists saw death in a decidedly eighteenth-century romantic light, as a way to keep loving, spiritual unions alive. The transatlantic evangelical views of death confirm the idea that mysticism and supernatural ideas still reigned throughout the eighteenth century. In America, this communion with saints was an important connection for African Americans who became converts, as this tradition resonated with African folk ancestral worship.[97] Death became an important moment to articulate a specific evangelical language and worldview, one that combined Methodist ideas about the love of fellowship, the ecstasy of religious communion, and a bifocal view of this world and the next.

For those who were left behind, death provided a moment to reflect on one's own readiness; for relatives and friends of the dying, their emotional response to death was a measure of their own religious state. Attachments to family members, if they were too emphatic, could signal an overinvestment in this world. Death of a family member was a religious test of one's faith in God. If the loss was particularly acute, evangelicals reminded each other to be "resigned" to God's will. Resigning oneself often meant not showing anger or questioning God. Yet, there was a balance between the emotional expression of grief and the religious resignation to God's will.

Many evangelicals did in fact dwell in the loss of their loved ones, and even questioned God as well. When the Virginia preacher Dromgoole lost his beloved child Neddy, he had a crisis of faith in that he was not willing to resign himself to this death.[98] Evangelical writings were saturated with tears, particularly the tears of men. Dromgoole was not alone in his romantic brooding over losing his child. Charles Wesley was another example of a prominent evangelical who was sentimental in writing about his children's deaths.[99] Being resigned to death did not mean being stoic, as evangelicals emphasized their feelings, sentimentality, and enduring connections to the dead family members.

Accounts of death were meant to provide a guide to the living, particularly unconverted family members. A common element of the "happy death" narrative was to illustrate how affecting the deaths of believers were to those present at their deathbeds, and to imply that their deaths would move their relatives, friends and neighbors toward conversion. Englishwoman Ann Manwaring, who died in 1800, when she was only twenty-seven, worried about the state of her husband's soul as she died.[100] Her "happy death" account related her unswerving devotion to religion.[101] She had been married at twenty-two to Charles Manwaring, after which she had a quick succession of children—four sons and one daughter in four years' time. All of the sons had died. After the narrative related this extraordinary account of loss, the author emphasized that Ann Manwaring remembered her religious duties before dying. She had important talks with each of her family members. To her husband she had an especially important message: "My dear, remember the words of a dying wife. . . . I am now on the confines of vast eternity, and I have no doubt, no fear. . . . Get your heart changed, and you will meet me in glory. Our four little ones are gone before, and I am following them to the right hand of God. . . . Would it not be dreadful if we should be separated, and you be found on the left hand of our Judge."[102] Dying Methodists commonly articulated concerns that they would be separated from loved ones on the other side. In order to be together after death, they had to be together in their religious lives. This lent even more weight to the importance of finding a religious match when marrying. This was the apotheosis of the necessity of faith, because nothing was more compelling to believers and nonbelievers than the prospect of finding or losing each other's eternal company.

Mary Bosanquet and John Fletcher were both well-known spiritual leaders in their own right when they married, so they would have no doubt about keeping each other's eternal company. Bosanquet was clearly devastated by the loss of her husband, writing that she was "exceeding sorrowfull." They had been married for less than four years, and his death was shockingly quick. In the months after his death in August of 1785, she was so depressed that she had stopped writing altogether. But in October of 1785, Mary Bosanquet Fletcher had her first vision of her husband: "one night being in great anguish of mind which I always felt sleeping as well as awake I thought I saw him coming to meet me—he ran toward me clasping me in his arms with great affection I started back crying, 'who, what is this—my dear husband is dead?' He relpyed: 'No I am not dead I live—I live!' . . . it was his dear Spirit Striving to bring me Comfort—he laid his head on my Shoulder and with the voice of tenderest pitty said—'I ant Dead I ant Dead' "[103] Her only spot of consolation in her loss of Fletcher was his repeated appearances from the other side. At first she was doubtful that these visions were real, but then she began to expect them and believed in them completely. Their marriage continued in the next realm; Mary saw her husband regularly in visions and dreams until her death in 1815. She repeatedly stroked his hand, received counsel from him, and relied on his appearances at every anniversary. While the completeness of Bosanquet's chronicle of her husband's appearances beyond death is unusual, it was not unexpected or ill-received in the evangelical community. Her ability to recall Fletcher from beyond the grave was known by others and seen as further proof of her spiritual power.[104] Although they had a short marriage, John Fletcher reappeared regularly to Mary Bosanquet from the afterlife in the twenty years that she outlived him. This was the ultimate love and soul match; he was present in life and in death.

In 1786, marking the first anniversary of her husband's death, Bosanquet set down her feelings on how marriages between spiritual loves persisted through death. She wrote:

> if it was in reallity as many suppose that seperate Spirits forget all they have known and loved here, his will be done—I was content, so my dearest love, and my own soul were Lost in His emensity and knew each other no more. . . . I then found as it were a conversation carried on in my mind—the question arose; what part of our union can heaven Desolve? Tis true it will take away all that was painfull such as our fears of each others hurt, of seperation etc., but what of the pleasant part can heaven Desolve? I answered from the bottom

of my heart *Nothing Lord Nothing* . . . it fixed in my soul an assurance of our *eternal Union* and it increased my tender affection toward my dear husband—so it seemed to [spread] it all around I felt it reflect as it were backwards and forwards to and from all the heavenly Host, all seemed dubly dear thro [that] indearing love I found to him. I did not go thro *this love* to Jesus—but *thro Jesus* to this love, in a manner far better felt than explained.[105]

Bosanquet confirmed that mourning her husband and persisting in loving him after death did not detract from her religiosity—to the contrary, spiritual unions reflected the love of God and magnified it.

Bosanquet's writings powerfully evoked the sense that the dead and the living were not in separate physical or spiritual worlds. John Fletcher was a good husband; even in death he remembered to appear on every anniversary of their wedding and of his death. Just before the third anniversary of his death, Fletcher visited her to tell her not to think about the scene of his death and the pain and suffering she must have witnessed. On the day of the anniversary itself, she had a waking vision of lying with Fletcher in his tomb.[106] On the fifth anniversary of his death, she meditated on the fact that she hoped her soul was saved, and she returned to the theme of their eternal union: "Lord are we not one? The head of the woman is the man—as the head of the man is Christ—and whom God hath joined together none can put asunder. Adam and Eve was never intended to be Seperated—and shall sin so overturn thy original design as that it cannot be restored by the Saviour—surely *No* as thou hast taken away the Sting of Sin So that part taken away—the Smart of Seperation, we are yet *one* and shall I not feel a communication from thyself passing thro that Channel? Lord make me Spiritualy minded, capable of being made to meet *to partake of the inheritance of the Saints in Light*."[107] Bosanquet, in her writings, incessantly sought some reassurance that these visits signified her own ultimate sanctification and the continued union with her husband after death. In fact, she later affirmed that she and Fletcher both felt that separation was not possible for the truly converted and that they refused to say in vows or elsewhere the familiar phrase "till death do us part" since theirs was "an eternal union."[108]

This romantic sentiment of soul mates in life and death was not limited to the bonds between husbands and wives. Bosanquet also dreamed of her first soul mate, Sarah Ryan, and was visited by her repeatedly after Ryan's death. Ryan was particularly present when Bosanquet was taking care of Fletcher in his final days in the summer of 1785. Bosanquet wrote, "Sister ryans Spirit also I have had since my affliction much Communion with— this began a few nights before my Dear loves last illness. Every night I dreamt I saw her by me and that she seemed to mourn over me. One morning before we rose I named it to my dear husband saying 'I wonder why I dream so of Sister R—— I have not done so for years." He speculated that Ryan had reappeared to comfort her for some loss, which Bosanquet saw later as a prophetic statement. Ryan had anticipated Fletcher's death and had come to comfort her.[109]

Evangelicals wrote about longing to visit their friends, their religious family, in the afterlife and about having visits from beyond the grave.[110] Bonds between the living and dead did not occur only between those who were married; intimate spiritual bonds, not just the legal ones, transformed into eternal bonds for believers. The religious family bonds between Methodists were so important, because these bonds would endure into the next realm. This could act as a powerful tool for cohesion to religious ideals, because the peril of losing one's soul was compounded by the loss of the entire Methodist fellowship for eternity.

Conclusions

The burning, melting ethos of the heart religion that Methodism promoted in its simplest form seemed in opposition to the placid and complacent domesticity of married life. Early Methodists questioned the purpose of marriage and its effect on the serious preachers and exhorters in the group. Looking over the period of the late eighteenth and early nineteenth centuries, Methodist attitudes toward marriage and family were shifting. Through the institution of marriage, Methodists negotiated the place of the individual within the Methodist family at large, alongside negotiating various levels of authority when they formed their own families. By the early nineteenth century, Methodists had begun to transform the image of their group, from home wreckers to home builders. Earlier models of ardent members, who remained celibate in the face of familial pressures, were less likely by the nineteenth century. Increasingly, marriage was a normative choice, even for preachers.

In the Methodist family, the path toward marriage was still tortuous and deliberative in the eighteenth century. While some Methodists demonstrated their careful consideration of parental authority, in other cases, parental consultation was diminished by the fact that many Methodists married later in their lives. As many eighteenth-century Methodists had separated from their families by converting, their choices to marry were less encumbered by parental directives.

Yet, Methodists never wrote about marriage or adulthood as a place for the obstinate, willful assertion of the self. Most of the narratives about courtship and marriages seemed almost to do away with considering the desires of the marriage partners. Methodists went to great lengths to emphasize how they considered the will of God over all else. Still, Methodists were also representing their own determination, by interpreting these signs, whether from parents or God. For instance, the remarkable dependency on dreams as signifiers in these narratives further underlined the power of divine will in these cases, but usually these dreams occurred to and were interpreted by the potential spouses. Methodist marriages confirmed individual sovereignty, despite the passive language, by demonstrating the individual's power in understanding God's will for their lives. As Charles Wesley looked back on their courtship, he saw "Delight on every step, every Circumstance in that whole Design of Providential *Love*." As Wesley's romantic language portrays, their language surrounding the concept of providence inculcated a sense of the importance of their spousal choices, the romantic and religious destiny behind choosing the correct soul mate.

The expressive religious language of Methodists, though countervailing eighteenth-century public discourse, was largely in tune with the nineteenth-century descriptions that imbued marital choices with a sense of romantic spirituality. Methodists' emphasis on suitable soul matches is the predominant way that Methodists contributed to the larger movement toward a romantic basis for marriage. Elements of individual spousal choice and finding spiritual matches remained and flourished in the nineteenth-century Victorian familial culture.

Chapter 7

One Family, Two Nations

In the late eighteenth century, the Methodist family grew on both sides of the Atlantic, and the transatlantic Methodist family acted as an imagined community of brothers, sisters, mothers, and fathers all working in concert to convert themselves and the world around them. In their narratives, transatlantic Methodist converts established a common language and struggled with a common set of religious and social goals for an ideal spiritual community. In the previous chapters we have seen that Methodists shared a religious culture that transcended locality. Through the eighteenth century, evangelical discourse and practice were remarkably similar on both sides of the ocean. The development of a romantic language that called for a union of like-minded evangelical souls was consistent throughout the eighteenth century. Methodists made decisions about sexuality, marriage, and family formation as individuals, but individuals who never stood apart from the larger evangelical familial network. Methodists exhibited the ways in which concepts of selfhood were changing during this period. While their language often confirmed individual sovereignty, it also confirmed evangelical submission of the individual will to divine and communal will.

This simultaneous commitment to individual and collective will was also seen in the political realm, as the Methodist family evolved through Revolutionary and post-Revolutionary developments in the Atlantic world. In this chapter, I examine how this transatlantic family dealt with questions of political organization, as the American preaching "sons" asserted themselves within the English-dominated Methodist leadership during the 1770s and 1780s. While leadership changes had started to divide the transatlantic family of Methodists politically, another significant element of difference between these two groups of Methodists was the growing number of African American Methodist converts in the post-Revolutionary period. In calling awakened sinners and redeemed alike to be active members of this family, evangelicals commonly evoked the sentiment that "God is no respecter of persons," regardless of their background, class, race, denomination, or nationality.[1] This concept underpinned the theological principle of free grace, the Arminian theology espoused by Wesleyan Methodists. In the Revolutionary and post-Revolutionary period, the ideal family was tested on these convictions. While British and American Methodists disagreed over principles of religious governance in the post-Revolutionary period, they agreed on an antislavery position that reflected the evangelical ideal of interracial unity through salvation. Historian Cynthia Lynn Lyerly frames this antislavery stance as a test of the principles of Methodist familial equality: "The rhetoric of 'brotherhood' and 'sisterhood,' so prominent in Methodism, must have rung truer for a sect whose leaders were in the main against slavery and who spoke out against physical abuse and neglect."[2] In the Revolutionary and post-Revolutionary period, the ideal evangelical family was tested on these principles. By 1790, American Methodist societies had formed a significantly biracial membership, while their abolitionist position was becoming less radical and increasingly ambivalent.

Their shared antislavery ideals were just one of the ways in which British and American Methodists remained united in their religious culture and practice, despite the fact that they adopted different leaders after the 1780s. In the 1770s and 1780s, the leadership struggles between Wesley and his American "sons in the Gospel" resulted in the establishment of Methodism as a separate denomination from the Church of England.[3] Yet, by the late eighteenth century, on both sides of the Atlantic, Wesleyan Methodism had become the predominant form of Methodist practice, and it survived challenges from various visionaries and splinter groups.

One dominant theme in American revolutionary ideology was defining the terms of the compact between rulers and followers. Many revolutionaries spoke ardently against the ideals of deference and paternalism that were the reigning modes of authority in Anglo-American culture.[4] Methodists on both sides of the Atlantic were keenly aware of Wesley's fatherly role and the deference he expected. His love of hierarchy led him to cling very tightly to his role as father to American and British Methodists until his death in 1791. Wesley promoted his ultimate authority within multiple arenas, from arranging preachers' circuits to deciding who and when Methodists should marry. His leadership was so natural, so dominant, that he held their allegiance and affection almost as unquestionably as a father would—

almost. The American sons did begin to question the rightfulness of Wesley's leadership and increasingly saw the power of "Dear Old Daddy" as anathema to republican politics, which had begun to infuse the American Methodist leadership by the 1780s. The preacher brotherhood was based on ideals of equality among preachers, ideals established within the Methodist framework. Yet, republican notions of brotherhood stood in philosophical opposition to Wesley's role as religious paterfamilias.

John Wesley did promote many democratic features in Methodism, including lay preachers, lay exhorters, bands, and classes. Yet, he was still interested in preserving a hierarchy of religious and political orthodoxy. During the Revolutionary War he wrote in favor of the monarch's rule over the colonies and against the cause of the patriots. He further commanded his American sons, the preachers, to stay out of the conflict. The conservative, often pro-monarchical politics of John Wesley complicated the establishment of Methodism in America during these Revolutionary years. Methodists were not, on the whole, revolutionaries in their political sentiments. In fact, most American Methodists were pacifists, and many chose to withdraw from the Revolutionary War, claiming to belong to neither side.[5] The American Methodist leader Francis Asbury was a primary example of this pacifist, neutral position, and he urged others to follow his lead. He made few direct comments about political matters; instead, he argued against the necessity of war and bewailed the fact that the Revolution seemed to distract people from religious causes. In many ways, refusing to take sides or being pacifist was interpreted as being loyalist, since this position was counter to patriotic assertions of the absolute necessity for war. During the Revolutionary War, Methodists were dissenters in both religion and politics.

In the Revolutionary period, Methodists also established themselves as a separate denomination. From the beginning of Methodist practice, John Wesley had maintained his ties to the Church of England as an ordained minister within the established church. Paradoxically, while Methodists diverged from many Anglican practices, a number of prominent Methodist preachers had been ordained within the Church of England. During the 1780s, the American Methodists separated from the British Methodists, because the American Methodists needed autonomy in order to serve their growing population by administering the sacraments, baptizing, and marrying their followers. The Americans' push for ordained ministers and sacramental authority prompted the formal separation of Methodists as a whole from their mother church, the Church of England. Before the Revolution, eighteenth-century English Methodists had been comfortable with their somewhat divided loyalties. On the one hand, Methodists were still members of the Church of England, and they felt love, loyalty, and deference to Mother England. On the other hand, Methodists were part of the transatlantic revivalism that supported the group's expansion throughout the Atlantic world and made Methodism distinct from its Anglican parent.

The Family Politic

In the seventeenth century, the idea of "family" served as a metaphor for good societal order. Political metaphors of the family were based on the family as a natural site of belonging, as one might belong to a community or nation. In this respect, the term "family" was a way to signify compulsory authority. This use of the term "family" would seem in opposition to late seventeenth- and eighteenth-century philosophers who sought to replace the compulsory bonds of family with the idea of voluntary contractual political participation.[6] Yet, the two ideas of authority and political participation existed alongside each other through the eighteenth century and survived the Revolutionary period.

The seventeenth- and eighteenth-century English family was generally a patriarchal institution, as was the political order. The family was central to political and social order, and the father was most often the ruler within the family. Family was also used metaphorically to describe the basis for political authority, particularly by invoking the terms of patriarchy. Fathers simply embodied authority in various political and social contexts. In 1633, Puritan author Matthew Griffith suggested that all rulers and leaders are "our Fathers but as they represent unto us the image of God's paternity."[7]

John Winthrop, as head of the Massachusetts Bay Colony, described the commonwealth as a composition of many individual families, each submitting themselves to the law of the governor as one would to the law of one's father.[8] Puritan leaders were especially keen to promote patriarchal authority as the basis for an orderly society and government.[9] Patriarchal rule both emanated from above and was confirmed from below. The equation of patriarchal rule, both in the body politic and the family, was reaffirmed in multiple Puritan writings.[10] Puritan John Udall wrote, "Every kingdom or household must be governed only by the laws of the king, or orders of the householders," confirming the centrality of the household to political order. Richard Greenham warned that the hierarchical order needed to translate to every level of Puritan life: "Care in superiors, and fear in inferiors, cause a godly government both private and public, family, church and commonwealth."[11]

Patriarchy as the basis for political authority was parental in nature, but absolute in its power. For instance, Robert Filmer defended the natural power of the monarch over his subjects as an inherently nonconsensual relationship, likening the complete control of parents over their children to that of a king and his subjects.[12] Filmer further outlined in his writings the ways in which wifely subordination was directed by the Bible.[13] The composite picture of the ideal family contained well-defined roles, an orderly chain of authority from nation and church to husband, wife, and other dependents.

As the seventeenth century progressed, theorists combated the compulsory qualities of social and political authority with more contractual language and consensual ideas about the power of fathers and rulers. English historian Susan Amussen describes this late seventeenth-century movement as "[t]he impulse to escape the [familial] analogy, either because of its limits or because of its absolutist implications."[14] Thomas Hobbes argued that both the king and the father in fact based their authority on contract.[15] John Locke, of course, attacked the Filmerian notions of authority, arguing that the familial metaphor did not apply to political power and that the assumption of a father/monarch's absolute power was unfounded. Furthermore, Locke argued that marriage was inherently contractual and absolute parental power only worked on infants.[16] Still, the ideas linking family and political order never completely died; Locke's vehement writings suggest he faced a significant challenge in erasing the familial basis for political order.[17]

Despite the intervention of Lockean individualism, the eighteenth-century republican body politic still relied on the image of individual families building the nation. Children in families would learn the design of a just, orderly world through observing the natural order embodied in their own families. Women's role in this republican family was to train children in the foundation of morality and ethics that would constitute the basis for their civic participation. As women were central to this order, they themselves would have to be monogamous, virtuous, and moral. While family remained a convincing metaphor for societal and political order, the family ideal changed. The eighteenth century witnessed a shift toward companionate marriage on both sides of the Atlantic. This companionate marriage ideal became the new metaphor for American post-Revolutionary order. Much like a harmonious marriage, the ideal republican political realm would not see an ugly fight between self-interested parties, but rather a consensual partnership between virtuous, respectful individuals.[18] For male citizens, the republican body politic was a body of brothers, freely relating to each other in the presumed absence of the despotic will of a monarch. They could be brothers without a father.

Within Methodist culture, there was a parallel struggle for authority within the terms of family. On one level, Methodists were equal brothers, but they also submitted to a father, politically and personally. While possessing a fairly democratic ethos on the lowest level, where all members of the laity felt themselves equalized in spirit, they had a well-developed hierarchy above them. They held to the ideal of a strong steward or leader, and during Wesley's time, he was the natural discipliner and father of the whole society. Unlike Baptists, who formed independent congregations and whose ministers had to satisfy their congregants or be dismissed by them, a central authority designated the circuits for Methodist preachers. In Wesley's time, he held this power to appoint preachers and configure their circuits. Wesley's position as father figure played out differently in America, where his physical absence called for others to serve in loco parentis. American preachers grappled with their relationship to Wesley as America was going through a Revolution against England, and simultaneously they formulated a distinctive brand of Methodism with its own structures. One of the distinctive features of American Methodism was Wesley's absence and the lack of natural hierarchy he regularly invoked among the British. Instead, American preachers enjoyed a prevailing ethos of being brothers rather than sons. During the Revolutionary period, they instituted more republican features. American Methodist preachers sought a representative leadership that was accountable to checks and balances by the preaching brethren as a whole.

"Family" was the central paradigm that pervaded the political conflict within transatlantic Methodism in the Revolutionary era. Largely, this was a struggle between Father Wesley and his "sons." Methodist women were not members of the preachers' conferences, the sites of these struggles. During the Revolutionary period, American Methodists focused on forming a legitimate power structure and navigating their relationship to British Methodists. Parallel to the political processes that segregated women's voices from the discussions of citizenship in the formation of the American nation, male leadership within Methodism was naturalized during this period. As Methodists became more organized, they sought to formalize the boundaries of lay leadership, which in many cases also limited female leadership. Even as Wesley was overthrown as the official patriarch in American Methodism, the group strengthened its essentially patriarchal organization as a whole, by focusing on who would become the male leaders in America. Although they stressed the democracy of the preachers, they formalized and legitimated the secondary status of women within this group. After Wesley's death in 1791, both American and English Methodists took up the task of codifying leadership, and the possibilities of female leadership narrowed considerably. When Wesley was "king," he benevolently, if quietly, allowed that some women were worthy of the call to preach and were true Mothers in Israel. However, in the following generation, when American Methodism was firmly established, there were no sanctioned female preachers.

Organizing American Methodists

Up to the 1770s, American Methodism had a small official membership and was largely led by the laity. Starting in 1771, Wesleyan Methodists began to systematize the American societies in earnest. The first step was to send over licensed preachers and a supervisor to oversee all the preachers and societies that had already formed without John Wesley's assistance. English Preachers Richard Boardman and Joseph Pilmore had come to America in 1769, but immediately realized the magnitude of their work and petitioned Wesley for help in providing preachers to the American societies. In August of 1771, at a preachers' conference in Bristol, Francis Asbury volunteered for service in America.[19] A scant two months later, he arrived in Philadelphia with fellow itinerant Richard Wright. Asbury threw himself into "disciplining" American societies, because he thought the previous leadership had been especially lax. In New York, Methodists were allowing folks outside the society to infiltrate the select bands and other meetings. In an attempt to be ecumenical, the leaders had blurred the lines between members and nonmembers.[20] Bands and classes were intimate groups, and the lack of discipline meant a violation of these familial spheres.

In order to organize American societies, Asbury reasonably sought to control this most basic level of Methodist belonging. Asbury further assessed that the predominantly urban organization of Methodist societies

Figure 11. *The Revd. Francis Asbury, Bishop of the Methodist Episcopal Church in the United States*, engraving by B. Tanner after a painting by J. Paradise (Philadelphia, 1814). Courtesy of the Library of Congress.

in America ignored the largely rural population of the colonies. He sought to bring together the two regions of Methodism that had been growing independently prior to this time, one area focused around Maryland and Delaware and the other in New York and Philadelphia.[21] Due to Asbury's demonstrated organizational acumen, Wesley anointed him as supervisor of all American preachers in October of 1772.

Asbury had scarcely held this leading position, before Wesley handed over the supervisory role to Thomas Rankin, who was named General Assistant by Wesley in 1773.[22] Rankin was older and had more experience than Asbury, but perhaps more importantly, he was closer to Wesley and more likely to adhere to Wesley's wishes. Shortly after arriving in America in 1773 with a directive to make American Methodism shipshape, Rankin convened the first conference of preachers. He directed preachers to follow the printed guidelines of the Methodist *Discipline* more closely and to keep closer accounts of membership numbers. He repeatedly wrote in his diary about the lack of regulation of the various societies he encountered as he toured the American colonies from the middle of 1773 through August 1777 (when he retreated to England during the Revolution).[23] Soon after his arrival he wrote, "From what I see and hear, and so far as I can judge, if my brethren who first came over had been more attentive to our discipline, there would have been, by this time, a more glorious work in many places of this continent. Their love-feasts, and meetings of society, were laid open to all their particular friends; so that their number did not increase, and the minds of our best friends were thereby hurt."[24] In New York and Philadelphia, he complained of women's extravagant dress, and the lack of order.[25]

Rankin outwardly blamed Asbury for what he perceived as American Methodism's failure to thrive. He opined that Asbury was an effective preacher but a deficient leader. He wrote in his journal in December of 1774, "Brother Asbury preached this evening, and not without the Divine blessing. Next day we talked over different matters respecting the work and also removed some little and foolish misaprehensions, that had taken place in his mind."[26] Rankin held the power of Wesley's blessing and was closer to the esteemed leader than Asbury was; this power gave him the right to be condescending and absolute in his leadership style.

Rankin and Asbury were two spiritual brothers fighting over their father John Wesley's affections, yet they also represented different modes of leadership in the Revolutionary period.[27] Even by the time Rankin arrived,

Asbury had become "American" in some important ways. He was not distinguished in his education and therefore more readily associated with the lay preachers who served with him than with the well-educated ministers who ruled English Methodism. Throughout his life, he traveled extensively through rough terrain as an itinerant preacher, even after he became bishop of American Methodists. Rankin, on the other hand, believed in ruling from above, and he was critical of American preachers. According to Asbury, Rankin "assumed too much authority over the preachers and people."[28]

At the same time that American Methodists were beginning to become organized, strained relations between England and America developed. According to Asbury, the essence of John Wesley's counsel to American Methodists during the war was "to have nothing to do with the affairs of this world if he could help it, and mind the business of our spiritual calling."[29] In this way, Wesley followed English liberal Enlightenment theorists. If religion should be separate from government, then Methodists should also stay out of the Revolutionary War. Wesley thought that all Christians should be neutral in politics, which was derived from his pietistic Moravian connections and also from his parents' nonjuror and dissenting religious stance.[30] In March of 1775, signaling a withdrawal from "the affairs of this world," Wesley recalled all the English preachers, including Asbury. Wesley demanded that Asbury return as soon as possible, and Wesley also counseled the remaining Americans preachers to act as "peace-makers" and be neutral in the conflict. Overall, they should be united as a group, following Rankin's leadership. Charles Wesley also urged American Methodists to be "like-minded with me. I am of neither side, and yet of both; on the side of New England and old. Private Christians are excused, exempted, privileged, to take no part in civil troubles."[31] Most American preachers responded to John Wesley's various recalls by leaving America between 1774 and 1778, as the war started to encroach upon the middle colonies.[32]

Asbury disobeyed the call to leave America during the Revolution, interpreting this recall of preachers as a reflection of Wesley's and Rankin's desire to stay within the fold of both the mother country and the mother church. Writing to an English preacher, Asbury complained, "It appeared to me that [Rankin's] objective was to sweep the continent of every preacher that Mr. Wesley had sent to it and of every respectable travelling preacher from Europe who had graduated among us, whether English or Irish. He told us that if we returned to our native country, we should be esteemed as such obedient, loyal subjects that we should obtain ordination in the grand episcopal Church of England and come back to America with respectability after the war was ended."[33] Wesley made repeated appeals to Asbury to leave the colonies,[34] but Asbury refused and wrote, "I can by no means agree to leave such a field for gathering souls to Christ, as we have in America. It would be an eternal dishonour to the Methodists . . . neither is it the part of a good shepherd to leave his flock in time of danger: therefore, I am determined, by the grace of God, not to leave them, let the consequence be what it may."[35]

Wesley did not practice what he preached to American Methodists, regarding the need to remain above the political fray and focus solely on spiritual matters. In 1775, he published *A Calm Address to Our American Colonies*, which caused Americans to become more suspicious of Methodists' political stance. Wesley had copied, with little alteration, a pamphlet previously published by Samuel Johnson that was staunchly monarchical. The pamphlet argued that the Seven Years' War, the ostensible cause for increased taxes and the root of the conflict, was an example of how the mother country protected America. Raising taxes to pay for that war was reasonable and well within Parliament's prerogative. Wesley urged Americans to acquiesce as subjects of the king and to accept British authority. Displaying a deeply rooted Tory philosophy, he argued that the English ideals of liberty were already well at work in American society. Wesley wrote, "What more religious liberty can you desire, than that which you enjoy already? May not every one among you worship God according to his own conscience? What civil liberty can you desire, which you are not already possessed of? Do you not sit without restraint, every man under his own vine? Do you not, every one, high or low, enjoy the fruit of your labour? This is real, rational liberty, such as is enjoyed by Englishmen alone; and not by any other people in the habitable world."[36]

Wesley's pamphlet circulated widely; forty thousand copies were sold in the first three weeks it was out in England. He also published a number of other addresses and pamphlets in the same pro-monarchical vein.[37] By publishing this pamphlet, Wesley effectively turned every neutral American Methodist into a suspected loyalist. In short, Wesley's *Calm Address* made life more difficult for American Methodists during the Revolution.[38]

John Wesley's publication was not the only event that cast doubt on Methodist loyalties after 1775. American Methodists were not active supporters of the patriot cause. In fact, some prominent Methodists, including

Rankin's assistant, Martin Rodda, had been outspoken in their support of the loyalists. Other Methodists proclaimed neutrality or, like Asbury, claimed that their nonjuror status exempted them from participating in any political cause.[39] In 1777, Rodda actively joined the loyalist ranks by distributing loyalist material (particularly the royal proclamation) while on his preaching circuit. Rodda was arrested and narrowly escaped execution before returning to England with the help of a fellow Methodist.[40] In 1775, preacher Philip Gatch was nearly blinded after being tarred and feathered by a mob in Maryland. Other preachers faced similar violence on their circuits.[41] In 1776, some Methodist preachers, including Gatch, were jailed for not participating in the militia, though they were released when a Maryland council concluded that these lay preachers were covered by an exemption from military service for all ordained clerics.[42] Patriots were generally very suspicious of Methodists, claiming that many Methodists were loyalist spies. Many Americans saw Methodists as inherently duplicitous in the Revolutionary War, hiding their true weakness and political cowardice "under the mask of religion."[43]

Methodists thought these accusations and violent responses were a misreading of their true stance, which was pacifism and neutrality on religious grounds.[44] The violent feelings and actions of war opposed the religious spirit Asbury hoped to inspire. He was disappointed that more people did not see the parallel between earthly struggles and those in the next world.[45] After noting the commotion in Baltimore over the recent arrival of a British man-of-war in 1776, he wrote in his journal, "Alas for fallen man! He fears his fellow creatures, whose breath is in their nostrils, but fears not Him who is able to destroy body and soul in hell. If fire and sword at a small distance can so alarm us, how will poor impenitent sinners be alarmed when they find, by woeful experience, that they must drink the wine of the wrath of God, poured out without mixture?"[46] The real battle, as Asbury and other revivalists struggled to remind those living through the Revolutionary War, was between God and their souls. In this view, this earthly war was just a passing trifle and not worth so much energy and emotion. By trivializing the political war on the ground, Asbury emphasized the bonds that transcended these political rifts, such as those between English and Americans in the larger evangelical family.

The war did have significant effects on the Methodists, despite some of their best efforts to ignore it. In September of 1777, Rankin made a hasty departure from Maryland, when he believed his life was in danger. When

Rankin left Maryland, British troops had just landed on the shore, and patriots were rounding up Methodists in eastern Maryland. Yet, the Methodists had refused to fight with them. Rankin decried "the conduct of these patrons of liberty against the peaceable inofensive people!" The treatment of Methodists as suspected Tories during the war seemed only to confirm the negative view Wesley held of American independence. "The Rebels in Scotland did not even hang or Shoot those who refused to Join with them," Wesley wrote on the reverse of Rankin's letter. "But if they had what mercy had than been compared to the death inflicted by the Rebels in America? Can Englishmen Still open their Mouth in favor of those worse than Indian Savages."[47] Wesley saw it as a war of true Englishmen against these Revolutionary Americans, and he hoped that political and cultural transatlantic English allegiances would carry the day.

"So we are left alone," Asbury wrote glumly in his journal after Rankin's departure from Maryland in September of 1777.[48] Since 1773, sixty American and English preachers had itinerated in the American connection. After March of 1778, only one licensed itinerant, Asbury, now remained, and less than half of the unlicensed preachers were still on their circuits. The war had nearly obliterated Methodist leadership.[49] Despite this isolation and confinement, during the Revolution, Asbury became a powerful leader over a growing body of American Methodists.

Unlike many denominations during the war, Methodists experienced a healthy rate of growth; they actually tripled their numbers in only eight years. They went from just under 5,000 members in May 1776 to almost 9,000 in 1777, and 10,500 in 1781. At the end of the war in 1784, their numbers had increased to 15,000 members. During the war, Asbury was continually drawing up new circuits and appointed ninety new preachers between 1774 and 1784.[50]

How did American Methodists manage to thrive in the face of maltreatment and neglect from Wesley, alongside a public perception of counterrevolutionary politics? The answer lay largely in the fact that Methodists had an ecumenical stance toward other religious denominations, a position that served them well as the religious environment shifted during the Revolutionary War.[51] Methodists were able to recruit their members from a wide variety of different denominations. In the South, the Anglican Church was struggling to retain its already weak hold over the area, and Methodists easily stepped into the breach. Their itinerant structure was well suited to areas that lacked churches, which included much of the South. While the cannons of war were sounding, leaders in America sent triumphant accounts to Wesley of their spectacular growth in areas like Virginia.[52] By the end of the Revolutionary War, the South accounted for a stunning 89 percent of Methodist members.[53]

During this period of this growth, young energetic southern preachers stepped into the breach left by the withdrawal of English Methodist preachers. Asbury relied on American-born preachers who were not daunted by the challenges of wartime evangelicalism—preachers like Freeborn Garrettson. Garrettson became an itinerant at the very start of the war in 1776, and Asbury appointed him to oversee Methodist work in other parts of the South and middle colonies. Garrettson's preaching circuit was the Delmarva Peninsula area, which had a huge concentration of Methodists. In 1779, while Asbury was hiding out in Delaware, nervous of being persecuted as an English Methodist, Garrettson acted as his agent in many ways, traveling to Philadelphia, Maryland, and New Jersey to bolster those societies.[54]

From 1779 to 1780, the struggle between American and English authority continued in Methodist societies. In April 1779 an "irregular" conference recognized Asbury's leadership and resolved "that brother *Asbury* ought to act as *general assistant* in America." The conference decided that this should be the case "because [he was] originally appointed by Mr. Wesley."[55] The primary motive for this irregular meeting, occurring before the regularly scheduled conference would take place, was for Asbury and the northern preachers to form a preemptive assertion of authority, based on Wesleyan principles. A crisis had been brewing throughout the war, because Methodists depended upon the Church of England to fulfill the sacraments so that Methodists could take communion and have baptisms for children. With the scattering of the Church of England during the war, Methodists suffered from this loss, and particularly in the South, where the Church of England had deteriorated in areas by not keeping pace with new population expansion.[56] Southern preachers, led by Robert Strawbridge, were convinced that it was their right to administer sacraments. Soon after this conference of primarily northern preachers, Garrettson traveled to Virginia and North Carolina to "help convince preachers and people of the Wesleyan viewpoint" that there should be no ordinations conferred or sacraments given, and Asbury should be the leader for all Methodists, north and south.[57]

The next month, on May 18, 1779, southern preachers met together in Fluvanna, Virginia, without the northern preachers (and without Asbury), and decided to administer sacraments and baptism until the next scheduled preachers' conference in 1780.[58] The question was whether preachers could claim the status and powers of ordained ministers. When the southern preachers answered affirmatively, they made a statement against Wesley's authority and Anglicanism, in both religious and political matters. It was also a statement supporting democratic decisions among Methodists and the revolutionary spirit of the times.[59] As the southern preachers saw it, they constituted the majority of preachers, and they should have the final word on how to resolve these thorny questions of independence from British Methodism. It marked a turning point in the emergence of American Methodism as a separate entity.

A chasm had opened between Methodists of the North and the South. Southern preachers' independence signaled a rejection of not only the authority of northern preachers, but also of Asbury, Wesley, and perhaps English Methodism altogether. As Jesse Lee wrote, "There was great cause to fear a division, and both parties trembled for the ark of God, and shuddered at the thought of dividing the Church of Christ."[60] There was a real concern that schisms would form, and these divisions would weaken American Methodism.

The northern and southern preachers remained divided for almost a year. During that time, the South saw dramatic increases in membership, which only confirmed to them that their independent actions were correct.[61] In April of 1780, a meeting of northern preachers and Asbury passed a number of resolutions. One of the first resolutions was against slavery. The other major resolution was to declare that they viewed the southern preachers "as no longer Methodists in connection with Wesley and us till they come back."[62] The northern preachers dreaded the thought of losing such a thriving society of Methodists and splitting the formerly strong fellowship of preachers. Once Asbury could travel again, his first business was to arrange compromise between the two groups of preachers. In 1780, Asbury, Freeborn Garrettson and William Watters went to the Virginia conference to convince the southerners to revoke the previous measures supporting sacramental independence, and they agreed to suspend these actions. In 1782, after much debate and a last-minute reversal of voting by the southern preachers, the conferences reunited and unanimously chose Asbury to act as General Assistant, which they were careful to say was "according to Mr. Wesley's original appointment." Finally, in 1783, Wesley officially backed him as the General Assistant in America.[63] This was a just reward for Asbury valiantly supporting Wesley at a crossroads in the formation of American Methodism. Eventually, though, even Wesley had to concede that Americans were on their way to forming an independent church, completely separate from the Church of England, and somewhat separate from Wesley as well.

Independence and the Birth of Organized American Methodism

Despite these conciliatory moves on both sides of the ocean, Asbury felt that the Revolution had sundered his relationship with his father Wesley and his English brothers. He wrote retrospectively that his "greatest sorrow" was "that our dear father [Wesley] from the time of the Revolution to his death grew more and more jealous of myself and the whole American connection; that it appeared that we had lost his confidence almost entirely."[64] How did the Americans supposedly lose Wesley's confidence? Asbury again blamed elder brother Rankin, concluding that Rankin had poisoned Wesley against American Methodists.

Wesley was certainly insecure about his power over the Americans. In October 1783, he wrote in an open letter to American Methodists that there were English preachers working in America who had gone without his permission. Wesley insisted that any English preacher going to America had to have his permission to do so, as well as accept the local authority of Asbury and the American conference of preachers.[65]

Despite Wesley's need for control of the American leadership, by 1784, he understood that the American Methodists should have some sort of separate and independent status. There were logistical reasons for forming an independent American church; the issues of sacraments and ordination of new ministers had become difficult ones, threatening to divide the American connection. The expansion of American societies had left them disorganized, and Asbury requested a different form of government that would address the specific needs of American Methodists.[66] But the primary reason was that Wesley realized that the American Revolution had separated England and America, perhaps irrevocably.

Wesley still hoped that the American leadership would be largely British and connected to British Methodist leaders. In September of 1784, Wesley attempted to extend his influence and resolve some of the issues of sacramental authority by sending a new leader for the Americans, the Reverend Thomas Coke. The establishment of a Methodist superintendent further cemented American Methodism as a separate, dissenting religion—distinct from American Anglicans and the Church of England. This departure for American Methodists marked a departure for Methodists as a whole. Upon granting sacramental powers to the Methodist superintendent in America, both the British and American Methodists took a further step of separation from the Church of England.

American Methodists increasingly moved away from their unquestioned allegiance to their mother church and their father Wesley. In a declaration of independence, the American preachers did not immediately fulfill Wesley's wishes by instating Thomas Coke; instead, an irregular conference of preachers met in Baltimore to decide whether to accept Coke as the superintendent.[67] At this 1784 Christmas Conference, preachers declared a fair amount of autonomy. The clash between the British and American Methodist cultures became evident when Coke expected to be confirmed as superintendent, which was akin to being bishop in the Anglican Church, only to see the American preachers assert their own authority. They formed themselves as the Methodist Episcopal Church and made "the elected superintendent amenable to the body of ministers and preachers."[68] Their superintendent had to undergo a democratic confirmation by the whole body of preachers. The conference elected Coke and Asbury as cosuperintendents and made the power structure of Methodism more democratic than Wesley had directed. The superintendent had veto power on major decisions, yet the conference could depose a superintendent if it saw fit. The conference limited both Wesley's power and his appointees' power by making their decisions subject to their preachers' approval. This conference established that no one could be named a superintendent, elder, or deacon without being backed by the superintendent and the majority of the conference.[69]

However, the American preachers still followed Wesleyan ideas and confirmed their position as his sons. One of the first things they did was to pledge allegiance to Wesley. "During the life of the Rev. Mr. Wesley, we acknowledge ourselves his sons in the gospel, ready in matters belong to church government to obey his commands."[70] The preachers underlined the republican nature of their leadership, even while affirming the essential structure and leadership that Wesley had desired. Though they declared their independence in many ways, the preachers still sought to maintain their emotional and cultural ties to British leadership and to Wesley.

When Asbury arrived at the first meeting of the new Methodist Episcopal Church in January of 1785, as if he were dressed for a special ordination, wearing "full canonicals, gown, cassock, and band," American preacher Jesse Lee expressed surprise and "no little mortification" to see him so turned out.[71] The new American church wanted a clear hierarchy, but they were also suspicious of leaders that would assume a despotic or lordly position above the brethren of preachers.

The first test of the newly organized American Methodists came when Wesley wrote to Coke in September of 1786, directing Coke to call a general conference meeting in Baltimore during the following year, in order to appoint English preacher Richard Whatcoat as a cosuperintendent.[72] The preachers met and agreed that this directive was objectionable mainly because Wesley was "not qualified to take the charge of the connection."[73] In a statement of protest, the American preachers erased the Wesleyan allegiance clause and Wesley's name altogether from the *Discipline*. At the same time, they sent a letter to Wesley, requesting he visit America. Their father had presumed to be a parent in absentia, much as the British government had, and the sons were making a gesture toward holding Wesley accountable. Coke was also in trouble with the American preachers for being too willing to follow Wesley's commandments, and for doing this as a British minister. The preachers made Coke sign an agreement that he would not make any decisions involving the governance of American Methodists when he was in England.[74]

All of these decisions made by the American preachers mortified Wesley, who explicitly faulted Asbury for not modeling the behavior of a good son to him and for allowing the American preachers to remove his name from the *Discipline*. Wesley expected Asbury to lead like him, to demand that the preachers defer to Asbury and to Wesley as their ultimate father. He wrote Whatcoat, "It was not well judged of Brother Asbury to suffer, much less indirectly encourage, that foolish step in the late Conference. Every preacher present ought, both in duty and in prudence, to have said: 'Brother Asbury Mr. Wesley is your father, consequently ours, and we will affirm this in the face of all the world.'"[75] If Asbury had treated Wesley as a father to follow and obey, the American preachers would have done so too, Wesley reasoned. The conference did eventually acquiesce to Wesley in electing Whatcoat as bishop and wrote Wesley back into the *Discipline* in 1789, naming him as a leader (alongside Coke and Asbury). However, the Americans never reinstated the language that acknowledged Wesley as their father and ultimate leader.

Wesley's relationship with American leadership continued to be strained in the final years of his life. Alongside his presumptions of power over the Americans, Wesley's Tory political statements had ultimately alienated him from his American sons. Asbury wrote to Jasper Winscom in 1788, "There is not a man in the world so obnoxious to the American politicians as our dear old Daddy, but no matter, we must treat him with all the respect we can and that is due him."[76] The mode of leadership that Wesley had presumed was part and parcel of the issues of the Revolution. In his love of king and country, Wesley had internalized the ideology of paternal power, the expectation of deference, and the unquestioning right to authority. If his American sons loved and valued their father, they would submit to his decisions. While Asbury and other American preachers claimed they loved and cherished their "dear old Daddy," they saw that he was hopelessly out of step with the American ethos of governance from below. Furthermore, in forcing a separation of Methodists from the Church of England, American Methodists were prying apart another familial association. American preacher Thomas Haskins had termed all Methodists as the "generous and dutiful sons of the Episcopal church."[77] For American Methodists there were now fewer ties, dutiful or otherwise, to the Church of England.

In the end, they did not fully reform themselves as a band of brothers without their father Wesley. American Methodists underlined their adherence to the English organization of appointments from above and power located in the leadership, rather than with the lay preachers. There was one attempt to completely republicanize the organizational methods of Methodism, when a leading preacher, James O'Kelly, voiced dissatisfaction with some of the seemingly autocratic decisions by Asbury. Asbury wanted to streamline decision making and sought to create a governing council. When O'Kelly tried to introduce a measure allowing the preachers to have more say in their appointments, he was overruled. O'Kelly left to form the Republican Methodist Church in 1793, which drew away Methodists in southern Virginia and North Carolina. O'Kelly argued against the lack of representation in the decisions of the mainline American Methodist connection. He carried republican rhetoric into the religious sphere, decrying the consolidating tendencies of the office of bishop and Asbury in particular. The leaders of the American conference defended their organization and power structure against O'Kelly's criticisms; they maintained that all preachers were represented, but that some higher office and power was necessary.[78]

How revolutionary were the American Methodists? In the arena of democratic reform of religious hierarchies, they were mixed. O'Kelly's Republican Methodists were seeking a more direct embodiment of the American republican ethos within the governing structures of Methodism. Yet, at its heart, Methodist organization still relied on leadership from above, still held to the Anglican office of bishop, mitigated by the more democratic institutions of the preachers' conferences. While lay preaching had its undeniably democratic features, valuing individual inspiration over the privileges of education and training, lay preachers were not the leaders of American Methodists. Coke and Asbury were English born and had been ordained within the Church of England. Within the English culture of leadership, John Wesley was the unquestioned patriarch, able to make autocratic decisions on circuit assignments, decisions that were rarely questioned by the preachers whose lives they affected.

These political shifts were largely concerned with the leading class of American Methodism, whether it would have an English or American culture and whether the leadership itself would be unified across the Atlantic. Glaringly absent from these discussions were women; within preacher's conferences, this was the case on both sides of the Atlantic. Despite some differences between the two cultures, British and American political ideology was in fairly close agreement that women were excluded from leadership positions. The language of leadership within Methodist circles barred women from the fraternity of preachers. Wesley asserted his rights as a father to expect political adherence from his sons, and this sort of obedience in organizational matters was never demanded of Methodist women. In fact, this particular use of the rights of the father, as employed by both Father Wesley and his American sons, was solely political and alternated between the masculine codes of obedience and rebellion.

Race and the Transatlantic Family

The struggle for leadership in the Revolutionary era revealed a desire among American evangelicals to draw lines between their organization and that of English evangelicals, and this rebellious move was centered in the young preachers of the South and the Middle Atlantic region. Not coincidentally, these were areas that included large populations of African American Methodists, as well as the greatest area of growth for Methodist societies in the late eighteenth century. One of the most promising revolutionary prospects for Methodism in the late eighteenth century was in the group's growing body of African American believers. The primary revolutionary impulse of early American Methodism came in the group's desire to expand the notions of family and to include blacks and whites in the same family.

In 1773, Thomas Rankin (in his capacity as English superintendent of American Methodism) wrote a letter from New York to the York Society of Methodists in England, in order to report to his countrymen on the status of Methodist societies in America. There were many things going wrong in American Methodism, as he saw it, but one thing was very right: the conversion of African American Methodists.[79] Rankin sought to link York to New York, but he simultaneously highlighted one of the key differences between English and American Methodism, the growing proportion of African Americans in the American societies. One of Rankin's initial duties as superintendent was to assess the state of American societies and their capacity for growth. While he wrote repeatedly that American Methodists everywhere were disorganized, in need of proper discipline and leadership, what they did not lack was enthusiasm and growing numbers. African Americans were largely responsible for both. In his 1773 letter, Rankin reported, "I am now visiting the classes in this Place, and I have Reason to Bless God for the Consolation and also particular among the Blacks in whome there appears much of the Simplicity of the Gospel, Maney of them are happy in a pardoning God, and some of them [are] . . . White Souls in Black bodies."[80]

One gets the sense from Rankin's assessment of black religiosity that he thrilled at the growth and enthusiasm of these societies, but that he also viewed black Methodists as curious and particular to American culture. As an English person, he saw this as an American innovation, and Rankin's tone was always that of the English traveler abroad; in his journals, he noted American flora, fauna, and people with the same curious, observant tone of a travel narrative. While Rankin maintained a rather condescending tone toward all things American, describing them as alternately crude, chaotic, and exotic, he was also one of the many Methodist leaders who seriously challenged slavery.

The period following the Revolution saw remarkable growth among Methodists as a whole and African American Methodists in particular. In 1800, African American Methodists accounted for over 20 percent of the group.[81] Methodism attracted slave and free African Americans by offering a strong sense of association and communal identity. While the First Great

Awakening had converted steady numbers of African Americans, their numbers remained an inconsequential proportion of the larger evangelical societies. Following the American Revolution, however, African Americans converted in much larger numbers and began to form their own groups, especially within Baptist and Methodist societies.[82]

Theologically, post-Revolutionary evangelical revivals promoted the idea of salvation as subject to human will, in contrast to the dominant Calvinism of the First Great Awakening; importantly, Arminianism countered the idea that one is born into a particular fate regarding salvation. In this way, one can see its radical challenge to the negation of humanity in the theory and practice of racial slavery, which marked certain people from birth as lesser beings. Early Methodist commitment to antislavery was a radical aspect of this transatlantic group and a particular challenge to the growing normalcy of slavery in the American South.

By the 1770s, John Wesley had become an active supporter of abolitionism. He corresponded regularly with Granville Sharp, one of the leaders of the early abolitionist movement in England. Wesley wrote to Sharp in 1787, "Ever since I heard of it first, I felt a perfect detestation of the horrid Slave Trade."[83] Wesley saw religious sensibility and slaveholding practice in opposition to each other, and he believed that in perfecting people's religious souls, they would naturally see the truth of the evil of slavery. He had contact with a few slaves during his mission in Georgia in the 1730s. During this time, he formulated his desire to convert African Americans, whom he saw as central to his evangelical mission and to his earliest vision of Methodism.[84] His writings, particularly the pamphlet *Thoughts Upon Slavery*, marked a turn in early English abolitionism toward using sentimental language to evoke a response in the reader.[85] Methodists applied religious sensibility to the realm of antislavery efforts, a potent combination that endured through antebellum-era abolitionism.

The British movement toward abolitionism was in an entirely different context from the American movement. In the 1770s, Charles Wesley had championed the case of two former slaves, Little Ephraim Robin John and Ancona Robin John, who had successfully petitioned for their freedom in England. While it may have been revolutionary for an ordained minister to cross these lines, this was an isolated case for Charles Wesley. He had taken the Robin Johns into his familial fold and saw their case as principled but also personal.[86] After the American Revolution, a public movement had begun in England to end the slave trade and slavery itself in the 1780s and

1790s. At this time, Olaudah Equiano was among the few public Afro-British voices, and his published narrative became a sensation in 1789.[87] Equiano had been greatly influenced by George Whitefield's preaching, and he had become a part of the Calvinist Methodist movement.[88] John Wesley read and supported Equiano and other antislavery writers. Wesley was reading Equiano's slave narrative on his deathbed, and he wrote to famed British abolitionist William Wilberforce to discuss the text in his last letter before his death in 1791.[89]

Early American Methodists shared this ethos of antislavery activism, though the context of slavery in America was decidedly distinct from that of England. By the time of American Methodists' rise in the late eighteenth century, American colonies, north and south, had become deeply invested in the institution of slavery. American Methodists formed a significant protest against slavery, alongside their British leaders. Rankin, Wesley, and other Methodist leaders were critical of the hypocrisy they saw in American revolutionaries who owned slaves but sought liberty for themselves.[90] These antislavery ideals percolated through Methodist societies, particularly within the English-born leadership of early Methodism in America. Methodists challenged the slaveholding South in the late eighteenth century. They did this by holding services and open-air meetings where black and white congregants were encouraged to undermine the segregation of slave and free, black and white in the American South, and by choosing challenging themes from biblical texts in their sermons that stressed the evils of slavery and the potential power of slaves.[91] Francis Asbury and Thomas Coke, the bishops of American Methodists, believed slavery was a "great evil," and the central document of American Methodism, the *Discipline*, continued to underline Methodist opposition to slavery through the late 1700s.[92]

As a consequence, in the 1770s and 1780s, American Methodists made an effort to demand that their members emancipate all the slaves they held. Circuit preachers agreed to not hold slaves. Southern preacher Freeborn Garrettson seemed to answer that call when he freed all of his slaves after he had a vision that God urged him to emancipate them. Garrettson addressed his family, slave and free, as they assembled for prayer, and dramatically announced on the spot, "Lord, the oppressed shall go free," renouncing their bondage immediately. By his account, Garrettson was not following the English leadership or the broader abolitionist movement; he said he was solely inspired by his vision of God's will on the matter.[93] In

1780, the Methodist *Discipline* leaders argued that slavery was "contrary to the laws of God, man, and nature, and hurtful to society, contrary to the dictates of conscience and pure religion."[94] In 1784, the leadership promised to expel any Methodist member who did not free their slaves within two years. Presbyterians and Baptists followed suit by issuing antislavery statements in the late 1780s.[95] In 1785, Methodists also moved to make political change by collecting signatures for an antislavery petition they submitted to the Virginia Assembly, though this effort made little headway and provoked Virginia's proslavery advocates to work harder to safeguard their interests. These efforts revived the specter of Methodists' Toryism, and proslavery advocates questioned the American credentials of the Methodist movement. One of the proslavery petitioners labeled Methodists "Enemies of our Country, Tools of the British Administration," and another called Asbury and Coke and other Methodists "contemptible Emissaries and hirelings of Britain." They equated antislavery with anti-Americanism, contending that the Revolution had in fact secured their rights to slaveholding.[96]

By 1790, Methodist societies had become biracial. Itinerants preached to both black and white audiences. The idea of white and black converts seeing themselves as one religious family had a revolutionary, egalitarian promise. In some areas, they were mixed, and in others, they were separate societies.[97] African American Methodists outnumbered the whites gathered to hear a preacher on his circuit in many places in the South. There were sizable African American Methodist groups in Maryland, Virginia, and North Carolina. In many of these gatherings, preachers noted the enthusiasm that African Americans showed toward evangelical religion.[98]

In the late eighteenth century, white evangelicals had mixed responses to the enthusiastic and growing number of African American Methodists. Some white Methodists described African American practices as improper and made an effort to control the powerful surge of religiosity that African American converts exhibited. When Freeborn Garrettson preached to a congregation in Virginia in 1776, a woman "cried out so loud as to make the church ring: the people being unacquainted with such things, strove to get out; but the ailes, and every place were so crouded that they could not."[99] In 1801, at a chapel in Delaware, "blacks were so enthusiastic that their movements brought the gallery crashing down on the whites below."[100] In early nineteenth-century revivals, African Americans started to innovate with this open, lay-oriented revival space. They also emphasized lay participation and the importance of visions, music, and other aspects indigenous to African spirituality.[101]

William Colbert was an inexperienced itinerant preacher in 1790, when he took up a circuit in Maryland. He wrote repeatedly about meeting with African American classes, and often spoke in glowing terms of their serious devotion in love feasts and other meetings. When he preached outdoors, black and white members met together. When he preached indoors, however, there was racial segregation: the white folks sitting indoors, and the black folks meeting outside the doors of the meetinghouse. He described one such meeting in 1790:

> the white society was much opposd to the noise and was for going away, but was prevented by a power that came on [the exhorter], and was so wrought on that he took hold on one of his brothers that stood by to keep from falling. . . . I stood at the door of a partition: the black people were behind me and the white before—I wanted to see a move among them, therefore I exerted myself and sure enough, there was a move for the blacks behind began to shout aloud jump and fall—the whites look wild, and go off. I am sorry that prejudice moved so many to day. A young woman among them that went off said that she would come no more, and that she believed I should kill myself, the meeting did not last long, and I returned to Isaac Smiths. I am young and inexperienced in the work of the ministry, and I expect not guarded enough.[102]

Colbert did not commit suicide as the woman helpfully suggested. Instead, Colbert was one of the more radical preachers, insisting on calling African Americans brethren and sisters, despite objections from white converts.[103]

Colbert's accounts portray the deep association between African American congregations and slave insurgency for white southerners. Evangelical African Americans' physical enthusiasm frightened white Americans. African American Methodists often refused to be contained by the segregationist measures in churches and meetinghouses. After 1800, in the wake of Gabriel's Conspiracy, a suspected slave plot in Virginia, there was an increasing nervousness on the part of white southerners regarding black religiosity and its potential for inciting insurrection.[104] In the same year, though, Methodists made one last strong political stand regarding antislavery. They published a broadside, *The Address of the General Conference of the Methodist Episcopal Church, to All Their Brethren and Friends in the United States*, urging their members and sympathizers to petition for gradual emancipation laws in all states that had none.[105] The political reaction was swift and uniform in decrying this broadside as an incitement to slave insurrection.[106]

Methodists worked in other ways to transmit a message of egalitarian ideals between their black and white brethren, particularly through the promotion of black preachers. Francis Asbury toured in Virginia with Harry Hosier, an inspired black preacher. Hosier regularly appeared alongside white Methodist preachers, drawing throngs of white and black converts on their circuits and occasionally outraging white audiences. However, black male and female preachers did not commonly become official preachers with their own Methodist circuits, but rather, like white female preachers, were given the roles of exhorters or lay speakers. Occasionally, these black male exhorters threatened to upstage their white counterparts, since they were more compelling to black audiences.[107]

Evangelicalism was not a strong enough force to erase the boundaries of racial segregation and increasingly definitive ideas about the natural order of races in America. Evangelicals' push to recognize black preachers and to repudiate slaveholding members held a strong potential, but in the case of Methodists, they overturned their own radical principles within a relatively short period of time, caving to vociferous objections by slaveholding members and Methodist leaders who saw this abolitionist stance as wrongheaded and unnecessarily alienating to southerners. Methodist leaders had to step down from their previously promised excommunication, replacing their prior radicalism with a program of "education and moral suasion."[108] By the antebellum period, evangelicalism conformed to some of the more conservative elements of southern society by underlining the existing social and political structures. Many evangelical groups in the early nineteenth century also supported a proslavery reading of the Bible and a hierarchy of society, men over women, free over slave, white over black.[109]

In the post-Revolutionary era, the increased attention to "family" conversion meant that there was more attention to the souls of black slaves and servants who were in the service of white Methodist families. In 1811, Georgia Methodist Charles Hill wrote to the Reverend Daniel Shine that he regretted hearing that Shine's sister was not yet reborn, but Hill happily reported that he had converted his "black family" (his slaves) and hoped that his wife would soon follow in their footsteps.[110] The accommodation of slaveholding southern families within Methodist societies meant that slavery was central to Methodist identity in the South by the first decades of the nineteenth century.

In the antebellum South, Methodism aided and abetted the rise of a new wave of paternalism, infused by the notion that whites needed to shepherd slave souls through conversion to evangelical Christianity. Evangelical ideas about emotional sentimentalism, so present in religious enthusiasm, fueled the establishment of emotional qualities for the family life of an ideal slave master. Methodist slave masters embodied religious ideals through their inculcation of paternalist norms, taking slaves as part of their family, encouraging religious conversion among their slaves, and treating their dependents with generosity. This shift away from earlier notions of patriarchy likewise mirrored the larger political transition, where families were seen less as places of coercive rule and more as sites for emotive sustenance. Yet, clearly the ideal, sentimental Victorian family and its emotional bonds did not extend to include slaves within the affective bonds of plantation households. While some historians argue that modest gains were made in the treatment of slaves through the principles of paternalism, no one would argue that Methodist suasion of planters was a step forward for slaves overall.[111]

White Methodists who retained the ideal of an evangelical community free of slavery were part of a movement of abolitionist evangelicals into new territories of post-Revolutionary expansion, especially Ohio. Philip Gatch relocated his family to Ohio in 1801 so that he could get out of "a Land of Slavery." He freed his slaves before moving to Ohio, but some of the younger slaves moved with him because their status as freed slaves would have been challenged in Virginia.[112] He boasted to friends that he had many familial converts, black and white: "one of our Children and A Black Boy of our Family got converted, our three Oldest Daughters profess religion My Wife I hope is devoted to God."[113] Gatch was committed to the antislavery cause, and he continually pressed his relatives and friends to join him in nonslave territory. In the early nineteenth century, other abolitionist Methodists relocated to Ohio and established a small evangelical network there.[114] Gatch's commitment to antislavery and this ideal of an egalitarian interracial family, based on evangelical spiritual equality, seemed to be sincere. At his death, he left part of his land in Ohio to the four former slaves who had moved with his family.[115]

However, for some white evangelicals, the desire to leave slaveholding societies was rooted in the racist desire to avoid black people altogether. Peter Pelham, another western migrant, repeatedly wrote to Virginia preacher Edward Dromgoole that the "land of liberty" is a much better place for perfecting one's soul. In 1808, he wrote that he had never regretted the move and "enjoy[ed] so much peace in being freed from a Land of Slavery and having no blacks about me in my family."[116]

African American converts themselves realized the potential radicalism within evangelical religiosity. Instead of waiting for the white leadership to recognize them, many formed their own congregations. Richard Allen was a powerful preacher, who rose up through the ranks to become the first African American ordained by the Methodist Episcopal Church in 1799. Allen was increasingly frustrated with the acceptance of slaveholding Methodists, and he separated to form the African Methodist Episcopal Church (AME) in 1816. His church was centered in Philadelphia and soon there were AME congregations in New York, Long Island, and Baltimore as well. Though black Methodists were once the majority of members in the Methodist churches in Baltimore, as more African Americans joined with Allen's church, they became a minority within the white-led Methodist churches. Virginia had high numbers of all-black Baptist churches. These churches were highly oriented to the community of believers and tended to be less hierarchical than their white counterparts.[117] Still, as the case of Jarena Lee points out there were significant limits for women's leadership within these churches. In 1819, Lee sought to be confirmed as a female preacher within the AME Church, but she faced opposition from Allen and the AME Church as a whole. Lee managed to act as an unofficial itinerant preacher, traveling thousands of miles and giving hundreds of sermons each year.[118] While black women were not given leadership roles, they had more meaningful, active lay roles in church business and lay leadership than their white counterparts.[119] By the antebellum period, the African Methodist Episcopal Church realized more of the radically egalitarian possibilities than the largely white Methodist Episcopal Church, and the AME achieved its goals ultimately through its separation.

Conclusions

By the time of John Wesley's death in 1791, Wesleyan Methodism had become a major presence on the American and English religious landscape. Once planted in America, Methodist societies would grow phenomenally

Figure 12. Richard Allen, artist unknown, engraving based on print by John Sartrain, ca. 1850–90. Courtesy of the Drew University Methodist Collection.

during the early national period and claim half a million members by 1830. By 1850, two-thirds of all churchgoers were either Baptist or Methodist.[120]

As American Methodism developed and became somewhat independent of the English establishment, the ties were always there. They shared a common evangelical ethos, language, print culture, and personnel. In the establishment of American Methodism as a church, with its own powers of ordination, both English and American Methodism became formalized as a separate entity from the Church of England. Wesley continued to be an almost mythical figure in American Methodism before and after his death in 1791. Laity and preachers read his sermons, essays, and letters, and they followed his suggested reading lists.

In the realm of political conflict, the degree to which this power struggle was termed as a struggle between fathers and sons is reflected in many of the letters between American and English leadership. Throughout the eighteenth century, the ideas of paternalism were strongly imbedded in authority. The Revolutionary period saw contestation over the terms of fatherhood; Wesley was the wise father at times, the doddering, presumptuous father at others. Yet, the power of the term "father" survived this struggle, and American Methodists would go on to call both Asbury and Wesley their spiritual fathers well into the nineteenth century.

American preachers emphasized the roles of brotherhood, as they resisted the absolute power of the father in the role of Wesley. In the post-Revolutionary period, the American leadership resented the idea of more hierarchy. That resentment extended to Wesley's appointed leaders, who, they suspected, were more English and therefore more likely to be Wesley's obedient sons in deciding matters of governance. Certainly, it also became clear that American preachers saw themselves as distinct from their English brethren. Opposition to English interference and Wesley's absolute leadership eventually brought the American Methodist family together. The North and South had been divided within the preachers' conferences at the end of the Revolutionary War, but they joined together with a sense of purpose and some solidarity over their independence from England. Yet, in many ways, culturally and organizationally, English and American Methodism were more alike than different. The structure and form of American Methodist practice was almost exactly as Wesley had desired.

The cultural differences that did become more pronounced through the nineteenth century were ones of popular religious expression. American evangelicals remained more comfortable with ecstatic expressions of religiosity than their English counterparts, ironically so, considering that ecstatic religious expression had deep roots in the English revivals of the 1730s and 1740s. As the American camp meeting and its phenomenal success in the early 1800s demonstrate, American evangelicals were happy to exploit the entertainment value of religion, when they found a popular practice. On the British side, they feared the potential backlash of employing these means of stirring up religious sentiment. At the base of some of these cultural differences was the matter of race. African Americans were central in the continuing success of camp meetings, as well as being central supporters in the continuing ecstatic religious culture in American evangelicalism.

Religious historian Don Mathews contends that African American conversion "did offer blacks a means of establishing their claim upon the Christian care, respect, and love of their newfound comrades [white evangelicals]."[121] To be sure, these claims were somewhat limited. Mathews points out that evangelical culture privileged individual experience; this culture relied upon conversion narratives and the links these narratives made between different members of the evangelical community, black and white. This religious community did have revolutionary possibilities, but African American Methodists made more of these claims to equality than did their white brethren.

American Methodism doubled and tripled its membership into the beginning of the nineteenth century. Much of this fact had to do with African American retention of the early evangelical fervor alongside the frontier revivals of the nineteenth century. African American Methodism represented some of the most socially and expressively radical elements of Methodism, particularly as the African Methodist Episcopal Church split from Methodist Episcopal Church and led its own religious organization.

Methodism demonstrated its ability to grow with the young nation along the western areas of Kentucky, Tennessee, Georgia, and Ohio, where antislavery Methodists like Gatch and Shine chose to resettle. American Methodist practice did have a culture distinct from its English counterpart by the 1800s, when camp meetings and new revivals continued to attract new converts, especially in those newly settled western areas. The antebellum South is where Methodism left its lasting influence, though, and in that legacy, there was a fairly compromised version of Methodism. Split from its early transatlantic antislavery heritage, it became a respectable denomination for slaveholders. It was only after this antislavery stance was softened that Methodism expanded its membership exponentially in the antebellum South.[122]

Conclusion

The early years of Methodism were an experimental period for laity and leadership alike. Together they forged a new culture, an evangelical family that supported individuals and transformed their families. At its core, this book argues that early Methodists saw themselves as a family, both reflecting and reformulating eighteenth-century notions of family. The Methodist family formed a challenge to eighteenth-century English and American society. Methodists minimized their blood family ties to assume new identities as spiritual brothers, sisters, mothers, and fathers with distinctive social practices. This perfected family was an eternal family, which would be reconstituted in the next world.

The Methodist family practices influenced ideas about family that were emerging in this period of social and emotional transitions within Anglo-American society. For one, the infusion of evangelical religious ideals in marital choice was significant. The prior religious marital model of the Puritan helpmeet promoted female subservience to the male head of household. In the ideal eighteenth-century evangelical family, both men and women worried about their religious usefulness after marriage. In eighteenth-century Methodist literature, there were no references to the ultimate subservience of female religiosity to the husband's in marriage. This element bolstered the companionate marriage ideal, a significant component in the emergence of modern familial practices. As well, by relying upon providential signs, evangelicals' search for their religious soul mates supported the emergence of the romantic ideal of love-based marriages. In many ways, the search for God's approval was akin to the search for a sign of true love.

The modern sense of falling in love, though, had a different cast in the evangelical Methodist context. God was not an irrational force like romantic love, but rather rational, and through providential signs, individuals could discover their role in a sensible design. In this way, Methodists sublimated their own individual desires to a larger plan for their lives and to the

Figure 13. *John Wesley, That Excellent Minister of the Gospel, carried by Angels into Abraham's Bosom. Well done, good and faithful Servant. Enter thou into the Joy of thy Lord. St. Matthew, Ch. 25*, artist unknown (London: Robert Sayer, 1791). © Trustees of the British Museum.

common good of the religious family more generally. Yet, Methodist forms of courtship paradoxically reinforced individuality by disregarding human input in favor of divine knowledge or approval, because divine knowledge could only be accessed through the individual's interior sense of divine will. Evangelicals sought signs of God's approval in these matters, imbuing spousal choice with a sense of mystical rightfulness. It sometimes took months to ascertain the rightfulness of a match as they waited for God's approval, and then the matter would be settled suddenly due to a dream, a vision, or simply an overwhelming change in the individual's assessment of the match. In the context of Methodist selfhood, this meant that individual actions and decisions were seldom random but, rather, embedded in understanding and acting on religious authority.[1]

Finding a suitable match meant turning to providence, God, and spiritual mentors, instead of parents. In this way, children were increasingly making their own choices regarding spousal selection, like many of their eighteenth-century contemporaries. As Methodists described their courtships in their letters and journals, they tuned out people who would otherwise have been the normative authorities in these life decisions, their friends and family. Still, evangelical marriages were not wholly individualistic during this period. Their choices were often carefully embedded within Methodist lines of authority. Yet the outcome was fairly radical: men and women resisted parental and societal pressure to marry in order to follow their own spiritual callings.

The alternative social ways of the Methodist family were part and parcel of the evangelical rejection of the existing family ties in favor of a new family with alternative social norms. These new social norms were not easy to follow; being in the "narrow way" meant sacrifice for eighteenth-century Methodists. While the anti-Methodist press attempted to paint Methodist sexuality as loose and dangerous, Methodists themselves were very careful about their sexual choices. The popular press characterized Methodists as dangerous and cultish, likely to draw a child into madness and sexual depravity. These characteristics all pointed to the position of Methodists as dissenters, and as a deviant family apart, not to be trusted by mainstream society. Methodists emphasized that their choices to step outside the customs of their natal families and to follow their spiritual callings was taking the hard road; they preferred their difficult holy lives to the soft ways of indulgent and thoughtless living. The decision to reformulate one's life in the Methodist way must have been difficult for many converts, but it was a necessity. The painful rupturing of one's old life was a crucial antecedent to rebirth and regeneration into a new life.

When converts loosened their traditional familial bonds, they gained a new life within the larger connection of the Methodist family. The Methodist family expanded the concept of family during the long eighteenth century. It was a voluntary association of like-minded people, a chosen kin network that substituted for or elaborated on natal families. This religious family stepped into a gap, providing economic, social, and emotional support where necessary. Individuals did not have to leave their families altogether or join Methodist households to reap the benefits of their chosen religious family, but they did become part of a larger support network than their blood families could provide.

While the Methodist family was modeled in many ways on the nuclear family, it was also significantly different. This new religious family, though conforming to a nuclear family in many ways, put greater emphasis on the children, since Methodist brothers and sisters had more power than in a patriarchal family. Wesley's political and social clout, both as a governing father to the itinerants and as a personal father to all Methodists, should not be underestimated. However, the Methodist basis for decision making, the emphasis on providence, and the ways in which divine will was made known through individuals—all these elements mitigated religious patriarchal authority in favor of individual authority.

As the Methodist family grew during the nineteenth century, Methodists transformed themselves from a dissenting social association into a full-fledged church and distinct denomination. The ultimate outcome of the crisis of sacraments and ordinations, provoked by American Methodists in 1785, was that Methodists on both sides of the Atlantic realized that they were now officially separate from the Church of England. Their increased focus on institution building, fueled by their increasing numbers, reduced the intimacy and flexibility of the eighteenth-century family. The first three decades of the nineteenth century saw the greatest success of American Methodism as wave after wave of new members converted through the backcountry revivals and urban evangelicalism that made up the Second Great Awakening.

John and Charles Wesley had not conceived of Methodism as a full-fledged church.[2] From the early years of Methodism, starting in the Holy Club and the mission work in America, the Wesleys saw this project as a social organization, an intimate voluntary association that existed in tandem with the Church of England, to help individuals perfect their spiritual lives. The formation of the American Methodist Episcopal Church in 1785 sparked a significant, if inevitable, break with the initial plan of Methodism as a social entity. It still retained that vital core of social fellowship and familial religious ideals, but as full institutionalization took hold, some of those elements became de-emphasized, particularly after Methodism began to gather much wider membership in the early nineteenth century.

By the nineteenth century, John Wesley was a lionized and well-regarded leader, but he was no longer the father of Methodists. Wesley's death in 1791 had a profound effect on the movement. After his death, leadership was open, but it was a relatively smooth transition to the formalization of the roles of the leaders who would succeed him. While his death is an easy marker for the beginning of institutionalization and increased conservatism, some elements had begun well beforehand, with the separation of American leadership. Deborah Valenze has convincingly argued that Wesley's death marked the beginning of a more conservative period of Methodism in England. However, Valenze also argues that Methodist "fringe" sects developed a distinctive brand of worship. These branches of Methodism protested against middle-class norms of religion and work, especially the changes associated with the onset of the industrial revolution.[3] In this way, one can see the seeds of eighteenth-century radical Methodist ideas, especially in the arenas of class and gender, surviving well into the nineteenth century. In America, those countercultural seeds developed in the nineteenth-century African Methodist Episcopal Church, which promoted black leadership and built its own churches. As well, in the nineteenth century, the anti-elitist populist element of Methodism remained in place in the American Methodist Episcopal Church. While women were still formally barred from preaching, white men could rise up to the rank of preacher without formal education or upper-class refinement.[4]

Many of the expressive elements of early Methodism, particularly the romantic religious ecstasy that contemporaries found so abhorrent, took on a different form in the nineteenth century. As observers of nineteenth-century camp meetings were quick to note, converts flailed and groaned, sighed and pitched themselves around the benches. Ecstatic physical reactions to the Holy Spirit still occurred, especially in nineteenth-century American Methodist meetings. In the eighteenth century, men and women expressed emotions and sexual fervor that was normally deemed inexcusably excessive and imprudent within the public arena, particularly as they expressed their love and devotion to fellow Methodists and preachers. This element of romantic religious feeling, bound as it was to sentimentalism, promoted affective relationships between Methodist family members. As the nineteenth century became more oriented toward the family as a domestic unit, Methodist religious familial ideals found expression in the affective bonds of the nuclear family. It was during the early nineteenth century that Methodists instituted widely popular Sunday Schools, formalizing the expectation that Methodists would form their own families and catechize their children. As the Methodist family became more formalized and institutional, the radicalism of its voluntary social organization faded, and these romantic, sentimental bonds found outlet in the more traditional sense of the Methodist household, a bounded nuclear unit.

Many of the conservative, bourgeois elements of the Wesleyan Methodist movement persisted in mainstream Methodism in the nineteenth century, dominating social practice and religious organization. Wesleyan Methodism on both sides of the Atlantic became inherently Victorian and bourgeois in its organization. The Methodist family in the nineteenth century did not challenge standard cultural practices; instead, it flourished within Victorian culture. In the nineteenth century, mainstream Methodist societies reflected and reinforced a period of increasingly domestic ideals for women and hardening of racial structures.[5] As the nineteenth century progressed, Methodism moved from dissent to mainstream and helped define the ethos of modern Christian life in America.

Abbreviations

DUL	Drew University Library and General Commission on Archives and History of the United Methodist Church, Madison, N.J.
DUSC	Duke University Rare Book, Manuscript, and Special Collections Library, Durham, N.C.
MARC	Methodist Archives and Research Centre, John Rylands University Library of Manchester, Manchester, England.
SHC	Southern Historical Collection, Wilson Special Collections Library, University of North Carolina at Chapel Hill.
VHS	Virginia Historical Society, Richmond, Va.
Letters	*The Letters of the Rev. John Wesley, A.M.*, John Telford, ed. London: Epworth Press, 1931.
Works	*The Bicentennial Edition of the Works of John Wesley*. Frank Baker and Richard P. Heitzenrater, gen. eds. Nashville: Abingdon Press, 1976–.
	Vol. 1. *Sermons I*. Ed. Albert C. Outler, 1984.
	Vol. 2. *Sermons II*. Ed. Albert C. Outler, 1985.
	Vol. 3. *Sermons III*. Ed. Albert C. Outler, 1986.
	Vol. 4. *Sermons IV*. Ed. Albert C. Outler, 1987.
	Vol. 9. *The Methodist Societies: History, Nature, and Design*. Ed. Rupert E. Davies, 1989.
	Vol. 11. *The Appeals to Men of Reason and Religion and Certain Related Open Letters*. Ed. Gerald R. Cragg, 1989.
	Vol. 18. *Journals and Diaries I (1735–1738)*. Ed. W. Reginald Ward and Richard P. Heitzenrater, 1988.
	Vol. 19. *Journals and Diaries II (1728–1743)*. Ed. W. Reginald Ward and Richard P. Heitzenrater, 1990.

Vol. 20. *Journals and Diaries III (1743–1754)*. Ed. W. Reginald Ward and Richard P. Heitzenrater, 1991.

Vol. 21. *Journals and Diaries IV (1755–1765)*. Ed. W. Reginald Ward and Richard P. Heitzenrater, 1992.

Vol. 22. *Journals and Diaries V (1765–1775)*. Ed. W. Reginald Ward and Richard P. Heitzenrater, 1993.

Vol. 23. *Journals and Diaries VI (1775–1786)*. Ed. W. Reginald Ward and Richard P. Heitzenrater, 1995.

Vol. 25. *Letters I (1721–1739)*. Ed. Frank Baker, 1980.

Vol. 26. *Letters II (1740–1755)*. Ed. Frank Baker, 1982.

Works (Jackson)   *The Works of John Wesley*. Ed. Thomas Jackson. 14 vols. London: Wesleyan Conference Office, 1872. Reprint, Grand Rapids, Mich.: Zondervan, 1958–59.

Notes

Introduction

1. Robert Drew Simpson, ed., *American Methodist Pioneer: The Life and Journals of the Rev. Freeborn Garrettson, 1752–1827* (Rutland, Vt.: Academy Books, 1984), 3.

2. Thomas Cooper, Account, 1741, Early Methodist Volume, MARC. Many Methodist narratives confirm the idea that converts felt personally implicated by preachers' sermons. See also Bruce Hindmarsh, *The Evangelical Conversion Narrative: Spiritual Autobiography in Early Modern England* (Oxford: Oxford University Press, 2005), 143–45.

3. Simpson, *American Methodist Pioneer*, 42.

4. Ibid., 49.

5. Some of the critical histories that have established the importance of the rise of American Methodism include: Frank Baker, *From Wesley to Asbury: Studies in Early American Methodism* (Durham, N.C.: Duke University Press, 1976); Nathan Hatch, *The Democratization of American Christianity* (New Haven, Conn.: Yale University Press, 1989); Russell Richey, *Early American Methodism* (Bloomington: Indiana University Press, 1991); Christopher H. Owen, *The Sacred Flame of Love: Methodism and Society in Nineteenth-Century Georgia* (Athens: University of Georgia Press, 1998); John H. Wigger, *Taking Heaven by Storm: Methodism and the Rise of Popular Christianity in America* (New York: Oxford University Press, 1998); Nathan O. Hatch and John H. Wigger, eds., *Methodism and the Shaping of American Culture* (Nashville, Tenn.: Kingswood Books, 2001).

Recent histories have been impressive in their attention to analyzing the social meanings of Methodism's growth in America. See especially Cynthia Lynn Lyerly, *Methodism and the Southern Mind, 1770–1810* (Oxford: Oxford University Press, 1999); Christine Heyrman, *Southern Cross: The Beginnings of the Bible Belt* (New York: Alfred A. Knopf, 1997); Dee E. Andrews, *The Methodists and Revolutionary America, 1760–1800: The Shaping of an Evangelical Culture* (Princeton, N.J.: Princeton University Press, 2000).

Histories regarding George Whitefield and the rise of Calvinist Methodism during the First Great Awakening have been important to establishing the full range of Methodist ideas in America. See Frank Lambert, *"Pedlar in Divinity": George Whitefield and the Transatlantic Revivals, 1737–1770* (Princeton, N.J.: Princeton University Press, 1994);

Frank Lambert, *Inventing the "Great Awakening"* (Princeton, N.J.: Princeton University Press, 1999); and Harry S. Stout, *The Divine Dramatist: George Whitefield and the Rise of Modern Evangelicalism* (Grand Rapids, Mich.: W. B. Eerdmans, 1991).

6. Scholars of British Methodism have been industrious in the past forty years. David Hempton's prodigious work alone has opened up the landscape of English Methodism wonderfully. See particularly David Hempton, *The Religion of the People: Methodism and Popular Culture, c. 1750–1900* (London: Routledge Press, 1996) and *Methodism: Empire of the Spirit* (New Haven, Conn.: Yale University Press, 2005). Other essential histories of English Methodism include: Robert F. Wearmouth, *Methodism and the Common People of the Eighteenth Century* (London: Epworth Press, 1945); Frank Baker, *John Wesley and the Church of England* (Nashville, Tenn.: Abington Press, 1970); Bernard Semmel, *The Methodist Revolution* (New York: Basic Books, 1973); Deborah Valenze, *Prophetic Sons and Daughters: Female Preaching and Popular Religion in Industrial England* (Princeton, N.J.: Princeton University Press, 1985); Henry Rack, *Reasonable Enthusiast: John Wesley and the Rise of Methodism* (London: Epworth Press, 1989); Gail Malmgreen, *Religion in the Lives of English Women, 1760–1830* (London: Croom Helm, 1986); Richard P. Heitzenrater, *Wesley and the People Called Methodists* (Nashville, Tenn.: Abingdon Press, 1995); and Gareth Lloyd, *Charles Wesley and the Struggle for Methodist Identity* (Oxford: Oxford University Press, 2007).

7. Recent works have also sought to redefine the history of marriage and family, such as Stephanie Coontz's *Marriage, a History: How Love Conquered Marriage* (New York: Penguin Press, 2006) and Nancy Cott's *Public Vows: A History of Marriage and the Nation* (Cambridge, Mass.: Harvard University Press, 2000).

8. See Randolph Trumbach, *The Rise of the Egalitarian Family: Aristocratic Kinship and Domestic Relations in Eighteenth-Century England* (New York: Academic Press, 1978); Amanda Vickery, *The Gentleman's Daughter: Women's Lives in Georgian England* (New Haven, Conn.: Yale University Press, 1998), 39–41; and Lawrence Stone, *Family, Sex and Marriage in England, 1500–1800* (New York: Harper and Row, 1979). Stone is a leading proponent of this wave of romantic marriage. Though Stone's work has been largely criticized for the extent to which it generalized early modern English families, his narrative of the rise of the romantic model has been more widely confirmed. See E. P. Thompson, "Happy Families," *New Society* 41 (1977): 499–501; and Alan Macfarlane, review of Stone's *Family, Sex and Marriage*, *History and Theory* 18 (1979): 103–26. For descriptions of the American shift toward romantic marriage, see particularly: Carl Degler, *At Odds: Women and the Family in America from the Revolution to the Present* (New York: Oxford University Press, 1980), 9–14; Daniel Scott Smith, "Parental Control and Marriage Patterns: An Analysis of Historical Trends in Higham, Massachusetts," *Journal of Marriage and the Family* 35 (August 1973); Daniel Blake Smith, *Inside the Great House: Planter Family Life in Eighteenth-Century Chesapeake Society* (Ithaca, N.Y.: Cornell University Press, 1980); Jay Fleigelman, *Prodigals and Pilgrims: The American Revolution Against Patriarchal Authority, 1750–1800* (Cambridge, Mass.: Cambridge University Press, 1982); and Cott, *Public Vows*, 16–20.

9. Coontz's *Marriage, a History* is a sweeping and persuasive cross-cultural survey. Coontz largely casts eighteenth-century religious groups as fighting against the current, denying the importance of marriage because it risked individuals becoming obsessed with their partners, rather than with God. See Coontz, *Marriage, a History*, 150.

10. See Phyllis Mack, *Visionary Women: Ecstatic Prophecy in Seventeenth-Century England* (Berkeley: University of California Press, 1992), 56, 85–86. American Quakers endured the same aspersions in the seventeenth and eighteenth century. See Barry Levy, *Quakers and the American Family: British Settlement in the Delaware Valley* (New York: Oxford University Press, 1988). Perhaps witchcraft was the ultimate form of unorthodox religious practice, and Puritans ascribed insatiable and devilish sexual behaviors to female witches. Carol Karlsen, *The Devil in the Shape of a Woman: Witchcraft in Colonial New England* (New York: Norton, 1987), 156–59.

11. Richard Green, *Anti-Methodist Publications Issued During the Eighteenth Century* (London: C. H. Kelly, 1902).

12. For specific examples of the sexual deviance attributed to Methodists, see Albert M. Lyles, *Methodism Mocked: The Satiric Reaction to Methodism in the Eighteenth Century* (London: Epworth Press, 1960).

13. Nancy Cott, "Eighteenth-Century Family and Social Life Revealed in Massachusetts Divorce Records," *Journal of Social History* 10 (Fall 1976): 20.

14. Ruth H. Bloch, "Changing Conceptions of Sexuality and Romance in Eighteenth-Century America," *William and Mary Quarterly*, 3rd ser., vol. 60, no. 1 (January 2003): 13.

15. For a good overview of this shift, see Peter Laslett, *The World We Have Lost* (New York: Charles Scribner's Sons, 1965). His book is a synthesis of the work by the Cambridge Group for the History of Population and Social Structure. See D. E. C. Eversley, Peter Laslett, and E. A. Wrigley, *An Introduction to English Historical Demography from the Sixteenth to the Nineteenth Century* (New York: Basic Books, 1966), for the results of the Cambridge Group. See also Peter Laslett's "Size and Structure of the Household in England over Three Centuries," *Population Studies* 23 (1969): 199–223, and E. A. Wrigley, "Family Limitation in Pre-Industrial England," *Economic History Review* 19 (1966): 82–109.

16. See Jon F. Sensbach, *Rebecca's Revival: Creating Black Christianity in the Atlantic World* (Cambridge, Mass.: Harvard University Press, 2005), particularly for the ways in which Moravians were attracting nonelite diverse peoples. Aaron Fogleman establishes the broad missionary scope of the Atlantic realm of Moravians in his *Jesus Is Female: Moravians and Radical Religion in Early America* (Philadelphia: University of Pennsylvania Press, 2007).

17. Naomi Tadmor discusses the parameters of the word "connection" in the eighteenth-century context; see Tadmor, *Family and Friends in Eighteenth-Century England: Household, Kinship, and Patronage* (Cambridge: Cambridge University Press, 2001), 131–32.

18. Important works that have examined the evangelical family terms more centrally include Andrews, *The Methodists and Revolutionary America*; Heyrman, *Southern Cross*, especially 117–205; Susan Juster, *Disorderly Women: Sexual Politics and Evangelicalism in Revolutionary New England* (Ithaca, N.Y.: Cornell University Press, 1994), 113–22; Lyerly, *Methodism and the Southern Mind*; and Janet Moore Lindman, *Bodies of Belief: Baptist Community in Early America* (Philadelphia: University of Pennsylvania Press, 2008).

19. David Hempton, *Methodism and Politics in British Society, 1750–1850* (Stanford, Calif.: Stanford University Press, 1984), 13–14.

20. See Lindman, *Bodies of Belief*; Juster, *Disorderly Women*; and Rhys Isaac, *Transformation of Virginia, 1740–1790* (Chapel Hill: University of North Carolina Press, 1982), for Baptist familial titles and practices. For the English Quaker sense of family, see Mack, *Visionary Women*.

21. Juster, *Disorderly Women*, 123–25.

22. See especially Hester Ann Roe Rogers, Journals, 1:16, MARC.

23. Juster, *Disorderly Women*, 39.

24. Degler, *At Odds*, 5; Tadmor, *Family and Friends*, 116–17.

25. One significant modification to this picture of nuclear family continuity has been in understanding the role of kinship in family culture. Tadmor, for instance, points out that a significant number (while still a minority) of the households in Peter Laslett's landmark survey did include extended kin. Tadmor explains that kin were often rotating in and out of a particular household, making it difficult to determine the role of extended family members in households. Tadmor, *Family and Friends*, 36, 116. Peter Laslett, *The World We Have Lost—Further Explored* (London: Routledge), 93–94.

26. *Gentleman's Magazine*, June 1741, 11.

27. W. H. Daniels, *The Illustrated History of Methodism in Great Britain and America, from the Days of the Wesleys to the Present Time* (New York: Methodist Book Concern, 1880), 390.

28. Philip Greven, *The Protestant Temperament: Patterns of Child-Rearing, Religious Experience, and the Self in Early America* (New York: Alfred A. Knopf, 1980), 124.

29. Juster, *Disorderly Women*, especially 5–6, 31, and 65–66; Lyerly, *Methodism and the Southern Mind*; and Heyrman, *Southern Cross*.

30. See Jean Miller Schmidt, *Grace Sufficient: A History of Women in American Methodism, 1769–1939* (Nashville, Tenn.: Abingdon Press, 1999), 29–32. In the final two decades of Wesley's life, he began to formally recognize female preaching, although he understood it as an "extraordinary call." Methodist historian Paul Chilcote finds that female preaching was fairly widespread in the early years; he counts forty-two female preachers before 1803, the year that female preaching was distinctly and officially discouraged within Wesleyan Methodism. Paul Chilcote, *John Wesley and the Women Preachers* (Metuchen, N.J.: Scarecrow Press, 1991).

31. The line between preaching and exhorting was often a thin one. Some promi-

nent Methodist exhorters called their work preaching at times, and Wesley acknowledged women preachers. How exactly did their work really differ from what was called exhorting? Exhorting seemed to exist primarily as an auxiliary to preaching and to occur within closed Methodist meetings. Women were more likely to call their speaking preaching when it was independent of men preaching and when it occurred in public spaces or in front of large crowds.

32. This growing conservatism has been described in a number of ways in English and American Methodist histories. In the English context, E. P. Thompson's *The Making of the English Working Class* (London: Gollancz, 1963) has described this social conservatism and the intense Methodist hierarchy as having a gradual, insidious effect on the working classes. Valenze's *Prophetic Sons and Daughters* also describes mainstream Methodism as growing increasingly bourgeois in focus and leadership after the 1790s.

33. Greven, *Protestant Temperament*, 3–17 and 26–35.

34. Recent studies of George Whitefield have established the necessity for viewing Methodism in a transatlantic context. See Stout, *Divine Dramatist*, and Lambert, *Pedlar in Divinity*.

35. Frank Baker argues that John Wesley considered Whitefield a Methodist agent in America and that he remained a close friend to brothers Charles and John Wesley. See Baker, *From Wesley to Asbury*, 70–71. Other scholars have highlighted the differences between Whitefieldian and Wesleyan Methodism, in terms of theology and competition for influence and members. See especially Frank Lambert, *Inventing the "Great Awakening,"* 165–67. Henry Rack has argued that while there was a personal affinity between Whitefield and the Wesley brothers, their followers often lobbed attacks at one another. See Rack, *Reasonable Enthusiast*, 282–86.

36. There are some notable examples of works that have crossed the Atlantic divide. Frank Baker wrote about the connections between American and English Methodism, before the word "transatlantic" was fashionable. See Baker, *From Wesley to Asbury*. Rack's biography of John Wesley includes a chapter about American Methodism, primarily from the perspective of John Wesley's brief stint there as a missionary in the 1730s. See Rack, *Reasonable Enthusiast*, 108–23. W. R. Ward, *The Protestant Evangelical Awakening* (Cambridge: Cambridge University Press, 1992), is an impressively exhaustive history of the connections between eighteenth-century European and American revivalism. A recent foray into transatlantic waters is David Hempton's work on a transatlantic Methodism, particularly on the formation of Methodism as a missionary religious movement. See Hempton, *Methodism: Empire of the Spirit*.

37. For examples of important studies of religion in the American South, see Lyerly, *Methodism and the Southern Mind*; Heyrman, *Southern Cross*; Isaac, *Transformation of Virginia*; and William Henry Williams, *The Garden of American Methodism: The Delmarva Peninsula, 1769–1820* (Wilmington, Del.: Scholarly Resources, 1984).

38. See Sylvia Frey and Betty Wood, *Come Shouting to Zion: African American Protestantism in the American South and British Caribbean to 1830* (Chapel Hill: Univer-

sity of North Carolina Press, 1998); Heyrman, *Southern Cross*; and Lyerly, *Methodism and the Southern Mind*.

39. Recent examples of transatlantic religious history include Hempton, *Methodism: Empire of the Spirit*; Rebecca Larson, *Daughters of Light: Quaker Women Preaching and Prophesying in the Colonies and Abroad, 1700–1775* (New York: Alfred A. Knopf, 1999); and Susan Juster, *Doomsayers: Anglo-American Prophecy in the Age of Revolution* (Philadelphia: University of Pennsylvania Press, 2003). Recent Moravian histories have provided particularly rich models for transatlantic religious historians. See Sensbach, *Rebecca's Revival*; and Fogleman, *Jesus Is Female*. Transatlantic religious history was established in the late 1980s with a number of works, including Susan O'Brien, "A Transatlantic Community of Saints: The Great Awakening and the First Evangelical Network, 1735–1755," *American Historical Review* 91, no. 4 (October 1986): 811–32; Marilyn J. Westerkamp, *Triumph of the Laity: Scots-Irish Piety and the Great Awakening, 1625–1760* (New York: Oxford University Press, 1988); and Levy, *Quakers and the American Family*. Westerkamp's and Levy's studies focus on the translation and transplantation of Old World ideas to the New World. Richard Carwadine's work on nineteenth-century transatlantic evangelicalism reversed the usual current of Atlantic cultural transmission by demonstrating the influence that American revivals had on British religious ideas. See Carwadine, *Trans-Atlantic Revivalism: Popular Evangelicalism in Britain and America* (Westport, Conn.: Greenwood Press, 1978).

40. Lambert, *Pedlar in Divinity*, 52–94.

41. O'Brien, "Transatlantic Community of Saints," 823–29.

42. Frank Asbury to Jasper Winscom, 1788, in Francis Asbury, *The Journal and Letters of Francis Asbury*, ed. Elmer T. Clark, J. Manning Potts, and Jacob S. Payton (London: Epworth Press, 1958), 3:60–62.

43. Thompson, *Making of the English Working Class*, especially 350–400. His work was inspired by Elie Halévy's thesis in "The Birth of Methodism in England," first published in 1906. See Halévy, *The Birth of Methodism in England*, trans. and ed. Bernard Semmel (Chicago: University of Chicago Press, 1971). Also see Valenze, *Prophetic Sons and Daughters*; Andrews, *Methodists and Revolutionary America*, xi–xii.

44. Wesley expressed these views in his *Calm Address* (1775) and in letters to American itinerants. Wesley, *Letters*, 6:143, 181.

45. Semmel, *The Methodist Revolution*.

46. Andrews, *Methodists and Revolutionary America*, 3–9.

47. Jon Butler, *Awash in a Sea of Faith: Christianizing the American People* (Cambridge, Mass.: Harvard University Press, 1990).

48. Hatch, *Democratization of American Christianity*.

49. Butler, *Awash in a Sea of Faith*, 116–28.

50. Juster, *Disorderly Women*, 145–78.

51. For the purposes of this study, when I refer to "Methodism," I mean Wesleyan Methodism. In the eighteenth century, Wesleyan Methodists formed the main branch of Methodism, and no other offshoots had such high membership or sustained power and organization.

Chapter 1

1. "The Holy Club" moniker was not assigned by its members, but by opponents at Oxford. That title came from some "men of wit," as Wesley called them. See Wesley, *Works*, 18:129–30. Calling it a club, Henry Rack argues, was meant to belittle this venture, but it also points out how odd it was to be ardently religious at Oxford in this period. See Rack, *Reasonable Enthusiast*, 84–85.

2. There are many biographies of Wesley and histories of Methodism that include sketches of his early years, particularly analyzing that the Wesley family was primarily steeped in high church religious practice, and his father was a trained Anglican cleric. Wesley's maternal grandparents had been Calvinist Nonconformists, and his mother, Susanna Wesley, led worship at home, exposing John and Charles Wesley to Nonconformist ideas. See especially Rack, *Reasonable Enthusiast*, 45–57.

3. John Walsh, "Origins of the Evangelical Revival," in *Essays in Modern English Church History in Memory of Norman Sykes*, ed. G. V. Bennett and J. D. Walsh (New York: Oxford University Press, 1966), 133.

4. Ibid., 134–35.

5. Rack, *Reasonable Enthusiast*, 83–87; and Frederick C. Gill, *Charles Wesley, the First Methodist* (London: Lutterworth Press, 1964), 36–38.

6. Rack, *Reasonable Enthusiast*, 87.

7. Ibid., 81–84. "Methodist" was only reluctantly accepted by John Wesley as a name for this society.

8. Cheyne furthered a number of theories on healthy diets, advocating moderation and vegetarianism as cures for obesity and depression. See Anita Guerrini, *Obesity and Depression in the Enlightenment: The Life and Times of George Cheyne* (Norman: University of Oklahoma Press, 2000). Taylor's rules were incredibly influential on what would be established as Methodist practice and discipline. His first rule for holy living (out of twenty-three) was "Care of our time," and this particular guideline was also of fundamental importance to Wesley. See Jeremy Taylor, *The Rules and Exercises of Holy Living* (London, 1650) and *The Rules and Exercises of Holy Dying* (London, 1651). For more on the rise of the Holy Club, see Rack, *Reasonable Enthusiast*, 61–106.

9. Baker, *John Wesley and the Church of England*, 10–28.

10. Charles Wesley to John Wesley, January 20, 1727[/8]; January 5 [22, 1728/9]; and May 5, 1729, in Wesley, *Works*, 25:229–31, 233–36, 237–39. See also Rack, *Reasonable Enthusiast*, 85–86.

11. Gill, *Charles Wesley*, 35.

12. Andrews, *Methodists and Revolutionary America*, 14.

13. Linda Colley, *Britons: Forging the Nation, 1707–1837* (New Haven, Conn.: Yale University Press, 1992).

14. Patricia U. Bonomi, *Under the Cope of Heaven: Religion, Society, and Politics in Colonial America* (New York: Oxford University Press, 1986).

15. Butler, *Awash in a Sea of Faith*, 109–15.

16. Rack, *Reasonable Enthusiast*, 35–37. For connections between evangelicalism and Catholicism, see Ronald Paulson, *Hogarth's Graphic Works* (London: Print Room, 1989), 175–78: *Methodism and Popery Dissected and Compared* (London: Fielding and Walker, 1779); and Joseph Trapp, *The True Spirit of the Methodists, and Their Allies, (Whether Other Enthusiasts, Papists, Deists, Quakers, or Atheists) Fully Laid Open* (London: Lawton Gilliver, 1740).

17. There was a perception that the Church of England was losing its hold on members, but in reality, there was no formal splintering of the church. The numbers of dissenters in the late seventeenth and eighteenth centuries were not inordinately large. Keith Thomas, for instance, points out that the actual membership of Quakers (who were the most numerous of radical dissenters in the seventeenth century) was fairly small—30,000–40,000 by 1660, or less than 1 percent of the total population. Even the largest group of dissenters in early eighteenth-century England, the Presbyterians, constituted a modest proportion of the population, 3.3 percent, or 179,350 "hearers," according to Michael Watts. See Keith Thomas, *Religion and the Decline of Magic* (New York: Charles Scribner's Sons, 1971), 146; and Michael R. Watts, *The Dissenters: From the Reformation to the French Revolution* (Oxford: Oxford University Press, 1978), 509. For more on dissent in eighteenth-century England and their numbers, see W. A. Speck, *Stability and Strife* (Cambridge, Mass.: Harvard University Press, 1979). For the rising establishment of Anglicans in America, see Butler, *Awash in a Sea of Faith*, 98–101. Butler argues that there was a simultaneous rise in religious authority and an Anglican "renaissance" in Virginia between 1680 and 1770. Rhys Isaac traces Anglican ascendancy in the building of brick churches, yet stresses the formality, rather than the fervor, of Anglican adherence. Isaac, *Transformation of Virginia*, 58–68.

18. Butler, *Awash in a Sea of Faith*, 104.

19. Andrews, *Methodists and Revolutionary America*, 14.

20. Hempton, *Methodism: Empire of the Spirit*, 13.

21. Doris Elisabett Andrews, "Popular Religion and the Revolution in the Middle Atlantic Ports: The Rise of the Methodists, 1770–1800" (Ph.D. diss., University of Pennsylvania, 1986), 5.

22. Wesley, *Works*, 18:137–38.

23. Ibid., 143.

24. Ibid., 150–51.

25. Ibid., 146.

26. See David Hempton, "John Wesley (1703–1791)," in *The Pietist Theologians*, ed. Carter Lindberg (London: Blackwell Publishing, 2005), 257–58.

27. Wesley, *Letters*, 1:150.

28. John Wesley, *The Journal of the Rev. John Wesley, A.M.*, ed. Nehemiah Curnock (London: Epworth Press. 1938), 1:435.

29. John Wesley to John Burton, October 10, 1735, in Wesley, *Works*, 25:439. Wesley maintains that his mission failed because local English leadership was not supportive of Wesley's Native American mission, though he maintains that Georgia's founder James Oglethorpe was supportive of this mission. Wesley, *Works*, 18:173.

30. This profile of Native Americans' willingness to be converted, of course, extends well beyond Wesley and originates well before his Georgia mission. Spanish Franciscans made similar assessments in the seventeenth century, regarding the Pueblos. See Ramón Gutiérrez, *When Jesus Came, the Corn Mothers Went Away: Marriage, Sexuality, and Power in New Mexico, 1500–1846* (Stanford, Calif.: Stanford University Press, 1991), 46–48, 92–94.

31. Wesley, *Works*, 18:193. Henry Rack notes that Wesley left the task of evangelizing Indians to fellow Anglican missionaries Charles Delamotte and Benjamin Ingham, but since neither spent a great deal of time in Georgia, and given Wesley's assessment, there seems to have been little progress in converting Native Americans by any Anglican missionary. Rack, *Reasonable Enthusiast*, 118. Andrews, *Methodists and Revolutionary America*, 18–19.

32. John Wesley, *An extract of the Rev. Mr. John Wesley's journal, from his embarking for Georgia, to his return to London, No. I and II* (London, 1797), 51–52 (April 27, 1737).

33. See Jon Sensbach, *A Separate Canaan: The Making of an Afro-Moravian World in North Carolina, 1763–1840* (Chapel Hill: University of North Carolina Press, 1998); and Sensbach, *Rebecca's Revival*.

34. Chilcote, *John Wesley and the Women Preachers*, 22.

35. Andrews, *Methodists and Revolutionary America*, 26.

36. Wesley, *Works*, 18:157.

37. Ibid., 9:25–45.

38. David Sherman, *History of the Revisions of the Discipline of the Methodist Episcopal Church* (New York: Nelson and Phillips, 1874), 449–50.

39. Chilcote, *John Wesley and the Women Preachers*, 22.

40. Andrews, *Methodists and Revolutionary America*, 15.

41. Adam Clarke, *Memoirs of the Wesley Family, Collected Principally from Original Documents*, 2nd ed., revised, ed. George Peck (New York: Lane and Tippett, 1848), 387.

42. Bartholomaeus Ziegenbalg, *Propagation of the Gospel in the East: Being an Account of the Success of the Danish Missionaries, Sent to the East-Indies, for the Conversion of the Heathen in Malabar* (London: J. Downing, 1714).

43. Andrews, *Methodists and Revolutionary America*, 16; Greven, *Protestant Temperament*, 36–38. Greven maintains that this Susanna Wesley's strict household was the prototype for evangelical households.

44. Walsh, "Origins of the Evangelical Revival," 134–35. Establishing the exact provenance of the Methodist band is somewhat difficult, because there were so many precedents to this idea. See Rack, *Reasonable Enthusiast*, 120.

45. Fogleman, *Jesus Is Female*, 87.

46. Patrick Tailfer, Hugh Anderson, David Douglas, et al., *A True and Historical Narrative of the Colony of Georgia in America, from the First Settlement Thereof, until the Present Period* (Charlestown, S.C.: P. Timothy, 1741).

47. Fogleman, *Jesus Is Female*, 86–87.

48. Gillian Lindt Gollin, "Family Surrogates in Colonial America: The Moravian Experiment," *Journal of Marriage and the Family* 31, no. 4 (November 1969): 652–53; Fogleman, *Jesus Is Female*, 8.

49. Fogleman, *Jesus Is Female*, 90.

50. Gillian Lindt Gollin, *Moravians in Two Worlds: A Study of Changing Communities* (New York: Columbia University Press, 1967), 69.

51. Otto Uttendörfer, *Zinzendorf und die Jugend* (Berlin: Furche Verlag, 1923), quoted in Gollin, "Family Surrogates," 653.

52. Gollin, *Moravians in Two Worlds*, 110–27.

53. Fogleman, *Jesus Is Female*, 88, 91–94.

54. See also Henry Rack's discussion of Wesley's personal shortcomings in this romance. Rack, *Reasonable Enthusiast*, 258.

55. J. Augustin Leger, *John Wesley's Last Love* (London: J. M. Dent, 1910).

56. Notes on the Journal of John Wesley, Frank Baker Papers, DUSC.

57. Bufford W. Coe, *John Wesley and Marriage* (London: Associated University Presses, 1996), 20. Legislation regulating marriage was passed in England in 1694 and 1712, and Wesley was a stickler for discipline. These laws stipulated a public reading of the banns and rules on applying for a marriage license. No officiant was allowed to celebrate a marriage in a private home without the published banns and a license. Wesley campaigned against the laxity of marriages performed in South Carolina and Georgia (including Hopkey's) in his time there, 1736–37.

58. Andrews, *Methodists and Revolutionary America*, 18.

59. Rack, *Reasonable Enthusiast*, 129.

60. Andrews, *Methodists and Revolutionary America*, 19.

61. Baker, *From Wesley to Asbury*, 11.

62. Rack, *Reasonable Enthusiast*, 123.

63. Hawkins had also reportedly physically attacked John Wesley after he tried to smooth things over. Armed with a pistol and a pair of scissors, Hawkins had to be restrained in order to stop her attempts to hurt Wesley. Wesley, *Works*, 18:410–414 (August 20–22, 1736). See also Rack, *Reasonable Enthusiast*, 116.

64. Gill, *Charles Wesley*, 53.

65. Charles Wesley, *The Journal of the Rev. Charles Wesley*, ed. Thomas Jackson (London: John Mason, 1849), 1:35.

66. Frank Baker also suggests that the Wesley brothers were not savvy about the colonial hierarchy and were "inexperienced" at judging people. Baker, *From Wesley to Asbury*, 11.

67. Tailfer et al., *A True and Historical Narrative*, 42.

68. Ibid., 43.

69. See John Wesley, *An Extract of the Rev. Mr. John Wesley's Journal From His Embarking for Georgia to His Return to London* (Bristol: S. and F. Farley, 1740). In the preface to this journal, Wesley states that he was forced to publish the journal due to a previous publication that had laid bare the scandal. Because the scandal was known

in England as well as America now, Wesley felt "an Obligation upon me to do what in me lies, in Obedience to that Command of God, *Let not the Good which is in within you be evil-spoken of.*"

70. Williams, *Garden of American Methodism*; Baker, *From Wesley to Asbury*, 28. Dee Andrews, *Methodists and Revolutionary America*, likewise focuses her work on the years 1760–1800 to describe the rise of American Methodists.

71. George Whitefield, *George Whitefield's Journals* (London: Banner of Truth Trust, 1960), 155.

72. Baker, *From Wesley to Asbury*, 22–25, 30–31. Baker largely sees the period of 1738 to 1766 as a fallow one for American Wesleyan Methodism. On the other hand, he argues that there may have been some progress made in Georgia, which Wesley had attributed to the Moravians, but Baker believed were the latent fruits of John Wesley's work. While Baker sees Whitefield as fanning the sparks of evangelical Methodism, Baker largely discounts Whitefield's contributions to American Methodism because he failed to build lasting societies.

73. Williams, *Garden of American Methodism*, 2.

74. Ibid.

75. For a good interpretation of Whitefield's theological stance, see Butler, *Awash in a Sea of Faith*, 186–87; and Stout, *Divine Dramatist*. Stout maintains that Whitefield's theological position changed following his revivals in America, becoming more emphatically Calvinist over time and in America.

76. Luke Tyerman, *The Life of the Rev. George Whitefield* (New York: Anson D. F. Randolph, 1877), 1:553.

77. Sylvia Frey, *Water from the Rock: Black Resistance in a Revolutionary Age* (Princeton, N.J.: University of Princeton Press, 1991), 26.

78. Frederick Dalcho, *An Historical Account of the Protestant Episcopal Church in South Carolina: From the First Settlement of the Province, to the War of Revolution* (Charleston, S.C.: E. Thayer, 1820), 336–37.

79. Frey and Wood, *Come Shouting to Zion*, 93; Allan Gallay, *The Formation of a Planter Elite: Jonathan Bryan and the Southern Colonial Frontier* (Athens: University of Georgia Press, 1989), 49–51.

80. Wesley, "Free Grace," in *Works*, 3:544–63.

81. Nelson Waite Rightmyer, *The Anglican Church in Delaware* (Philadelphia: Church Historical Society, 1947), 115.

82. Baker, *From Wesley to Asbury*, 70–71.

83. See ibid., 15–27, for evidence of Wesley's monitoring of American revivals during the 1740s and 1750s.

84. Andrews, *Methodists and Revolutionary America*, 23–24.

85. See Jonathan Edwards and John Wesley, *Thoughts Concerning the Revival of Religion in New England* (London, 1745); and Andrews, "Popular Religion and the Revolution," 17.

86. Wesley, *Works*, 11:374.

87. O'Brien, "Transatlantic Community of Saints"; Hindmarsh, *Evangelical Conversion Narrative*, 67–72. See also Michael Crawford, *Seasons of Grace: Colonial New England's Revival Tradition in Its British Context* (New York: Oxford University Press, 1991); and Richard Steele, *"Gracious Affection" and "True Virtue" According to Jonathan Edwards and John Wesley* (Metuchen, N.J.: Scarecrow Press, 1994).

88. Fogleman, *Jesus is Female*, 158–59.

89. Hempton, *Methodism: Empire of the Spirit*, 14.

90. Wesley, *Works*, 19:16.

91. Hindmarsh, *Evangelical Conversion Experience*, 162–63.

92. Andrews, *Methodists and Revolutionary America*, 25–26.

93. Wearmouth, *Methodism and the Common People*, 13.

94. Wesley, *Works*, 19:67.

95. Ibid., 9:15–23.

96. Baker, *John Wesley and the Church of England*, 114.

97. William Warren Sweet, *Religion on the American Frontier, 1783–1840*, vol. 4, *The Methodists: A Collection of Source Materials* (Chicago: University of Chicago Press, 1946), 34–35.

98. *Minutes of the Methodist Conferences, from the First Held in London, by the Late Rev. John Wesley, A.M., in the Year 1744* (London, 1812), 58–61.

99. Chilcote, *John Wesley and the Women Preachers*, 48–49.

100. See Andrews, *Methodists and Revolutionary America*, 247, tables 1 and 2. These numbers account for members of Philadelphia and New York Methodist societies, 1786–1801.

101. John Wesley, *Rules of Band-Societies* (London, 1738).

102. Sherman, *History of the Revisions*, 139.

103. Lyerly, *Methodism and the Southern Mind*, 14; Hempton, *Methodism: Empire of the Spirit*, 78.

104. Andrews, *Methodists and Revolutionary America*, 93.

105. Accounts in the Early Methodist Volume, MARC, repeat the importance of the ticket to early members. It is interesting to note that the material form of the ticket was becoming more common in the eighteenth century in the commercial sphere and that Methodists were the first religious group to employ a ticket as a means for membership. See James E. Kirby, Russell E. Richey, and Kenneth E. Rowe, *The Methodists* (Westport, Conn.: Greenwood Press, 1996), 166. Henry Abelove argues that the ticket was surprisingly important to some Methodists, who requested they be buried with their membership tickets. Henry Abelove, *The Evangelist of Desire: John Wesley and the Methodists* (Stanford, Calif.: Stanford University Press, 1990), 108.

106. Thomas Rankin, Journal, 1773–78, DUL.

107. Christine Heyrman establishes Baptists and Methodists as parallel groups with many similarities in their evangelical approach, even as they had striking differences organizationally. Heyrman, *Southern Cross*, 11–13, 104–6.

108. Andrews, "Popular Religion and the Revolution," 17.

109. Ibid.

110. Williams, *Garden of American Methodism*.

111. Hempton, *Methodism: Empire of the Spirit*, 18.

112. Baker, *From Wesley to Asbury*, 42. Heck had emigrated with her husband, Paul Heck, originally from Germany as part of a group who was granted land in Ireland. See Hempton, *Methodism: Empire of the Spirit*, 20.

113. See Baker, *From Wesley to Asbury*, 33–50; and Andrews, "Popular Religion and the Revolution," 18–23.

114. Hempton, *Methodism: Empire of the Spirit*, 20.

115. Frey and Wood, *Come Shouting to Zion*, 82.

116. Donald G. Mathews, *Religion of the Old South* (Chicago: University of Chicago Press, 1977), 66.

117. Frey and Wood, *Come Shouting to Zion*, 120.

118. Ibid., 119.

119. Lyerly, *Methodism and the Southern Mind*, 14.

120. Andrews, *Methodists and Revolutionary America*, 123.

Chapter 2

1. Andrews, *Methodists and Revolutionary America*, 114.

2. Wigger, *Taking Heaven by Storm*, 58.

3. See especially *Methodism Unmasked, or The Progress of Puritanism, from the Sixteenth to the Nineteenth Century: Intended as an Explanatory Supplement to "Hints to Heads of Families"* (London: J. Hatchard, 1802), which warns that Methodism threatened to destroy families and political order simultaneously. See also Joseph Nightingale, *A Portraiture of Methodism: Being an Impartial View of the Rise, Progress, Doctrines, Discipline, and Manners of the Wesleyan Methodists, in a Series of Letters Addressed to a Lady* (London: C. Stower, 1807) and *The Story of the Methodist-Lady, or The Injur'd Husband's Revenge: A True History* (London: John Doughty, n.d.).

4. Stith Mead, Letterbook, 15 (1792), VHS.

5. Mary Maddern to Charles Wesley, June 29, 1762, Early Methodist Volume, MARC.

6. Ibid.

7. Benjamin Abbott, *The Experience and Gospel Labours of the Rev. Benjamin Abbott: To Which Is Annexed a Narrative of His Life and Death by John Firth* (Philadelphia, 1801).

8. Leigh Hunt, *An Attempt to Shew the Folly and Danger of Methodism in a Series of Essays, First Published in the Weekly Paper Called the Examiner* (London: John Hunt, 1809), 46–47. As the title explains, this volume is a collection of essays that were previously published in a weekly London paper, which was published by Leigh and John Hunt. Leigh Hunt had joined his brother in publishing this paper in 1808, but had already established himself as a theater critic. Leigh Hunt is the presumed author of this collection of essays, based upon his publication of a series of essays in the

Examiner. In his autobiography, he complains that the *Edinburgh Review* did not publish a review of his anti-Methodist pamphlet, "though the opinions in it were, perhaps, identical with its own." Leigh Hunt, *The Autobiography of Leigh Hunt with Reminiscences of Friends and Contemporaries, in Three Volumes* (London: Smith, Elder, 1850), 1: 250–51.

9. John Wesley, in his opening editorial, called the Calvinist discourse unreasonable "with Arguments worthy of *Bedlam*." He claimed the Methodist manner, in contrast, was "inoffensive," drawn from the Bible and from reason, thereby refuting the usual equation between behavior at Bedlam and the ecstatic conversions of Methodists. *Arminian Magazine* (1778).

10. Michael MacDonald's essay "Insanity and the Realities of History in Early Modern England," *Psychological Medicine* 11 (1981): 11–25, and Roy Porter's *Mind-Forg'd Manacles* (London: Athlone Press, 1987) clarify the links between religious enthusiasm and charges of mental illness from the late seventeenth century through the eighteenth century. MacDonald's essay analyzes more closely the diagnostic association of mental illness and religious enthusiasm and the influence this had on wider currents in society. See also Michael Heyd, *Be Sober and Reasonable: The Critique of Enthusiasm in the Seventeenth and Early Eighteenth Centuries* (New York: E. J. Brill, 1995).

11. Porter, *Mind-Forg'd Manacles*, 67, quoting George Whitefield's account.

12. MacDonald, "Insanity and the Realities of History," 16–17.

13. Heyrman, *Southern Cross*, 35–37.

14. Michael MacDonald, *Mystical Bedlam: Madness, Anxiety and Healing in Seventeenth-Century England* (Cambridge: Cambridge University Press, 1981).

15. Mary Bosanquet Fletcher, MS Autobiography, 1:21–22, MARC.

16. Rhys Isaac delineates the rules for eighteenth-century Baptists and how these abraded the local customs of Virginian public society in *Transformation of Virginia*. Particularly, Isaac demonstrates the ways in which Baptist culture ran counter to Virginian sociability and masculine culture, especially Baptists' avoidance of cockfighting, gambling, drinking, and profanity. See Isaac, *Transformation of Virginia*, especially 143–77. Cynthia Lynn Lyerly demonstrates how Methodist rules also irritated eighteenth-century southern society in *Methodism and the Southern Mind*, 47–93.

17. John Wesley, *Rules of the Band Societies. Drawn up Dec. 25 1738* (London: Strahan, c. 1746). See also *The Nature, Design, and General Rules of the United Societies in London, Bristol, Kingswood, Newcastle upon Tyne, Fourth Edition* (London: Strahan, 1743). In the 1770s, these general rules began to appear in periodic publications that came out of the Conference of Preachers and were generally known as the *Discipline*. See *Minutes of Several Conversations Between the Rev. John Wesley, A.M. and the Preachers in connection with him Containing the Form of Discipline Established Among the Preachers and People in the Methodist Societies* (London: G. Whitfield, 1779). See also David Sherman, *History of the Revisions of the Discipline of the Methodist Episcopal Church* (New York: Nelson and Phillips, 1874).

18. See Wesley, *Rules of the Band Societies*; Hempton, *Methodism: Empire of the Spirit*, 110; Lyerly, *Methodism and the Southern Mind*, 73–93.

19. Hunt, *Folly and Danger of Methodism*, 46.

20. Other accounts that highlight this need for separation from friends can be found in the Early Methodist Volume, MARC; see, for example, Joanna Mussell to Charles Wesley, 1762; Mary Maddern, Account, June 29, 1762; and Thomas Cooper, Account, 1741.

21. Stith Mead, *A Short Account of the Experiences and Labours of the Reverend Stith Mead* (Lynchburg, Va., 1829), 34–42.

22. Stith Mead to William Mead, June 12, 1793, Mead Letterbook, VHS.

23. Stith Mead to William Mead, June 12, 1793, and September 1, 1794, Mead Letterbook, VHS.

24. William Mead, copy of property settlement, in Stith Mead Letterbook, 31–32, VHS.

25. David Hall, *Worlds of Wonder, Days of Judgment: Religious Belief in Early New England* (Cambridge, Mass.: Harvard University Press, 1989). Hall's work on Puritan literature reveals the roots of Methodist conversion narratives, which drew heavily upon seventeenth-century forms.

26. See Juster, *Disorderly Women*, 46–47, for a discussion of the similar role of conversion narratives within the Baptist evangelical framework.

27. David Hall contends that the mimetic form of Puritan devotional literature was proof that Puritanism was a popular religion in practice. Hall, *Worlds of Wonder*, 70. In the same vein, one could argue that the mimetic nature of Methodist conversion narratives points to the idea that nineteenth-century Methodism had come into its own as a popular religion with its distinctive form of literature. See the *Methodist Magazine* for evidence of the imitative quality of conversion narratives in the nineteenth century.

28. For a collection of conversion narratives written for Charles Wesley, which contains many early Methodist lay narratives, see Early Methodist Volume, MARC.

29. Evangelical conversion narratives mirror descriptions of rites of passage across many historical and cultural contexts. For the classic anthropological descriptions of this process, particularly the elements of separation, liminality, and reintegration, see Arnold van Gennep, *The Rites of Passage* (Chicago: University of Chicago Press, 1960); and Victor Turner, *The Ritual Process* (Ithaca, N.Y.: Cornell University Press, 1977). I would argue that there was liminality to early evangelicals as a whole, a separateness that they embraced on a communal, not just an individual, level. This draws upon Turner's notion that fringe groups can have group liminality. See Turner, *Ritual Process*, 111–13. See also Susan Juster's work on Baptists' experience of liminality. Juster, *Disorderly Women*, 19, 50–52.

30. Hindmarsh, *Evangelical Conversion Narrative*, 79.

31. Lyerly argues that women's participation in Methodism was particularly problematic in the American context. See Lyerly, *Methodism and the Southern Mind*. Women's participation in Methodism was frequently cited in anti-Methodist pamphlets as evidence of a troubling breakdown of the patriarchal family. As a result, pamphlets

addressed women directly as the susceptible target of Methodist groups. See Nightingale, *Portraiture of Methodism* and *Story of the Methodist-Lady*.

32. Mary Bosanquet Fletcher, MS Autobiography, 2:4, Fletcher-Tooth Collection, MARC.

33. Elizabeth Hayden to Mr. Dornford, February 10, 1789, Fletcher-Tooth Collection, MARC.

34. Caroline Walker Bynum, *Fragmentation and Redemption: Essays on Gender and the Human Body in Medieval Religion* (Cambridge, Mass.: MIT Press, 1991), notes the phenomenon of a reversal of roles between parent and child saint in the medieval period. In Bynum's study, though, it was only young men who performed the role of child saint, not women. In contrast, this role seemed reserved for women in Methodism, and I have yet to find an account that described a boy precociously leading the family toward religiosity before adulthood. For examples of this role reversal in Methodism, see especially Sarah Ryan's letters to her mother, Fletcher-Tooth Collection, MARC; Stith Mead, *A Short Account*; Elizabeth Hayden to Mr. Dornford, February 10, 1789, Fletcher-Tooth Collection, MARC; and Account of Emily Geddey, Fletcher-Tooth Collection, MARC.

35. Mrs. Clagget to Charles Wesley, July 24, 1738, Early Methodist Volume, MARC.

36. I refer to her as Mary Bosanquet for this section, because it describes her childhood and young adult life, though she wrote this autobiography after she became Mary Bosanquet Fletcher. Because Hester Roe Rogers and Catherine Livingston Garrettson's accounts likewise deal with their unmarried lives almost exclusively, I employ their maiden names for these accounts.

37. Fletcher, MS Autobiography, 1:1.

38. Thomas M. Morrow, *Early Methodist Women* (London: Epworth Press, 1967), 65.

39. Fletcher, MS Autobiography, 1:1.

40. Ibid., 1:4.

41. Ibid., 1:6–11.

42. Morrow, *Early Methodist Women*, 68.

43. Ibid., 65.

44. Fletcher, MS Autobiography, 1:20.

45. Ibid., 1:25–26.

46. Morrow, *Early Methodist Women*, 69.

47. Fletcher, MS Autobiography, 1:21.

48. Ibid., 1:22–23. Eighteenth-century doctors frequently diagnosed strong nervous disorders as a lower level of mental illness, a disturbance of nerves that was sometimes also called the English malady. See Porter, *Mind-Forg'd Manacles*. George Cheyne, the eighteenth-century diet and health expert, wrote *The English Malady,* in which he relates this illness to excess of diet and consumption. Porter emphasized the feminizing associations with this particular brand of mental illness. See also Guerini, *Obesity and Depression in the Enlightenment*. Blistering, applying a sort of caustic plas-

ter, was a common treatment. Isolation was also common, although Roy Porter counters Michel Foucault's claims in *Madness and Civilization: A History of Insanity in the Age of Reason* (New York: Random House, 1965), which describes a post-Restoration frenzy of institutionalization (and isolation) of the mentally ill as "a great confinement." See Porter, *Mind-Forg'd Manacles*, especially 110–11.

49. Fletcher, MS Autobiography, 1:28.
50. Ibid., 1:29.
51. Ibid., 1:29–30.
52. Ibid., 1:32.
53. Morrow, *Early Methodist Women*, 75.
54. Fletcher, MS Autobiography, 2:4.
55. Ibid., 2:5–6.
56. Ibid., 2:32–34.
57. Mary Bosanquet Fletcher, Memorandum, 119, Fletcher-Tooth Collection, MARC.
58. Vicki Tolar Burton's work on Hester Roe Rogers outlines the significance of this diarist not only to Methodist culture but to women readers of all religious persuasions in the nineteenth century, especially in America. This journal went through dozens of reprints and various editions, becoming popular as a morality story within the romantic novelistic tradition. While nineteenth-century publishers heavily edited the printed volumes, one can see in the original journals how Roe's own voice was wonderfully dramatic and well shaped. Her story clearly provided irresistible fodder for the printing press. See Vicki Tolar Burton, "Perfecting a Woman's Life: Methodist Rhetoric and Politics in 'The Account of Hester Ann Rogers'" (Ph.D. diss., Auburn University, 1993).
59. For details of this industrial growth, see Gail Malmgreen, *Silk Town: Industry and Culture in Macclesfield, 1750–1835* (Hull: Hull University Press, 1985).
60. Hester Ann Roe Rogers, Journals, 1:7–8, MARC.
61. Ibid., 1:16.
62. Ibid.
63. Ibid.
64. Ibid., 1:48–52. In this passage, Mrs. Roe equates Hester's enthusiasm with madness.
65. Ibid., 1:17–18.
66. Ibid., 1:18–19.
67. Ibid., 1:19.
68. Ibid., 1:24.
69. Ibid.
70. Ibid., 1:34.
71. Ibid., 1:35.
72. Ibid., 1:63.
73. Diane Helen Lobody, "Lost in the Ocean of Love: The Mystical Writings of Catherine Livingston Garrettson" (Ph.D. diss., Drew University, 1990), 32.

74. Ibid., 34.
75. Catherine Livingston Garrettson, Autobiography, 3, DUL.
76. Catherine Livingston Garrettson, Journal I, December 2, 1787, DUL.
77. Garrettson, Autobiography, 8.
78. Ibid.
79. Garrettson, Journal I, November 27, 1787.
80. Ibid., December 2, 1787.
81. Ibid.
82. Garrettson wrote that she was afraid "I might do some act of violence in my phrensy that might cast me from my Blessed Savior forever." Garrettson, Journal I, December 2, 1787.
83. Her housekeeper had lent her Wesley's *Journal*, which included his experiences with Moravians in America and Germany. Wesley emphasized the level of emotional and spiritual steadiness Moravians displayed in the face of exile and persecution. See also Lobody, "Lost in the Ocean of Love," 148–49. Lobody includes a thorough discussion of Catherine Livingston Garrettson's reading habits during this period.
84. Garrettson, Journal I, December 27, 1787.
85. Ibid.
86. Garrettson, Journal III, April 15, 1788.
87. Garrettson, Journal III, April 25, 1788.
88. See, for instance, Garrettson, Journal IV, May 20, 1788, DUL.
89. Ibid., April 15, 1791. Wesley had died on March 2, 1791, but American Methodists had only just received word by mid-April. See Andrews, *Methodists and Revolutionary America*, 337 n. 51.
90. "To a young lady opposed by her relations," December 22, 1792, Mead Letterbook, 17, VHS.
91. Asbury, *Journal and Letters*, 1:748.
92. See Wesley, *Rules of the Band Societies*); and John Wesley, "The Danger of Increasing Riches," in *Works*, 4:177–86.
93. Fletcher, MS Autobiography, 10.
94. Lyerly, *Methodism and the Southern Mind*, 74–93; Andrews, *Methodists and Revolutionary America*, 155–84.

Chapter 3

1. Susannah Designe to Charles Wesley, March 18, 1742, Early Methodist Volume, MARC.
2. Sarah Ryan to Mary Bosanquet Fletcher, April 1762, Fletcher-Tooth Collection, MARC. Similar wording can be found in many narratives and letters. For example, see Hester Ann Roe Rogers, Journals, 2:109, July 17, 1781, MARC.
3. See Smith, *Inside the Great House*, 135–38; Trumbach, *Rise of the Egalitarian Family*, 111–13; and Roy Porter, *English Society in the Eighteenth Century* (New York: Penguin Books, 1990), 143–49.

4. This argument is closely related to Naomi Tadmor's description of nuclear family boundaries as being somewhat obfuscated by eighteenth-century kinship connections. See especially her explanation of "recognition and opacity" in *Family and Friends*, 122–32.

5. Michael MacDonald and Terrence Murphy, *Sleepless Souls: Suicide in Early Modern England* (Oxford: Oxford University Press, 1990), 260.

6. Ibid., 261.

7. Ibid., 260–61.

8. Degler, *At Odds*, 8–9. For more on the emergence of couples as the centerpiece of modern families, see Anya Jabour, *Marriage in the Early Republic: Elizabeth and William Wirt and the Companionate Ideal* (Baltimore: Johns Hopkins University Press, 1998).

9. Ruth H. Bloch, *Gender and Morality in Anglo-American Culture, 1650–1800* (Berkeley: University of California Press, 2003), 47.

10. See Tadmor, *Family and Friends*; and Tamara Hareven, "The History of the Family and the Complexity of Social Change," *American Historical Review* 91 (1991): 95–124.

11. See O'Brien, "Transatlantic Community of Saints"; and Lambert, *Pedlar in Divinity*.

12. See, for instance, John Valton, Diaries, 8:108 (May 9, 1784), MARC. The letters of Edward Dromgoole Sr. (Edward Dromgoole Papers, SHC) demonstrate how preachers maintained a steady correspondence with members of their circuit while "localized."

13. Lambert discusses the importance of evangelical press during this time period in *Inventing the "Great Awakening,"* 158. See also O'Brien, "Transatlantic Community of Saints." Dee Andrews has a different interpretation of the role of evangelical press in the sense of intimacy among Methodists. She argues that the publications were used, in the late eighteenth and early nineteenth centuries, as a sort of virtual preacher, to substitute for having a real preacher and to put some distance between Methodist preachers and their flock. See Andrews, *Methodists and Revolutionary America*.

14. John F. Wright, ed., *Sketches of the Life and Labors of James Quinn, Who Was Nearly Half a Century a Minister of the Gospel in the Methodist Episcopal Church* (Cincinnati: Methodist Book Concern, 1851), 47.

15. Stith Mead to Samuel Mead, September 24, 1794, Mead Letterbook, 83, VHS.

16. Jeremiah Norman, Diary, August 2, 1793, Stephen B. Weeks Collection, SHC.

17. William Spencer to Mary Gordon, May 22, 1796, Gordon-Hackett Family Papers, SHC.

18. Tadmor, *Family and Friends*, 131–32.

19. Ibid., 140.

20. Herbert Gutman, *The Black Family in Slavery and Freedom, 1750–1925* (New York: Pantheon Books, 1976), xxiii, 217. See also Brenda Stevenson, *Life in Black and*

White: Family and Community in the Slave South (New York: Oxford University Press, 1997). Stevenson paints a less sanguine picture regarding the ability of slave families to maintain nuclear bonds than Gutman.

21. See Lyerly, *Methodism and the Southern Mind*, 60–61.

22. Herbert J. Foster, "African Patterns in the Afro-American Family," *Journal of Black Studies* 14, no. 2 (1983): 201–32.

23. Mary Bosanquet Fletcher, Journal, August 6, 1799.

24. Chilcote, *John Wesley and the Women Preachers*, 126. See Mary Bosanquet Fletcher, MS Autobiography; and Account of Sarah Lawrence, Fletcher-Tooth Collection, MARC.

25. For evidence of this see Mary Bosanquet's Journals, especially September 1777. As Chapter 5 discusses, Bosanquet's finances and her devotion to "the family" precipitated, paradoxically, her desire to marry.

26. Chilcote, *John Wesley and the Women Preachers*, 126–27.

27. Isaac, *Transformation of Virginia*, 166.

28. Juster, *Disorderly Women*, 7.

29. Richey, *Early American Methodism*, 1–20.

30. Henry Abelove, *The Evangelist of Desire: John Wesley and the Methodists* (Stanford, Calif.: Stanford University Press, 1990), 85–103.

31. The image of the newborn babe did not originate with Methodist laity. The Methodist leadership, especially John Wesley and George Whitefield, spoke often of the need for regeneration or a new birth.

32. Mary Jane Ramsay to Charles Wesley, June 4, 1740, Early Methodist Volume, MARC.

33. This phrase can be found in various letters in the Early Methodist Volume, MARC: see, e.g., Margaret Austin to Charles Wesley, May 19, 1740; Sarah Barber to Charles Wesley, May 1740; see also Ann Chapman to Charles Wesley, November 3, 1772, in which Chapman uses a similar phrase, describing herself as a Wesley's *child* in Christ.

34. For more particular insight on the leadership differences between Charles and John Wesley, see Lloyd, *Charles Wesley and the Struggle for Methodist Identity*.

35. John Lednum, *A History of the Rise of Methodism in America, containing Sketches of Methodist Itinerant Preachers, from 1736 to 1785* (Philadelphia: Published by the author, 1859), 275.

36. Rom. 8:14–17, King James Version.

37. Ann Martin to Charles Wesley, 1740, Early Methodist Volume, MARC.

38. Joseph Carter to Charles Wesley, November 1741, Early Methodist Volume, MARC.

39. See particularly letters found in the Early Methodist Volume, MARC.

40. Ann Martin to Charles Wesley, 1740, Early Methodist Volume, MARC.

41. Mariah Price to Charles Wesley, May 18, 1740, Early Methodist Volume, MARC.

42. Ann Davis to Charles Wesley, April 25, 1766, Early Methodist Volume, MARC.

43. Mack, *Visionary Women*, 215–22, 246.

44. William Spencer to Mary Gordon, May 22, 1796, Gordon-Hackett Family Papers, SHC.

45. A. Gregory Schneider, *The Way of the Cross Leads Home: The Domestication of American Methodism* (Bloomington: Indiana University Press, 1993).

46. Lyerly, *Methodism and the Southern Mind*, 96–98.

47. Catherine A. Brekus, *Strangers and Pilgrims: Female Preaching in America, 1740–1845* (Chapel Hill: University of North Carolina Press, 1998), 133. Brekus notes that there were surprisingly few female Methodist preachers in the Revolutionary and early national era; among the more than one hundred female preachers in her study, only nine were Methodist.

48. Andrews, *Methodists and Revolutionary America*, 118.

49. Ibid., 119–22.

50. Lyerly, *Methodism and the Southern Mind*, 96–97.

51. Ibid., 106; Andrews, *Methodists and Revolutionary America*, 119.

52. Asbury, *Journal and Letters*, 3:431.

53. Brekus, *Strangers and Pilgrims*, 294–95.

54. William Andrews, ed. *Sisters of the Spirit: Three Black Women's Autobiographies of the Nineteenth Century* (Indianapolis: Indiana University Press, 1986).

55. Jarena Lee, *Religious Experience and Journal of Mrs. Jarena Lee, Giving an Account of Her Call to Preach the Gospel* (Philadelphia: Printed and published for the author, 1849; Digital Schomburg Collection, New York Public Library).

56. Frey and Wood, *Come Shouting to Zion*, 181.

57. Ward, *Protestant Evangelical Awakening*.

58. Chilcote, *John Wesley and the Women Preachers*, 117–40.

59. John Wesley to Sarah Crosby, March 18, 1769, in Zachariah Taft, *Biographical Sketches of the Lives and Public Ministry of Various Holy Women*, 2 vols. (London, 1825 and 1828), 2:55.

60. John Wesley to Sarah Crosby, June 13, 1771, in Taft, *Biographical Sketches*, 2:57–58.

61. Taft, *Biographical Sketches*, 45.

62. Brekus, *Strangers and Pilgrims*, 133.

63. Henry Moore, *Life of Mrs. Mary Fletcher, Consort and Relict of the Rev. John Fletcher*, 3rd ed. (London: Thomas Cordeux, 1818), 18.

64. Fletcher, MS Autobiography, 2:40–41.

65. Ibid., 3:1.

66. Ibid., 3:1–2.

67. Chilcote, *John Wesley and the Women Preachers*, 129.

68. Mary Bosanquet Fletcher, Account of Sarah Ryan, 87, MARC.

69. Fletcher, MS Autobiography, 3:9, and Journal, August 15, 1786, and October 25, 1785, MARC.

70. Mary Bosanquet Fletcher, Memorandum, 113, MARC.
71. John Valton, Diaries, 1:68 (May 4, 1764), MARC.
72. Ibid.
73. See Telford, *Wesley's Veterans: Lives of Early Methodist Preachers Told by Themselves* (London: Charles H. Kelly, 1913), 6:16. Valton describes Mr. Edwards's defamation of him as the devil's work, choosing diplomatic descriptions for the public record of his autobiography. There is some ambiguous marginalia, including one note, "My only Crime was the 'daring' to talk to Mr. —— concerning his growing cold, towards God. My impudence!" See Valton, Diaries, 1:70, MARC.
74. Valton, Diaries, 1:69 (May 9, 1764), MARC.
75. Ibid.
76. Ibid., 1:105–6 (August 26, 1765).
77. Ibid., 1:114–15 (September 16, 1765).
78. Ibid., 3:75–76 (June 23, 1766).
79. Colbert, Journals, October 11, 1794, DUL.
80. John Metcalf to Stith Mead, November 27, 1793, Mead Letterbook, 48, VHS.
81. Heyrman, *Southern Cross*, 147.
82. Chilcote, *John Wesley and the Women Preachers*, 198.
83. Historically, the ideas of brotherhood, fraternity, or brethren have enjoyed much more prominence than that of sisterhood. They carry different connotations regarding the idea of male groups: "brotherhood" and "fraternity" apply to secular or religious situations, while, according to the *Oxford English Dictionary*, "brethren" is reserved exclusively for the latter, after the seventeenth century.
84. Chilcote, *John Wesley and the Women Preachers*, 198–201.
85. See Juster, *Disorderly Women*, 20–21.

Chapter 4

1. Hunt, *Folly and Danger of Methodism*, 46.
2. Watts, *The Dissenters*, 434–43. Watts delineates how contemporaries compared Methodism to Puritan or dissenting churches and examines the limits of those comparisons on the grounds of Calvinist theology and practice.
3. Historians of southern evangelicals have emphasized particularly this evangelical opposition to societal norms in this period. See Heyrman, *Southern Cross*, 117–42; Lyerly, *Methodism and the Southern Mind*, 73–93; and Isaac, *Transformation of Virginia*, 105.
4. R. C. Monk, *John Wesley: His Puritan Heritage* (London: Epworth Press, 1966). For a comparison between the Puritan and Anglican influences on Wesleyan Methodism, see Walsh, "Origins of the Evangelical Revival," 138–60.
5. Stone, *Family, Sex and Marriage in England*, 422.
6. E. P. Thompson, "Time, Work Discipline, and Industrial Capitalism," *Past & Present*, no. 38 (December 1967): 56–97; Thompson, *Making of the English Working Class*. See also G. J. Barker-Benfield, *The Culture of Sensibility: Sex and Society in*

Eighteenth-Century Britain (Chicago: University of Chicago Press, 1992), 65–66. Barker-Benfield counters that there have been significant challenges to Thompson's narrative linking Methodism and repression. Many historians have illuminated the ways in which the working classes were themselves aspiring to consumerism and reforming their own patterns of work prior to industrialization. See particularly Neil McKendrick, "Home Demand and Economic Growth: A New View of the Role of Women and Children in the Industrial Revolution," in *Historical Perspectives: Studies in English Thought and Society*, ed. McKendrick (London: Europa, 1974), 152–210.

7. Hunt, *Folly and Danger of Methodism*, 47.

8. Nightingale, *Portraiture of Methodism*, 236.

9. Dee Andrews finds women the majority of converts in her survey of Middle Atlantic city membership rolls for Methodist societies. See Andrews, *Methodists and Revolutionary America*, 112–13; see also Heyrman, *Southern Cross*, 214–17.

10. Green, *Anti-Methodist Publications*.

11. Lyles, *Methodism Mocked*, 15–18. Alongside Anglican clergy, many anti-Methodist authors, surprisingly, were Methodists themselves, authoring tracts that disparaged rival Methodists and squabbling between the divides of Calvinism and Arminianism.

12. Hempton, *Methodism: Empire of the Spirit*, 87–94.

13. Lyles, *Methodism Mocked*, 93, 109.

14. Andrews, *Methodists and Revolutionary America*, 55–62; Heyrman, *Southern Cross*, 226. Wesley's loyalist political statements were not the only evidence that Methodists were potential loyalists; many Methodists objected to the war altogether or sided with loyalists.

15. Heyrman, *Southern Cross*, 226–29.

16. George Lavington, *The Enthusiasm of Methodists and Papists Compared* (London: J. and P. Knapton, 1754), 1:119.

17. See Mack, *Visionary Women*, 45–86 and 150–64.

18. Anne Hutchinson and Mary Dyer, for instance, were both labeled as religious and sexual deviants. Quakers and dissenting Puritans were also disproportionately targeted as witches, an accusation that carried a sexual charge as well. See Levy, *Quakers and the American Family*, 82–84. Elizabeth Reis, "The Devil, the Body, and the Feminine Soul in Puritan New England," *Journal of American History* 82, no. 1 (June 1995): 15–36, emphasizes the seventeenth-century association of female bodies and sin, especially in the case of witchcraft. See Amy Schrager Lang, *Prophetic Woman: Anne Hutchinson and the Problem of Dissent in the Literature of New England* (Berkeley: University of California Press, 1987), for discussion of Hutchinson and Dyer. See also Edmund Leites, *The Puritan Conscience and Modern Sexuality* (New Haven, Conn.: Yale University Press, 1986); Amanda Porterfield, *Female Piety in Puritan New England* (New York: Oxford University Press, 1992). Christine Heyrman emphasizes the long tradition of associating religious dissent and promiscuity was particularly aimed at women in the early modern period; see Heyrman, *Southern Cross*, 181.

19. Fogleman, *Jesus Is Female*, 137–52.

20. Cedric Cowing, "Sex and Preaching in the Great Awakening," *American Quarterly* 20, no. 3 (Autumn 1968): 624–44.

21. Heyrman, *Southern Cross*, 117–42; Isaac, *Transformation of Virginia*, 105.

22. Aaron Spencer Fogleman, "Jesus Is Female: The Moravian Challenge in the German Communities of British North America," *William and Mary Quarterly*, 3rd ser., 60, no. 2 (April 2003): 295–332; Fogleman, *Jesus Is Female*, 91–95.

23. Bruce Hindmarsh establishes some useful ideas about evangelical conversion, regarding the tendency for evangelicals to travel between different stages of conversion and never progress in a linear fashion. Hindmarsh, *Evangelical Conversion Narrative*, 12–13.

24. Barker-Benfield, *Culture of Sensibility*, 71.

25. Ibid., 282–85.

26. Edmund Gibson, *Observations upon the Conduct and Behavior of a Certain Sect Usually Distinguished by the Name of Methodists* (London, 1744), 4–13.

27. Ann Taves, *Fits, Trances, and Visions: Experiencing Religion and Explaining Experience from Wesley to James* (Princeton, N.J.: Princeton University Press, 1999), 20–46.

28. Hempton, *Methodism: Empire of the Spirit*, 37.

29. Samuel Johnson, *A Dictionary of the English Language*, 2nd ed. (London: W. Strahan, 1755–56), s.vv. "enthusiasm," "enthusiast." See Lawrence E. Klein and Anthony J. La Vopa, eds., *Enthusiasm and Enlightenment in Europe, 1650–1850* (San Marino, Calif.: Huntington Library, 1998), for the wider context of enthusiasm in Europe. "Enthusiasm" was a term applied outside of the religious arena as well. One can see the earlier roots of "enthusiasm" as an idea in Heyd, *Be Sober and Reasonable*.

30. Hunt, *Folly and Danger of Methodism*, 33–34.

31. Stout, *Divine Dramatist*, 247.

32. A good reference for works of Hogarth is Paulson, *Hogarth's Graphic Work*. The comparison of Methodism to Catholicism was particularly damning during this period, since anti-Jacobitism was also high in the 1760s. See Colley, *Britons*, 24.

33. Laurence Sterne, *The Sermons of Mr. Yorick* (London, 1760), 2:184.

34. John Wesley to Charles Wesley, December 11, 1762, in Luke Tyerman, *The Life and Times of the Rev. John Wesley, M.A., Founder of the Methodists* (London: Hodder and Staughton, 1870), 2:453–54.

35. Wesleyan Methodist Church Conference, *Minutes of some late conversations, between the Rev. Mr. Wesleys, and others* (Bristol, 1/65), 8, MARC.

36. Hempton, *Methodism: Empire of the Spirit*, 35–36.

37. Ibid., 34.

38. Karen Westerfield Tucker, *American Methodist Worship* (New York: Oxford University Press, 2001), 62–63.

39. Ibid., 65–68.

40. Lyles, *Methodism Mocked*, 89.

41. John Bew, *The Love-Feast: A Poem* (London, 1778), 28. In *Methodism Mocked*, Lyles cites *Fanatical Conversion*, a pamphlet that claimed that ministers spiked the eucharistic wine at love feasts with aphrodisiacs (supposedly uncovered by "a reformed Methodist Preacher"), 90.

42. Jeremiah Norman, Diary, Feb. 1797, 6: 395, SHC.

43. Mechal Sobel, *The World They Made Together: Black and White Values in Eighteenth-Century Virginia* (Princeton, N.J.: Princeton University Press, 1987), 199.

44. "Journal and Travels of James Meacham, Part I" (July 23, 1789), 88, DUSC.

45. Sobel, *The World They Made Together*, 206.

46. Timothy Hall, *Contested Boundaries: Itinerancy and the Reshaping of the Colonial American Religious World* (Durham, N.C.: Duke University Press, 1994), 45.

47. For the importance of camp meetings to settling Methodism on the American frontier, see Owen, *Sacred Flame of Love*. Donald Mathews also includes an important discussion of camp meetings in his *Religion in the Old South*, 51–52. Mathews stresses that camp meetings did not arise out of open-air preaching; rather he traces their genesis to a pan-evangelical revival in Kentucky in 1801. Earlier forms of camp meetings did exist, though, in Methodist quarterly meetings and Baptist meetings, when preachers congregated for business and inspiration.

48. Hatch, *Democratization of American Christianity*, 49–55.

49. Ibid.

50. Dennis Todd's *Imagining Monsters: Miscreations of the Self in Eighteenth-Century England* (Chicago: University of Chicago Press, 1995) takes Mary Toft's imaginative leap as a centerpiece of eighteenth-century enthusiasm. See also Ronald Paulson, *Hogarth's Graphic Works*.

51. See, for example, *Aristotle's Master-piece compleated in two parts: The first containing the secrets of generation, in all the parts thereof* (London: B. Harris, 1697). Mary Fissell demonstrates the development of medical opinion on the womb as a particular site for unholy entry into women's bodies. This idea becomes particularly prominent during the seventeenth century with the rise of reported "monstrous births" in both England and America. Mary Fissell, *Vernacular Bodies: The Politics of Reproduction in Early Modern England* (Oxford: Oxford University Press, 2004), 59–72.

52. Elizabeth Reis, "The Devil, the Body, and the Feminine Soul in Puritan New England," *Journal of American History* 82 (June 1995): 15–36.

53. Mack, *Visionary Women*, 27.

54. Barker-Benfield, *Culture of Sensibility*, 23–24.

55. As an interesting example of this, New England minister Charles Chauncy wrote a scathing diatribe against the work of Whitefield, aimed at convincing religious leaders in England that they had been misled in believing that Whitefield's revivals were successful. He dismissed revivalists as insignificant in number and identity, citing women and children as the most common dupes of enthusiastic performance. Charles Chauncy, *A Letter from a Gentleman in Boston to Mr. George Wishart . . .* (Edinburgh, 1742), 15.

56. Juster, *Disorderly Women*; Jan Lewis, "The Republican Wife: Virtue and Seduction in the Early Republic," *William and Mary Quarterly* 44, no. 4 (1987): 689–721; Nancy Cott, *The Bonds of Womanhood: "Woman's Sphere" in New England, 1780–1835* (New Haven, Conn.: Yale University Press, 1977).

57. Hunt, *Folly and Danger of Methodism*, 96–97.

58. *The Methodists, an Humorous Burlesque Poem: Address'd to the Rev. Mr. Whitefield and His Followers* . . . (London, 1739).

59. Author of *The Saints* [William Combe], *Sketches for Tabernacle-Frames: A Poem* (London, 1778).

60. Hunt, *Folly and Danger of Methodism*, 54–55.

61. Ibid., passim

62. *The Story of the Methodist-Lady, or The Injur'd Husband's Revenge* (London: John Doughty, 1770).

63. Ibid., 3–4.

64. Ibid., 11.

65. Lyles, *Methodism Mocked*, 68–69.

66. *Story of the Methodist-Lady*, 12.

67. Ibid., 17.

68. Ibid., 25.

69. Ibid., 26.

70. Ibid., 27–28.

71. Lyerly, *Methodism and the Southern Mind*, 94–118.

72. Hunt, *Folly and Danger of Methodism*, 56–57.

73. For instance, see Montesquieu's *Persian Letters* (1721).

74. As for the size of this magazine's audience and its overall importance as a cultural tool, it is difficult to determine its circulation in the period under examination. We do know that by Wesley's death in 1791, over 72,000 people in England were full-fledged members of "the Connection," and many English members would have read the magazine. When one takes into account reprinting abroad, especially in America where Francis Asbury had the magazine bound and printed for American Methodists, the circulation becomes much greater.

75. Hannah Hancock to Charles Wesley, April 1742, Early Methodist Volume, MARC.

76. Sally Eastland to Edward Dromgoole Sr., February 21, 1790, Edward Dromgoole Papers, SHC.

77. Sarah Jones to Edward Dromgoole Sr., undated, Edward Dromgoole Papers, SHC.

78. *Arminian Magazine*, March 1778, 228–29. Perrin used some phrases from Psalm 42: "As the hart panteth after the water brooks, so panteth my soul after thee, O God. My soul thirsteth for God, for the living God: when shall I come and appear before God?" (King James Bible).

79. *Arminian Magazine*, January 1782, 21.

80. Abelove, *Evangelist of Desire*.

81. Ibid., xi–xii.

82. Ibid., 8–9, passim.

83. *Arminian Magazine*, March 1778, 218–19. We have to presume Perrin is referring to John Wesley's ministering, given his publication of this letter in the *Arminian* and given the fact that there is no extant manuscript version of this letter. Since Perrin wrote some of her most intimate and interesting letters to Charles Wesley, though, this could refer to Charles Wesley's ministerial career.

84. Sarah Perrin had grown up as a Quaker, and so she brought a Quaker sense of authority to her Methodist life. Her Quaker upbringing would have exposed her to the concept of spiritual authority through individual embodiment of the divine spirit.

85. *Arminian Magazine*, March 1778, 221.

86. Ibid., 223–24.

87. Gareth Lloyd, "Sarah Perrin (1721–1787): Early Methodist Exhorter," *Methodist Magazine* 41, no. 3 (2003): 79–88.

88. See the illustration *The Enthusiastic Widow; the Popular Preacher* (A. Hamilton: London, 1783); Lyles, *Methodism Mocked*; Green, *Anti-Methodist Publications*.

89. John B. Matthias, Journals, n.d., DUL.

90. John Hutchinson to Charles Wesley, September 29, 1751, Early Methodist Volume, MARC.

91. Ibid.

92. John Hutchinson to Charles Wesley, October 31, 1752, Early Methodist Volume, MARC.

93. 1 Sam. 18:3.

94. 2 Sam. 1:26.

95. Henry Smith, *Recollections and Reflections of an Old Itinerant* (New York: Lane and Tippett, 1848), 293.

96. Stith Mead, Letterbook, 1792, 10–11, VHS.

97. Stith Mead to John Kobler, December 15, 1794, Mead Letterbook, VHS.

98. For a contrast, showing the way that anti-Masonic literature satirized homosocial bonds between Masons, see Thomas A. Foster, "Antimasonic Satire, Sodomy, and Eighteenth-Century Masculinity in the *Boston Evening-Post*," *William and Mary Quarterly*, 3rd ser., 60, no. 1 (January 2003): 171–84. Masonic secrecy and same sex intimacy were elements of commonality with the Methodist groups examined here, yet there were also some key differences between these groups, including the lack of women in Masonic societies and Masons' centrality in political and civic participation.

99. For reproductions of the vagina as side wound in Moravian imagery, see Fogleman, "Jesus Is Female" (2003) and *Jesus Is Female* (2007).

100. John Wesley, *The Journal of John Wesley*, 8 vols., ed. Nehemiah Curnock (London: Epworth Press, 1938), 3:515.

101. Thomas Cooper to Charles Wesley, 1741, Early Methodist Volume, MARC.

102. Valton, Diaries, 4:25 (February 22, 1767), MARC.

103. Ibid., 47–48 (April 7, 1767).

104. Norman, Diary, 5:10 (August 12, 1794), SHC.

105. Ibid., 4:276 (n.d., ca. September 1796).

106. William Ormond, Journal, April 25, 1796, SHC.

107. Norman, Diary, 3:203–4 (n.d.), SHC.

108. This is a general trend one can see in the letters of the Edward Dromgoole Papers and in the journals of Myles Green and Jeremiah Norman. Donald Mathews confirms this tendency, beginning in the mid-1790s into the first decade of the nineteenth century. He relates it to the growing popularity of deistic writings and the general preoccupation with Federalist taxes, the Alien and Sedition Acts, and other pressing political events. Evangelicals had also enjoyed a great surge prior to this period in America, and so a leveling off may have been inevitable for a time. See Mathews, *Religion in the Old South*, 48–49.

109. Richard Godbeer, *Sexual Revolution in Early America* (Baltimore: Johns Hopkins University Press, 2002), 121.

110. Ibid., 120–21.

111. Norman, Diary, 6:464 (June 18, 1797), SHC.

112. Ibid., 1:6 (June 29, 1794).

113. Ibid., 1:10 (August 21, 1794).

114. Ibid., 1:6 (June 29, 1794).

115. Ibid., 1:92 (November 23, 1795).

116. Ibid., 1:35 (November 3, 1794).

117. Zachariah Yewdall, Journals, 1:63 (February 8, 1780), MARC.

118. Ibid., 1:173 (September 3, 1780).

119. Valton, Diary, 4:33–34 (March 12, 1767), MARC.

120. See Susan Juster, "Eros and Desire in Early Modern Spirituality," *William and Mary Quarterly*, 3rd. ser., 60, no. 1 (January 2003): 203–6, for a sensible approach to interpreting erotic religious writings more generally.

Chapter 5

1. Sarah Crosby, Diary, February 2, 1773, DUSC.

2. See Peter Brown, *The Body and Society: Men, Women, and Sexual Renunciation in Early Christianity* (New York: Columbia University Press, 1988).

3. John Demos, *A Little Commonwealth: Family Life in the Plymouth Colony* (Oxford: Oxford University Press, 1970); Richard Bushman, *From Puritan to Yankee: Character and Social Order in Connecticut, 1690–1765* (New York: W. W. Norton, 1967); Patrick Collinson, *The Birthpangs of Protestant England: Religion and Cultural Change in the Sixteenth and Seventeenth Centuries* (New York: St. Martin's Press, 1988). While this generality holds true for both American and English Puritanism, in Puritan America, there were higher rates of marriage and there may have been further emphasis on the holiness of marriage, compared to England. See Laurel Thatcher Ulrich,

Good Wives Image and Reality in the Lives of Women in Northern New England, 1650–1750 (New York: Oxford, 1983), 6.

4. Godbeer, *Sexual Revolution*, 242–43.

5. Laurence Foster, *Women, Family, and Utopia: Communal Experiments of the Shakers, the Oneida Community, and the Mormons* (Syracuse, N.Y.: Syracuse University Press, 1991), 22.

6. Ibid., 20.

7. Wesley never believed in celibacy as a prerequisite for holiness. In his published writings, Wesley was very clear to distinguish his thoughts on celibacy from those of Catholicism. He wrote that papist beliefs in the holiness of celibacy and the tainted nature of marriage were extreme and irrelevant for true spirituality. See his *Thoughts on a Single Life* (London: J. Paramore, 1765). In this work, his very first point is to disparage the Catholic tradition of denigrating marriage and ally himself with the Protestant sanctity of marriage. Yet, he uses this as a preface to go on and complicate things by claiming that there are many arguments in Corinthians that support the idea of remaining single if one is able and to marry if one cannot avoid acting on lust.

8. John Wesley to Zachariah Yewdall, May 26, 1781, in Wesley, *Works* (Jackson), 13:11; Coe, *John Wesley and Marriage*, 64.

9. 1 Cor. 21.

10. See John Wesley, *Thoughts on Marriage and a Single Life* (Bristol, 1743), 10–11. Wesley folds in St. Paul's commentary on bondage and slavery with marriage and celibacy.

11. John Wesley to Zachariah Yewdall, December 7, 1782, Wesley, *Works* (Jackson), 13:13.

12. Thomas Mann, Journals, January 1, 1806, SHC.

13. Heyrman, *Southern Cross*, 104–7. Unlike Methodists, Baptists did not promote itinerant preaching and in fact encouraged "settled" preachers, who would remain within a particular congregation.

14. Valton, Diaries, 4:37 (March 18, 1767), MARC.

15. Ibid., 3:98 (August 22, 1766).

16. Wesley, *Thoughts on a Single Life*.

17. Wesley, *Thoughts on Marriage and a Single Life*, 8–9.

18. Ibid., 12.

19. John Wesley, *Explanatory Notes Upon the Old Testament*, 3rd ed. (Bristol: William Pine, 1762), 3:135. Sensationalist writers often hurled anti-Catholic slurs at Methodists, accusing the latter of being thinly disguised papists in many practices. The implication was that Methodism was secretive, idolatrous, and above all a threat to the Church of England and true Protestantism.

20. Nicholas Noyes, "An Elegy upon the Death of Mrs. Mary Brown," in Cotton Mather, *Eureka the Virtuous Woman Found* (Boston, 1704), 5, quoted in Godbeer, *Sexual Revolution*, 59.

21. Godbeer, *Sexual Revolution*, 54–58.

22. John Wesley to Mrs. Martha Hall, November 17, 1742, in Wesley, *Works*, 26:90–91. Martha Hall was married to Westley Hall, a man who was once esteemed by John Wesley as a fellow Oxonian and convert, but during his marriage to Wesley's sister, he became a polygamist. Martha raised several of his children, who were the products of her husband's affairs with different servants; she had a very unhappy marriage to him. See John Wesley to Westley Hall, December 22, 1747, in Wesley, *Works*, 26:269–73.

23. William Colbert, Journals, DUL.

24. For other examples, see Early Methodist Volume, MARC, especially Sister Meacham, Account, 1765.

25. Zachariah Yewdall, Journals, 1:63 (February 8, 1780), MARC. See also Andrews, *Methodists and Revolutionary America*, 110.

26. Asbury, *Journal and Letters*, 3:19. See also Andrews, *Methodists and Revolutionary America*, 110.

27. Joan Webb to Charles Wesley, May 1742, Early Methodist Volume, 136, MARC.

28. Ibid.

29. Hindmarsh, *Evangelical Conversion Narratives*, 143–44.

30. Margaret Austin to Charles Wesley, May 19, 1740, Early Methodist Volume, 1, MARC.

31. Wesley, *Letters*, 6:163.

32. Lyerly, *Methodism and the Southern Mind*, 112–13.

33. Nathan Bangs, *The Life of the Rev. Freeborn Garrettson* (New York: J. Emory and B. Waugh, 1829), 225.

34. Lyerly, *Methodism and the Southern Mind*, 114.

35. *Methodist Magazine*, May 1797, 198.

36. See Leger, *Wesley's Last Love*, 1.

37. Ibid., 82.

38. The memoir Wesley left behind was an account that Wesley did not choose to publish himself. Apparently, Wesley's wife, Mary Vazeille Wesley, found it and held on to it after their marriage dissolved. Mary Vazeille Wesley's son Noah Vazeille then acquired it, before it was passed on to the British Museum and first published in 1848. Wesley's published journals contain few references to his romantic life, save the first journal, whose publication was in fact prompted by the scandal with Sophy Hopkey. This memoir contains a close account of the events of 1748, as he was grappling with the questions of celibacy and marriage to Grace Murray. See Leger, *Wesley's Last Love*, v–xiii.

39. Ibid., 66–68.

40. Ibid, 70–71.

41. Rack, *Reasonable Enthusiast*, 263.

42. Leger, *Wesley's Last Love*, 5. See also Abelove, *Evangelist of Desire*, 19.

43. Rack, *Reasonable Enthusiast*, 21.

44. Ibid., 263.

45. Abelove makes more of this class transgression as the reason behind Charles Wesley's protest of this marriage. See Abelove, *Evangelist of Desire*, 19–23.

46. Leger, *Wesley's Last Love*, 1.
47. Andrews, "Popular Religion and the Revolution," 67.
48. Wesley, *Works*, 20:380.
49. Identified as "Anonymous" in Early Methodist Volume, but identified by this author to be in Mary Vazeille's voice and hand. They appear to be makeshift journal entries, only a couple were found in this collection—they are casual slips of paper, where she wrote what appear to be very unaffected notes on her life with John Wesley.
50. See Henry Rack, "'But, Lord, Let It Be Betsy!' Love and Marriage in Early Methodism," *Proceedings of the Wesley Historical Society* 53 (February 2001): 1–13.
51. Mary Bosanquet Fletcher, Account of Sarah Ryan, Fletcher-Tooth Collection, 34–35, MARC.
52. Ibid., 9.
53. Ibid.
54. Ibid., 10–11.
55. Ibid., 12.
56. Sarah Ryan's presumption of a marriage to Benreken was not unusual. Well into the eighteenth century, formal declarations of intent signaled a de facto marriage, and many couples never bothered to become legally joined but considered themselves married. This is important in understanding why Mary Vazeille Wesley would have accused Ryan of polyandry and why Ryan would have felt the need to defend her past.
57. Fletcher, Account of Sarah Ryan, 13
58. Ibid.
59. Ibid., 21.
60. Ibid, 15.
61. Ibid.
62. Ibid., 23.
63. Ibid.
64. Ibid. Next to Ryan's description of submitting to her husband's abuse while focusing on God's mercy, Bosanquet Fletcher added the note: "what a fruit of faith was this!"
65. Ibid., 27.
66. Phyllis Mack, "Religion, Feminism, and the Problem of Agency: Reflections on Eighteenth-Century Quakerism," *Signs: Journal of Women in Culture and Society* 29, no. 1 (2003): 156.
67. This theme of misrepresentation emerges in multiple forms of eighteenth-century literature. The use of the mask in various novels, like Daniel Defoe's *Roxana* (1724) and Ann Radcliffe's *The Italian* (1797), symbolized the possibility of moral transgression when identities were unknown or concealed.
68. In the early 1800s, in America the most popular novel was Susanna Rowson's *Charlotte Temple* (1791), which played on the themes of women's susceptibility to rakes. See Coontz, *Marriage, a History*, 157–58.
69. Cathy Davidson, *Revolution and the Word: The Rise of the Novel in America* (Oxford: Oxford University Press, 1986), 118.

70. Daniel Defoe's *Roxana* (1724) and *Moll Flanders* (1722) exemplified the role of the woman led astray by economic exigencies, fate, and sheer desire. It was in the questions of sexuality and marriage that women were thought to be particularly susceptible to choosing the wrong path. While in Defoe's novels it is the women who lose their self-identity, or gain multiple identities, romances of the late eighteenth and early nineteenth centuries emphasized the malevolent force of this sort of chicanery and almost invariably portrayed men as the ones with masked and multiple selves. See, for instance, Frances Burney's *Evelina* (1778) and Ann Radcliffe's *The Italian* (1797).

71. Stone, *Family, Sex, and Marriage in England*, 30–33.

72. Ibid., 196–97.

73. Account of Sarah Ryan, 38.

74. Sarah Crosby, Diary, February 2, 1773, DUSC.

75. Account of Sarah Lawrence, Fletcher-Tooth Collection, MARC.

76. Chilcote, *John Wesley and the Women Preachers*, 118–31, 255–59; Taft, *Biographical Sketches*, 2:23–115.

77. Chilcote, *John Wesley and the Women Preachers*, 94.

78. William Bramwell, *Account of the Life and Death of Ann Cutler* (York: John Hill, 1827), 15; see also James Sigston, *A Memoir of the Life and Ministry of Mr. W. Bramwell, Lately an Itinerant Methodist Preacher* (London: James Nichols, 1822), 2:164.

79. Hatch, *Democratization of American Christianity*, 87.

80. Bangs, *A History of the Methodist Episcopal Church*, 3rd ed. (New York: T. Mason and G. Lane, 1839–41), 2:421–51.

81. Hatch, *Democratization of American Christianity*, 88. Wigger also discusses the "Bachelor Conference" in *Taking Heaven by Storm*, 33. Hatch cites no exact figures or original studies in his comparison of British and American rates of marriage; this seems to be a rough estimate on his part.

82. Wigger, *Taking Heaven by Storm*, 67. He bases this on figures provided by Jesse Lee and William Warren Sweet in their studies of Methodism: Lee, *A Short History of the Methodists, in the United States of America: Beginning with 1766, and Continued to 1809, to Which Is Prefixed a Brief Account of Their Rise in England in 1729, &c* (Baltimore: Magill and Clime, 1810); and Sweet, *Religion on the American Frontier, 1783–1840*, vol. 4, *The Methodists*.

83. Wigger, *Taking Heaven by Storm*, 38, citing Sweet.

84. Hatch, *Democratization of American Christianity*, 87–89. Hatch has traced the impetus for itinerancy to Asbury, whom he credits for expanding Methodism beyond its primary success in the seaport cities. Asbury had written to Jesse Lee, an itinerant, in 1797 that resources had to move "from the centre to the circumference."

85. Hatch, *Democratization of American Christianity*, 87.

86. William Colbert, Journals, 5:7 (February 25, 1804), DUL.

87. Wigger, *Taking Heaven by Storm*, 58. The years of hardest travel in Garrettson's itinerancy, 1776–93, are, not coincidentally, the years prior to Freeborn Garrettson's marriage to Catherine Livingston in 1793.

88. John H. Wigger, *American Saint: Francis Asbury and the Methodists* (Oxford: Oxford University Press, 2009), 3–5.

89. Ibid., 350–51.

90. Ibid., 304–6.

91. Asbury, *Journal and Letters*, 2:474; Baker, *From Wesley to Asbury*, 160. It is clear that Asbury inhibited his preachers from marrying, and he was dismissive of preachers who chose to marry, even those who were imminent like Coke.

92. Wigger, *American Saint*, 355–57.

93. Jeremiah Minter, *A brief account of the religious experiences, travels, preaching persecutions from evil men, and God's special helps in the faith and life, &c. of Jeremiah Minter* (Washington City: Printed for the author, 1817), 8.

94. Ibid., 5.

95. Ibid., 9–10.

96. Ibid., 13–14.

97. Ibid., 13.

98. Ibid.

99. Cynthia Lynn Lyerly, "A Tale of Two Patriarchs; or, How a Eunuch and a Wife Created a Family in the Church," *Journal of Family History* 28, no. 4 (October 2003): 490–509.

100. Valton, Diaries, 4:47–48 (April 7, 1767).

101. Coe, *Wesley and Marriage*, 58.

102. Chappell Bonner to Sister Rose Hill, September 11, 1810, SHC.

103. Luke Barlow, *Marriage Commended, and Adultery Condemned: A Sermon, Preached in the Methodist Chapel, Stafford, September 1st, 1816* (London: D. Procter, 1816).

104. Tyerman, *Life and Times of the Rev. John Wesley*, 2:551.

105. Wigger, *Taking Heaven by Storm*, 68.

106. Ibid.

Chapter 6

1. The charge of being antifamily came on the heels of conversions that did divide some families along religious lines. In anti-Methodist literature, the charge was that these divisions were part of the evangelical plan. In T. E. Owen's *Hints to the Heads of Families* (London: J. Hatchard, 1802) and *Methodism Unmasked, or The Progress of Puritanism, from the Sixteenth to the Nineteenth Century* (London: J. Hatchard, 1802), fathers were urged to step up in their roles as religious patriarchs and stop their children from joining Methodist societies.

2. Family prayer had its roots in Puritan devotional patterns. As a distinction, "family religion" in the eighteenth century emerged in the context of writers concerned with the splintering of families over religious matters, dissension, or apathy toward religion in general. In the eighteenth century, the earliest book to take "family religion" as its central concern was printed in 1736, *A Persuasive to Family Religion:*

And the Obligation Christian Parents Are Under to the Religious Education of Their Children (London: Richard Hett, Bible and Crown, 1736). This was clearly a popular subject; books with this theme went into several editions. See David Muir, *An Humble Attempt Toward the Revival of Family-Religion Among Christians* (London: David Muir, 1759); P. Doddridge, *A Plain and Serious Address to the Matter of a Family, on the Important Subject of Family-Religion*, 4th ed. (London: C. Hitch and L. Hawes, et al., 1761); and *The Family Instructor, in Two Parts: I. Relating to Family Breaches, and their obstructing Religious Duties; II. To the Great Mistake of missing the Passions in the Managing and Correcting of Children; with a great Variety of Cases, relating to setting Ill Examples to Children and Servants*, 8th ed. (London: H. Woodfall, W. Strahan, G. Keith, et al., 1766).

3. Andrews, *Methodists and Revolutionary America*, 107. Family prayer is mentioned more consistently in American Methodist preachers' journals than in British Methodist journals, according to my survey of these materials. American preachers described performing family prayers at each stop on their circuit with each family who hosted them. Gregory Schneider describes a shift toward domesticity on the part of mid-nineteenth-century Methodists. See Schneider, *The Way of the Cross Leads Home*.

4. Charles Wesley, *Hymns for Children* (Bristol: E. Farley, 1763), 9–10.

5. Sherman, *History of the Revisions of the Discipline*, 19; Robert Emory, *History of the Discipline* (New York: Carlton & Porter, 1843), 147–50.

6. American preacher Myles Green, for instance, notes meeting with children but very little else on the content of those meetings in 1789. See Myles Green, Journal, 2:10, DUSC.

7. Sherman, *History of the Revisions of the Discipline*, 211–13; Emory, *History of the Discipline*, 147–50.

8. American Methodist Episcopal Church, *Minutes of Several Conversions Between the Rev. Thomas Coke, LL. D., The Rev. Francis Asbury and Others . . . Composing a Form of Discipline for the Ministers, Preachers and Other Members of the Methodist Episcopal Church in America* (Philadelphia: Charles Cist, 1784). This *Discipline* references more fully the directive for preachers to meet with children.

9. See, for instance, *A Persuasive to Family Religion* (1736), and Muir, *An Humble Attempt Toward the Revival of Family-Religion* (1759).

10. Juster, *Disorderly Women*, 181–82.

11. John B. Matthias, Journal, n.d., DUL.

12. Proof of this is the life and example of Francis Asbury. As well, Thomas Coke's resignation as Bishop was seen as implicit in his marriage in 1805. Although Wigger presents convincing evidence that it was not only his marital state (and the ill health of his wife) that precipitated his losing his leadership role, but also the disaffection felt by American preachers toward Coke, who had never fully committed himself to American leadership. See Wigger, *American Saint*, 340–43.

13. Copy of Sarah Crosby Letter Book, 1760–74, Sarah Crosby to P——y T——r, September 22, 1768, Frank Baker Collection, DUSC.

14. See Trumbach, *Rise of the Egalitarian Family*. Stone's *Family, Sex and Marriage* essentially describes this wave of romantic marriage. It has been largely criticized for the extent to which it generalized early modern English families. See Thompson's "Happy Families" and Macfarlane's review of Stone's book. For descriptions of the American shift toward romantic marriage, see particularly Degler, *At Odds*, 9–14; Daniel Scott Smith, "Parental Control and Marriage Patterns"; Daniel Blake Smith, *Inside the Great House*; and Cott, "Eighteenth-Century Family."

15. Trumbach, *Rise of the Egalitarian Marriage*, 97. However, Trumbach's study primarily focuses on aristocratic families, where Lawrence Stone agrees, there was a limit on the degree to which individual choice was allowed free rein. Among the upper classes, the expectation was clearly that choices were limited to those of the same class, and economic concerns were certainly as important as ever. Trumbach confirms this limitation in *Rise of the Egalitarian Marriage*, 69–103.

16. Vickery, *The Gentleman's Daughter*, 39–41.

17. Stone, *Family, Sex, and Marriage*, 128. Stone, however, also stated that Anglican sermons in the 1630s and 1640s emphasized companionate "married love," which, alongside less involvement from extended family in marriage, ushered in the romantic marriage ideal. See Stone, *Family, Sex, and Marriage*, 102–3.

18. Ibid., 230.

19. Sherman, *History of the Revisions of the Discipline*, 228–29. See also Heyrman, *Southern Cross*, 140–41. Heyrman draws parallels between Baptist and Methodist strictures on marriage, particularly their desires to boost endogamous marriages.

20. John Wesley, *A Short Account of the Life and Death of the Rev. John Fletcher* (London: J. Paramore, 1786), 126.

21. Samuel Rogal, *A Biographical Dictionary of 18th Century Methodism*, vol. 1 (London: Edwin Mellen Press, 1997), 163.

22. Ibid., 19.

23. Mary Bosanquet Fletcher, Journal, October 6, 1777, Fletcher-Tooth Collection, MARC.

24. Ibid., June 20, 1781.

25. Bosanquet's journal chronicles her deep anxiety during this period about the debts that she owed, many incurred in setting up and maintaining her burgeoning orphanage. She worried that she would be forced to marry someone in order to pay off these debts. So when her brother offered assistance, she felt free to marry for her own sake, not for money.

26. Mary Bosanquet Fletcher, Journal, October 30, 1781, MARC.

27. Hester Ann Roe Rogers, Journals, 1:89–90, (n.d. [1776]), MARC.

28. Ibid., 2:173 (February 28, 1782).

29. Ibid., 3:41 (October 22, 1782).

30. Ibid., 3:93 (December 15, 1783).

31. Ibid., 3:97 (December 15, 1783).

32. Ibid.

33. Burton, "Perfecting a Woman's Life"; Susie Cunningham Stanley, *Holy Boldness: Women Preachers' Autobiographies and the Sanctified Self* (Knoxville: University of Tennessee Press, 2000).
34. Vickery, *The Gentleman's Daughter*, 81–82.
35. Heyrman, *Southern Cross*, 141.
36. Vickery, *The Gentleman's Daughter*, 40–41.
37. John Wesley, *Explanatory Notes Upon the Old Testament*, 3 vols. (Bristol: William Pine, 1765), 1:13.
38. John Wesley to Jane Hilton, October 8, 1768, in Wesley, *Letters*, 5:109.
39. John Wesley to Elijah Bush, September 11, 1781, in Wesley, *Letters*, 7:83–84.
40. John Wesley to Thomas Roberts, December 22, 1787, in Wesley, *Letters*, 8:35.
41. "On Family Religion" in Wesley, *Works*, Sermon 94, 3:336.
42. Wesley, *Works* (Jackson), 8:308.
43. Norman, Diary, 262, SHC.
44. Catherine Livingston Garrettson, Journal 5, May 15, 1789, DUL.
45. Heyrman, *Southern Cross*, 156.
46. Gareth Lloyd emphasizes this divide between the Wesleys. His work on Charles Wesley underlines the divisions of labor, and he fleshes out the important leadership of the underrated brother. He maintains that followers of Methodism turned to Charles more often for real, human leadership in a way, and a primary example of his leadership was his healthy family life. See Lloyd, *Charles Wesley and the Struggle for Methodist Identity*.
47. John Johnson, "Account of Himself," November 3, 1767, in Early Methodist Volume, 93, MARC.
48. Charles Wesley, *Journal*, 2:55.
49. See particularly the Early Methodist Volume, MARC.
50. Rack, *Reasonable Enthusiast*, 252; Lloyd, *Charles Wesley and the Struggle for Methodist Identity*.
51. Gill, *Charles Wesley: The First Methodist*, 125.
52. An early biographer called Vazeille "one of the three bad wives" of history, alongside Job's wife and Socrates' wife. See Robert Southey, *The Life of John Wesley* (London: Hutchinson, 1820). Martin Schmidt called Vazeille a "stupid choice." See Schmidt, *John Wesley: A Theological Biography* (New York: Abingdon Press, 1962). More recently, Henry Rack confirms this judgment in *Reasonable Enthusiast*, 252–53.
53. Rack, *Reasonable Enthusiast*, 253.
54. Ibid.
55. Gill, *Charles Wesley: The First Methodist*, 130.
56. Charles Wesley to Sarah Gwynne Jr., January 26, 1749, DDWES 1/40, MARC.
57. Charles Wesley, *The Journal of the Rev. Charles Wesley, M.A., Sometime Student of Christ-Church, Oxford. To Which are Appended Selections from his Correspondence and Poetry, with an Introduction and Occasional Notes*, ed. Thomas Jackson, 2 vols. (London: Wesleyan Methodist Book Room, 1849), 2:12 (April 19, 1748).

58. For instances of John's participation in the marriage agreement, see Charles Wesley to Sarah Gwynne Jr., January 26, 1749, DDWES 1/40, MARC, and Charles Wesley, *Journal*, December 17, 1748. He wrote to Sarah about his brother's constant support of the marriage in the winter of 1748. John Wesley had urged his brother to go to Garth and to negotiate in person with Sarah's mother, Sarah Gwynne Sr., in December of 1748. These negotiations were in fact the only thing standing in the way of their marriage, as the Gwynnes required proof that Sarah would be well provided for, especially if she outlived Charles. This was a definite possibility, considering the age gap between them. The Gwynnes' approval of the marriage hinged on the amount of the marriage settlement and allowing the publishing proceeds from some of Charles and John's books to go to Sarah, in order for her to have a personal income in the event of her husband's death.

59. Charles Wesley to Sarah Gwynne Jr., January 15, 1749, DDCW 5/20, MARC.

60. Charles Wesley to Sarah G. Wesley, n.d. [1756], DDWES 4/75, MARC. See also Charles Wesley, *Journal*, 2:46–47 (December 17, 1748).

61. Charles Wesley, *Journal*, 2:56 (April 8, 1749).

62. Ibid.

63. Ibid., 55.

64. See Charles Wesley to Sarah Gwynne Jr., [December 25 or 27, 1748], DDCW 5/10, MARC.

65. Charles Wesley, *Journal*, 2:57 (April 22, 1749).

66. Charles Wesley to Sarah Wesley, February 24, 1759, DDWES 4/4, MARC.

67. Charles Wesley to Sarah Wesley, July 10, [1764], DDWES 4/5; ibid., n.d., DDWES 4/17; ibid., n.d., DDWES 4/37; ibid., June 14, [1763], DDWES 4/77, MARC.

68. It is important to state here that his withdrawal from itinerancy was not only due to Charles Wesley's desire to focus on his family obligations. Luke Tyerman, in his biography of John Wesley, argued that Charles gave up the itinerancy to avoid conflicts with preachers in 1756. Tyerman, *Life and Times*, 2:271. Charles Wesley was increasingly alienated from the brotherhood of preachers and for a variety of reasons was not as skilled as his brother at leading the preachers. Wesley was also particularly opposed to becoming independent of the Church of England, and this opinion divided him from many preachers. See Lloyd, *Charles Wesley and the Struggle for Methodist Identity*, especially 111–33.

69. This assessment comes out of the voluminous letters between Charles Wesley and laity, particularly correspondence with important female laity; see particularly the letters to Charles Wesley collected in the Early Methodist Volume, MARC.

70. See George Downing to Charles Wesley, November 15, 1758, DDPr 1/22, MARC; Joseph Cownley, May 9, 1774, DDPr 1/104, MARC; Charles Wesley to Sarah Wesley, March 1, 1850, DDWES 4/57, MARC.

71. John Collinson to Charles Wesley, September 11, 1772, DDWES 1/114, MARC.

72. One of the accepted interpretations of Charles Wesley's marriage is that it spelled the end of his real leadership of English itinerants, though this conclusion has

been contested. Rack asserts that this has been a common assessment: "It has been generally supposed that his marriage and family had much to do" with his withdrawal from itinerancy, Rack, *Reasonable Enthusiast*, 254–55. Evangelical Anglican John Berridge commented in 1770 that "[m]atrimony has quite maimed poor Charles" (cited in Tyerman, *Life and Times of John Wesley*, 2:271 n. 1), but there is good reason to doubt this theory. Gareth Lloyd's recent reevaluation of Charles Wesley contradicts that he was secondary to the Methodist movement, sidelined by marriage. See Lloyd, *Charles Wesley and the Struggle for Methodist Identity*, passim. Wesley's retirement from itinerancy, growing dissatisfaction with the preachers' separation from the established church and his well-documented disagreements with fellow preachers made it difficult for him to be an effective leader after 1756. Luke Tyerman, in his biography of John Wesley, argued that Charles gave up the itinerancy to avoid conflicts with preachers in 1756. Tyerman, *Life and Times*, 2:271.

73. John Valton, Diaries, 9:101–3 (December 20, 1786), MARC.

74. Ibid., 9:230 (August 17, 1787).

75. Robert Lindsay to Edward Dromgoole, March 4, 1783, Dromgoole Papers, SHC.

76. Robert Lindsay to Edward Dromgoole, May 1784, SHC.

77. Matthias, Journal, DUL.

78. In reference to American salaries and support of preachers' wives, see Andrews, *Methodists and Revolutionary America*, 111; see also Sweet, *Religion on the American Frontier*, 4:49–50, 136. For the British connection's decisions, see Heitzenrater, *Wesley and the People Called Methodists*, 275–76.

79. Sherman, *History of Revisions of the Discipline*, 253–55. See Andrews, *Methodists and Revolutionary America*, 111, and Sweet, *Religion on the American Frontier*, 4:49–50, for discussions of the variability of payment and preachers' debates regarding the payment of wives.

80. James B. Finley, *Sketches of Western Methodism: Biographical, Historical, and Miscellaneous* (Cincinnati: Printed at the Methodist Book Concern, for the author, 1855), 22–92.

81. Ibid.

82. Andrews, *Methodists and Revolutionary America*, 111.

83. Richard Sneath, "Diary," in Hazel B. Simpson, *The History of the Bethel Methodist Episcopal Church, Gloucester County, New Jersey* (Vineland, N.J.: Standard Publishing, 1945), 44, 54.

84. Ibid., 60.

85. Ibid.

86. Ibid., 80–87.

87. Edward Dromgoole Sr., "On the Death of My Son Edward," in Diary, 18–19, Edward Dromgoole Papers, SHC.

88. Dromgoole to Thomas Chew, September 17, 1784, Edward Dromgoole Papers, SHC. See also Colbert, Journals, DUL.

89. Dromgoole, Diary, 21.

90. Dromgoole to Chew, September 17, 1784.

91. Sweet, *Religion on the American Frontier*, 4:124.

92. Valton, Diaries, 10:54, MARC.

93. Manuscript of Thomas Lyell's Autobiography, part C, ca. 1805, Albert Smedes Papers, SHC.

94. Ibid.

95. Mary Bosanquet Fletcher, Journal, December 22, 1802, Fletcher-Tooth Collection, MARC.

96. Porter, *English Society in the Eighteenth Century*, 279.

97. Sobel, *The World They Made Together*, 171–77.

98. Dromgoole, "On the Death of My Son Edward," 18–19.

99. See particularly Charles Wesley's hymns and poetry on the death of his children. Regarding the loss of his daughter Martha Maria in 1755 he wrote that she was "[o]nly born to cry and grieve." Charles Wesley, *Hymns for the Use of Families, and on Various Occasions* (Bristol: William Pine, 1767), 74.

100. Cornelius Bayley, *An Account of the Death of Ann Manwaring; Who Died Feb.4, 1800; in the Twenty-Seventh Year of Her Age* (Manchester: Sowler and Russell, 1800), MARC.

101. Ibid., 5.

102. Ibid., 14–15.

103. Mary Bosanquet Fletcher, Journal, October 25, 1785, Fletcher-Tooth Collection, MARC.

104. When Thomas Cooper wrote to Bosanquet in 1806, he described Bosanquet as the matriarch of English Methodism, extolling her as "a saint of such extraordinary piety, long usefulness & unequalled character." He also cited her marriage and prophecies, particularly dwelling on her "remarkable intimacies with dear Mr. F. after his ascension." Thomas Cooper to Mary Bosanquet Fletcher, October 24, 1806, Fletcher-Tooth Collection, MARC.

105. Mary Bosanquet Fletcher, Journal, August 15, 1786, Fletcher-Tooth Collection, MARC.

106. Ibid., August 5, 1788 and August 15, 1788.

107. Ibid., August 14, 1790.

108. Ibid., November 12, 1799.

109. Ibid., October 25, 1785.

110. See for example, Valton, Diaries, 1:68 (May 4, 1764), MARC.

Chapter 7

1. The King James Bible states, "Then Peter opened his mouth, and said, Of a truth I perceive that God is no respecter of persons" (Acts 10:34). Wesley's notes on this passage were, "*I perceive of a truth*—More clearly than ever, from such a concurrence of circumstances. That *God is not a respecter of persons*—Is not partial in his

love. The words mean, in a particular sense, that he does not confine his love to one nation; in a general, that he is loving to every man, and willeth all men should be saved." John Wesley, *Explanatory Notes upon the New Testament* (New York: Lane and Tippett, 1847), 304.

2. Lyerly, *Methodism and the Southern Mind*, 51.

3. Francis Asbury called himself John Wesley's "dutiful son in the Gospel." See Francis Asbury to John Wesley, March 1784, *Arminian Magazine* 9 (1786): 682. Controlling Americans from afar was a challenge as American Methodists developed their own leadership in the 1770s and 1780s. Sweet, *Religion on the American Frontier*, 4:34–35.

4. See Fliegelman, *Prodigals and Pilgrims*; Gordon Wood, *The Radicalism of the American Revolution* (New York: Vintage Books, 1991); Mary Beth Norton, *Liberty's Daughters: The Revolutionary Experience of American Women, 1750–1800* (Ithaca, N.Y.: Cornell University Press, 1980); and Lewis, "The Republican Wife."

5. Andrews, *Methodists and Revolutionary America*, 3–4.

6. John Locke was the leading theorist of this idea of the voluntary contractual basis for political authority. See John Locke, *Two Treatises on Civil Government*, ed. Peter Laslett (Cambridge: Cambridge University Press, 1960).

7. Matthew Griffith, *Bethel, or A Forme for Families* (London, 1633), 45.

8. Edmund S. Morgan, *The Puritan Family: Religion and Domestic Relations in Seventeenth-Century New England* (New York: Harper and Row, 1966).

9. See Marilyn J. Westerkamp, "Puritan Patriarchy and the Problem of Revelation," *Journal of Interdisciplinary History* 23, no. 3 (Winter 1993): 573.

10. Christopher Hill, *Society and Puritanism in Pre-Revolutionary England* (New York: St. Martin's, 1997). See Hill's arguments regarding the links between patriarchal theory and familial order, 395–401.

11. John Udall, *A Demonstration of Discipline* (1588), 65, and Richard Greenham, *Workes* (1612), 12, quoted in Hill, *Society and Puritanism in Pre-Revolutionary England*, 398.

12. See Robert Filmer, *Patriarcha and Other Political Works*, ed. Peter Laslett (Oxford: Basil Blackwell, 1949).

13. See Mary Beth Norton, *Founding Mothers and Fathers: Gendered Power and the Forming of American Society* (New York: Alfred A. Knopf, 1996), 59.

14. Susan Amussen, *An Ordered Society: Gender and Class in Early Modern England* (Oxford: Basil Blackwell, 1988), 63.

15. Thomas Hobbes, *Leviathan, or The Matter, Form, and Power of a Commonwealth Ecclesiastical and Civil* (1654). See Amussen's discussion of Hobbes in *An Ordered Society*, 63.

16. Locke, *Two Treatises on Civil Government*, 324–25.

17. See Amussen's analysis of Locke's writings in *Ordered Society*, 64–66. Amussen argues that the concept of family as the basis for political order faded in the eighteenth century, with concerns over hierarchy and order being muted by confidence in law as the political stabilizer. Still, it seems as if gendered models of political participation,

particularly in the American arena, drew upon ideas about marriage and parental authority well into the nineteenth century.

18. See Lewis, "The Republican Wife"; and Cott, *Public Vows*, 21.

19. Bangs, *History of the Methodist Episcopal Church*, 1:47–61; and Abel Stevens, *History of the Methodist Episcopal Church in the United States of America* (New York: Carlton and Porter, 1867), 1:51–91.

20. Asbury, *Journal and Letters*, 1:28.

21. Asbury's challenge in joining together these disorganized areas in the early 1770s was formidable. See Wigger, *American Saint*, 47–59.

22. Kirby, Richey, and Rowe, *The Methodists*, 3.

23. Thomas Rankin, Journal, 1773–78, transcription by Francis Tees, DUL.

24. Ibid., 2 (ca. June 12, 1773).

25. Ibid., 4 (June 14, 1773) and 9 (December 5, 1773).

26. Ibid., 20 (December 4, 1774).

27. From Asbury's perspective, Rankin, whom he nicknames "Diotrephes," took advantage of his close counsels with Wesley and convinced him to distrust American Methodists and Asbury in particular. See Francis Asbury to Joseph Benson, January 15, 1816, Early Preachers Collection, MARC.

28. Quoted from Nathan Bangs's assessment of Asbury. See Bangs, *History of the Methodist Episcopal Church*, 1:86.

29. Francis Asbury to Joseph Benson, January 15, 1816, Early Preachers Collection, MARC. Asbury had written an earlier letter to Benson in 1777 that included a number of the observations he repeated in this later letter, with a significant difference. In the 1816 letter, he more clearly articulates that he thinks Rankin poisoned Wesley into being "jealous" and obstructive toward American preachers.

30. Nonjurors held that their religious consciences made it impossible to take any state or political oaths, and that would include oaths that were often prerequisites to learning or teaching at a university, to becoming a member of the clergy in some regions, or to joining in any public or political cause. Rack, *Reasonable Enthusiast*; Andrews, "Popular Religion and the Revolution," 14–18.

31. John Wesley to Thomas Rankin, March 1, 1775, in Wesley, *Letters*, 6:142–43.

32. Kirby, Richey, and Rowe, *The Methodists*, 4.

33. Francis Asbury to Joseph Benson, January 15, 1816, Early Preachers Collection, 2/3, MARC.

34. John Wesley to Thomas Rankin, August 13, 1775, in Wesley, *Letters*, 6:173.

35. Asbury, *Journal and Letters*, 1:161 (August 7, 1775).

36. John Wesley, *A Calm Address to Our American Colonies* (London, 1775), 15.

37. Andrews, *Methodists and Revolutionary America*, 50.

38. In 1776, Francis Asbury wrote that Wesley's *Calm Address* sparked anti-Methodist criticism during the war. Asbury, *Journal and Letters*, 1:181.

39. Asbury claimed that his nonjuror status made it impossible for him to preach in Maryland in 1778, so he went to Delaware, where no oath was necessary. See Asbury, *Journal and Letters*, 1:267 (April 12, 1778).

40. Simpson, *American Methodist Pioneer*, 4.
41. Andrews, *Methodists and Revolutionary America*, 58–59.
42. Ibid., 56.
43. Baker, *From Wesley to Asbury*, 65; Heyrman, *Southern Cross*, 230.
44. Rankin, Journal, 68–69 (July 1–27, 1777), DUL. Rankin wrote that he supported the American cause, but opposed war for any reason.
45. Asbury, *Journal and Letters*, 1:184 (April 23, 1776).
46. Ibid., 1:180 (March 7, 1776).
47. Thomas Rankin to John Wesley, September 17, 1777, PLP 86.17.10, MARC.
48. Asbury, *Journal and Letters*, 1:249 (September 22, 1777).
49. Andrews, *Methodists and Revolutionary America*, 55.
50. Numbers are from Gordon Pratt Baker, *Those Incredible Methodists: A History of the Baltimore Conference of the United Methodist Church* (Baltimore: Baltimore Conference, 1972).
51. Andrews, "Popular Religion and the Revolution," 5.
52. See Devereux Jarratt, *A Brief Narrative of the Revival of Religion in Virginia. In a Letter to a Friend* (London: R. Hawes, 1778).
53. Simpson, *American Methodist Pioneer*, 7.
54. Wigger, *American Saint*, 98–103; Simpson, *American Methodist Pioneer*, 96–97.
55. Jesse Lee, *Short History of the Methodists*, 67.
56. Andrews, *Methodists and Revolutionary America*, 63; Wigger, *American Saint*, 114–15.
57. Simpson, *American Methodist Pioneer*, 6.
58. See Baker, *From Wesley to Asbury*, 39; and Andrews, *Methodists and Revolutionary America*, 63–64.
59. Kirby, Richey, and Rowe, *The Methodists*, 4.
60. Lee, *Short History of the Methodists*, 70.
61. William Watters, *A Short Account of the Christian Experience and Ministereal Labours of William Watters, Drawn Up by Himself* (Alexandria, Va.: S. Snowden, 1806), 80.
62. Lee, *Short History of the Methodists*, 72.
63. Kirby, Richey, and Rowe, *The Methodists*, 4.
64. Francis Asbury to Joseph Benson, January 15, 1816, Early Preachers Collection, MARC.
65. Asbury, *Journal and Letters*, 1:450; Thomas B. Neely, *A History of the Origin and Development of the Governing Conference in Methodism, and Especially the General Conference of the Methodist Episcopal Church* (New York: Hunt and Eaton, 1892), 211.
66. American Methodist Episcopal Church, *Discipline* (1784).
67. Kirby, Richey, and Rowe, *The Methodists*, 6.
68. Lee, *Short History of the Methodists*, 94.
69. Ibid.
70. American Methodist Episcopal Church, *Discipline* (1784), 3.

71. Leroy M. Lee, *The Life and Times of Jesse Lee* (Richmond: John Early, 1848), 149.

72. John Wesley to Thomas Coke, September 6, 1786, in Wesley, *Letters*, 7:190–91.

73. Lee, *Short History of the Methodists*, 126.

74. Ibid., 125.

75. John Wesley to Richard Whatcoat, July 17, 1788, *Works* (Jackson), 2:23.

76. Lee, *Short History of Methodists*, 124–27.

77. Thomas Haskins, "The Journal of Thomas Haskins," typescript, 45–47, DUL.

78. See Dee Andrews' discussion of O'Kelly's schism in *Methodists and Revolutionary America*, 204–7. She compares O'Kelly's position to anti-Federalism and the Methodist Episcopal Church as largely Federalist in its power structure.

79. Rankin, Journal, 103, DUL.

80. Thomas Rankin to York Society, June 24, 1773, MARC.

81. Lyerly, *Methodism and the Southern Mind*, 56. These numbers are probably also conservative, accounting for the fact that slavery would have obscured the numbers and that it is difficult to measure Methodist membership in this period. See also Hempton, "Methodist Growth in Transatlantic Perspective," in Hatch and Wigger, *Methodism and the Shaping of American Culture*, 60–61.

82. Mathews, *Religion in the Old South*, 31.

83. John Wesley to Granville Sharpe, October 11, 1787, in Wesley, *Letters*, 8:17.

84. Wesley, *Works*, 18:255.

85. Brycchan Carey, "John Wesley's 'Thoughts Upon Slavery' and the Language of the Heart," *Bulletin of the John Rylands University Library* 85, no. 2 (2004): 269–84.

86. Robin Johns to Charles Wesley, 1774, DDWC I: 2/3–12, MARC. These letters were published in the *Arminian Magazine* in 1783. See also Randy J. Sparks, *The Two Princes of Calabar: An Eighteenth-Century Atlantic Odyssey* (Cambridge, Mass.: Harvard University Press, 2004).

87. Olaudah Equiano, *The interesting narrative of the life of Olaudah Equiano, or Gustavus Vassa, the African*, 2 vols. (London: Printed and sold for the author, 1789).

88. Vincent Carretta, *Equiano, the African: Biography of a Self-Made Man* (New York: Penguin Books, 2005), 171–75.

89. John Wesley to William Wilberforce, February 24, 1791, in Wesley, *Letters*, 8:265.

90. Rankin, Journal, 145, DUL.

91. Lyerly, *Methodism and the Southern Mind*, 52–53.

92. American Methodist Episcopal Church, *The Doctrines and Discipline of the Methodist Episcopal Church in America* (Philadelphia: Henry Tuckniss, 1798), 169–171.

93. Simpson, *American Methodist Pioneer*, 47–48.

94. Sherman, *History of Revisions of the Discipline*.

95. Mathews, *Religion in the Old South*, 69.

96. Lyerly, *Methodism and the Southern Mind*, 125.

97. Williams, *Garden of American Methodism*; Hempton, "Methodist Growth in Transatlantic Perspective," 59–60.

98. Jeremiah Norman, Diary, 395 (n.d.), Stephen Weeks Collection, SHC; Rankin, Journal, 103, DUL.

99. Simpson, *American Methodist Pioneer*, 58.

100. Williams, *Garden of American Methodism*, 115.

101. Ibid.

102. Colbert, Journals, 4:4–5, DUL.

103. Lyerly, *Methodism and the Southern Mind*, 50.

104. James Sidbury, *Ploughshares into Swords: Race, Rebellion, and Identity in Gabriel's Virginia, 1730–1810* (Cambridge: Cambridge University Press, 1997), 78–81, 129.

105. *The Address of the General Conference of the Methodist Episcopal Church, to All Their Brethren and Friends in the United States* (Baltimore: Methodist Episcopal Church, 1800).

106. Lyerly, *Methodism and the Southern Mind*, 127–28.

107. Frey and Wood, *Come Shouting to Zion*, 124–25.

108. Mathews, *Religion in the Old South*, 69.

109. Frey and Wood, *Come Shouting to Zion*, 140.

110. Charles Hill to Daniel Shine, April 9, 1811, Shine Family Papers, SHC.

111. Philip D. Morgan, "Three Planters and Their Slaves: Perspective on Slavery in Virginia, South Carolina, and Jamaica, 1750–1790," in *Race and Family in the Colonial South*, ed. Winthrop D. Jordan and Sheila L. Skemp (Jackson: University Press of Mississippi, 1987), 37–79.

112. Under Virginia law, slave owners were responsible for any slave they manumitted until the slaves were twenty-one years old. Lyerly, *Methodism and the Southern Mind*, 119.

113. Philip Gatch to Edward Dromgoole Sr., Edward Dromgoole Papers, February 11, 1802, SHC.

114. Peter Pelham to Edward Dromgoole Sr., Edward Dromgoole Papers, March 8, 1808, SHC.

115. Lyerly, *Methodism and the Southern Mind*, 119.

116. Pelham, Dromgoole Papers, SHC.

117. Frey and Wood, *Come Shouting to Zion*, 181.

118. Jarena Lee, *Religious Experience and Journal*, 51.

119. Frey and Wood, *Come Shouting to Zion*, 181.

120. Hatch, *Democratization of American Christianity*, 3.

121. Mathews, *Religion of the Old South*, 67.

122. Frey, *Water from the Rock*, 24.

Conclusion

1. Phyllis Mack makes a parallel argument in her work on eighteenth-century Quaker women. See Mack, "Religion, Feminism and the Problem of Agency."

2. Frederick Dreyer, "A 'Religious Society Under Heaven': John Wesley and the Identity of Methodism," *Journal of British Studies* 25, no. 1 (January 1986): 65.

3. See Valenze, *Prophetic Sons and Daughters*.

4. See Hatch, *Democratization of American Christianity*.

5. Schneider, *The Way of the Cross Leads Home*, xvi–xxiii. Valenze's *Prophetic Sons and Daughters* agrees with the assessment of mainstream Wesleyan Methodism in the English context.

Index

Abbott, Benjamin, 46, 83
Abelove, Henry, 81, 119–20, 238n105, 256n45
Abolitionism. *See* antislavery
African American Methodists: conversion of, 26, 33, 35, 41–42, 105, 187, 206–8, 212–13; and death, 181; enthusiasm of, 42, 105–6, 210–11, 217; as family members, 4, 79–80, 188, 210–11, 217; kinship of, 79–80; leaders of, 13, 86–87, 214; meeting with white Methodists, 40, 42, 210–11, 214; women among, 86–87, 214. *See also* Allen, Richard; African Methodist Episcopal Church; antislavery
African Methodist Episcopal Church, 214, 217, 222
Allen, Richard, 83, 87, 214–15
Amussen, Susan, 191, 266n15, 266–67n17
Andrews, Dee, 13, 20, 44, 144, 245n13, 249n9, 269n78
Anglicans. *See* Church of England
antimarriage. *See* marriage, arguments against
anti-Methodist publications, 3, 96–119, 121, 124–25, 131–32, 259n1
anti-Methodist violence. *See* mobs
antislavery, 3, 188, 208–14, 217
antisocial attitudes of Methodists, 5, 45–50, 62–69, 70–71, 77, 96–99, 154, 220
Arminian Magazine, 46–47, 86, 118–21, 240n9, 253n83, 269n86
Arminianism, 13, 35, 43, 83–84, 188, 208, 249n11
Asbury, Francis, 38–39, 252n74, 258n84, 266n3, 267n27, 267n29; and African Americans, 106, 209–10, 212; as father, 1, 83, 216; on female preaching, 86; and formation of the AME, 202–6; and itinerants, 93, 139, 153; on marriage, 152–54, 171, 180, 259n91,

260n12; and the preacher recall, 196–97; during the Revolution, 189, 193–202, 267n21, 267n38–39; on wealth, 70
Attempt to Show the Folly and Danger of Methodism, An (1809), 46, 96, 110–11, 114, 117–18, 239–40n8
Austin, Margaret, 140, 246n33
authority: of individual convert, 2, 14–16, 28, 53–54, 58, 69–70, 120–21, 220–21; of legal families, 9–10, 29, 141, 190–92; of Methodist family, 6–7, 9–10, 14–15, 92–93, 115; of spiritual fathers, 6–7, 83, 91, 93; of spiritual mothers, 6–7, 85–88, 156; in spousal choice, 161–71, 185–86, 266–67n17; of John Wesley, 37–38, 135–37, 188–90, 192–97, 201–6, 216, 221

"Bachelor Conference," 151, 258n81
Baker, Frank, 31, 231n35–36, 236n66, 237n72
Baptists, 22, 106, 192, 255n13; familial language and, 6, 81, 85; gender and, 9, 14; growth of, 1, 39, 41, 214, 216; social discipline of, 49, 96, 99, 133, 160, 164, 240n16, 261n19
Bennet, Grace. *See* Murray, Grace
Bennet, John, 143
Bloch, Ruth, 4
Boardman, Richard, 193
Bosanquet (Fletcher), Mary: adopting Sarah Lawrence, 80–81, 150; childhood of, 56–57; and madness, 48, 58; and marriage to John Fletcher, 163–66, 182–85, 246n25, 261n25; joining Methodist culture, 49, 57–60; as Methodist leader, 54, 80, 85–86, 93, 156, 265n104; orphanage of, 59, 80–81, 88, 164–66, 261n25; and Sarah Ryan, 59, 88–89, 146; separating from family, 53–54, 57–59, 70–71
Bray, Thomas, 22

brother, 91–95, 248n83; covenant, 123–24; egalitarian meaning of, 6, 81–83; preacher as, 37, 152, 188–92, 195, 205, 216; as term of friendship, 122–24
Budd, Samuel, 152
Burke, William, 177–78
Bush, Elijah, 169
Butler, Jon, 14, 234n17

Calm Address to Our American Colonies, A (1775), 197
Calvinism, 33–35, 39, 209, 227n5, 233n2, 237n75, 240n9, 248n2
camp meetings, 98, 107–8, 124, 171, 217, 222, 251n47
Catholicism, 2, 89; and celibacy, 134–36, 138, 255n7; compared to Methodism, 21, 62, 99, 102, 234n16, 250n32, 255n19
celibacy: America and England compared, 151–52; debate over, 15, 133–35; among itinerants, 73, 124, 135–39, 151–57; temporal, 135–36, 146, 150–51, 163; for women, 133–36, 139–41, 146, 150–51, 156
Cheyne, George, 19, 233n8, 242n48
Chauncy, Charles, 101, 251n55
children: disobedience of, 52, 54, 56, 58, 63–64; in Methodist families, 159–60, 163, 174–80; spiritual authority of, 53. *See also* death, of children
Church of England: compared to Methodism, 9, 128, 136, 158–59, 169; establishment in America, 21–22, 234n17; Methodists belonging to, 26–27, 39–40, 85–86, 189–90, 200, 221–22; Methodist challenge to, 1–2, 21–22, 40–41, 48, 98, 106–7, 234n17; Methodists' separation from, 188–90, 201–6, 216, 221; missionary work of, 18, 22–23, 35, 42, 234n29, 235n31; tolerance in, 20–22
circuits (of preachers): assignment of, 37, 92–94, 151, 175–78, 188, 192, 199, 206; difficulty of, 44, 123–24, 151–52, 156–57, 176–80; and the Methodist family, 17, 75–78, 80–82, 91, 106, 159–60, 260n3, 245n13. *See also* local preachers; preachers
Clagget, Mrs., 53
Clapham, Ann, 166
Clarissa (1748), 148–50
class: middle, 3, 60, 71, 222; upper, 30, 49, 57–59, 64–66, 69–71, 93, 119–20, 261n15; working, 3, 13, 70–71, 97, 114, 128, 149, 248–49n6

class meetings: of African Americans, 207, 211; for children, 160; formation of, 26–27, 37–40; and Methodist family, 43, 75, 78, 193; women's leadership of, 9, 69, 85–86, 133
Coke, Thomas, 153–54, 202–4, 206, 209–10, 259n91, 260n12
Colbert, William, 92, 139, 152, 211
Colley, Linda, 20
communities: eighteenth-century, 4, 12, 73, 190; Methodist, 4–5, 30, 36–37, 40, 68, 75, 94–95, 100, 187; Moravian, 3, 5, 24, 26, 28–30, 36–37; Puritan, 11; Shaker, 134; slave, 79
Continence of a Methodist Parson, or Divinity in Danger, The (1776), 111–12
conversion, 5, 9, 18, 35–38, 42–43, 250n.23; and ecstatic behavior, 95, 100, 104, 240n.9; of families, 159–61; individual nature of, 134; Methodist family's importance in, 1, 40, 72–95; parents' views of children's, 6, 104; psychological implications of, 45–48, 67, 69, 78, 94–95; as rupturing nuclear families, 6–7, 44–71, 100, 115–16, 141, 158, 259n.1
conversion narratives, 10, 15, 18, 35–36, 50–52, 69, 179, 217; accounts of marriage in, 140; differences between men's and women's, 52, 125; and familial language, 1, 76, 83–84; sensual language in, 118; stages of, 51–54
conviction of sin, 45–47, 51, 68
Cooper, Thomas, 125, 227n2, 265n104
Cott, Nancy, 4, 162
courtship, 97, 140–44, 152, 161, 164–73, 186, 220
Credulity, Superstition, and Fanaticism: A Medley (1762), 102–3, 106, 109, 250n32
Crosby, Sarah, 57–58, 81, 87, 94, 133, 150, 161
Cutler, Ann, 150–51

Davidson, Cathy, 149
Davis, Ann, 85
death, 59, 69, 83, 160; of children, 138–39, 175, 178–79, 265n99; and conversion, 23, 50, 66, 140–41; and Methodist family, 88–89, 177, 180–85
Defoe, Daniel, 149, 257n67, 258n70
Degler, Carl, 162, 228n8, 261n14
Delaware, 40–41, 195, 200, 210, 267n39
Designe, Elizabeth (Betty), 145
Designe, Susannah, 72

Dickins, John, 122
Discipline, Methodist: and families, 159–60, 260n8; and rules for preachers, 195, 204; and slavery, 209–10; and social strictures, 38, 49, 139, 163–64, 170–71, 240n17
dissent, 2–3, 45–50, 99–100, 135, 220–23, 234n.17, 249n.18; in America, 21–22, 203; in England, 19–22
dreams, 47, 62, 123, 126; of dead Methodists, 89, 180–85; as providence, 15, 143, 165–68, 170, 186, 220
Dromgoole, Edward: correspondence with, 118, 176, 214, 245n12; and decision to leave itinerancy, 176; as leader, 80; family of, 163, 176, 178–79, 182

Eastland, Sally, 118–19
ecstatic discourse, 3, 100, 116–24, 130–32, 134, 145, 162, 216–17
Edwards, Jonathan, 33, 35–36
egalitarianism, 6, 13, 81–82, 92–93, 188–89, 209–14, 217
Embury, Philip, 40
English civil war, 20, 47
enthusiasm: American, 105–9; definition of, 101–2, 250n29; and gender, 109–16, 130–32; and mental illness, 240n10, 243n64; satire of, 34 , 102–3, 106, 109, 251n50; John Wesley's view of, 36, 104. *See also* African American Methodists, enthusiasm of
Episcopalians. *See* Church of England
Equiano, Olaudah, 209
exhorters: African American, 105, 212; celibacy of, 135, 139, 157; definition of, 9, 77, 230–31n31; examples of, 54, 120–21, 146, 163; marriage of, 163, 185; publications of, 119–21; role in Methodist family, 74–75, 77, 84–87, 93, 150–51; and John Wesley, 119, 135, 139, 144
Explanatory Notes Upon the New Testament (1762), 138

Faithful Narrative of the Surprising Work of God, A (1737), 35
family: early modern, 73–74, 228n8, 261n14; emotional ties within, 73–74, 178, 213; as metaphor, 1, 4–7, 16, 190–92; modern, 2, 7–8, 16, 73–74, 218, 245n8; nuclear, 6–9, 72–74, 79–80, 95, 158, 221, 230n25, 246n20; Victorian, 7–8, 74, 186, 213, 223; voluntary bonds of, 6–7, 27, 38, 91, 95, 221–23.

family prayer, 158–59, 259–60n2–3
father: authority in Methodist family, 6–7, 83, 91, 93; in blood families, 8, 50, 53, 58–59, 71; God as, 7, 58, 70, 77, 84–85, 121; spiritual role in Methodist family, 1, 66, 69, 78, 82–85, 90–91. *See also* patriarchy; Wesley, Charles, as father to Methodists; Wesley, John, as father to American preachers; Wesley, John, as father to Methodists
Female Brethren, 94
femininity. *See* gender
Fetter Lane Society, 36
Filmer, Robert, 191
First Great Awakening, 8, 10, 21, 33–36, 39, 41, 208, 227–28n5
Fletcher, John, 89, 163–66, 181–85
Fletcher, Mary Bosanquet. *See* Bosanquet, Mary
Fluvanna Conference, 200–201
Fogleman, Aaron, 30, 229n16, 253n99
Foundery Society, 38, 80, 142, 156
fraternity, 6, 77, 81–82, 93–94, 151–52, 206, 248n83

Garrettson, Catherine. *See* Livingston, Catherine
Garrettson, Freeborn: conversion of, 1; emancipating slaves, 209; as preacher, 44, 141, 152, 200–201, 210; and his relationship to Catherine Livingston, 69, 163, 170; and his relationship to Methodist family, 1, 6
gender: and conversion narratives, 52; and ecstatic language, 116–19, 121–24, 130–32, 145; among men, 8–9, 49, 71, 82, 110, 115–16, 121–24, 149, 206, 240n16; among women, 8–9, 49, 110, 116–19, 130–31, 145
Gentleman's Magazine, 8, 98
Georgia, 18, 23–35, 38, 80, 149, 208, 236n57, 237n72
Godbeer, Richard, 127
Great Awakening. *See* First Great Awakening
Green, Richard, 98
Greven, Philip, 8, 9, 235n43
Griffith, Matthew, 190
Gutman, Herbert, 79, 246–47n20
Gwynne, Sarah, 121, 171–75, 263n58

Hall, Timothy, 107
Harris, Howell, 19
Haskins, Thomas, 205
Hatch, Nathan, 14, 151–52, 258n81, 258n84

Hawkins, Beata, 31, 236n63
Hayden, Elizabeth, 53, 242n34
Heck, Barbara, 40, 239n112
Hempton, David, 5–6, 22, 40, 228n6, 231n36
Heyrman, Christine Leigh, 9, 168–69, 238n107, 249n18, 255n13, 261n19
Hill, Charles, 212–13
Hindmarsh, Bruce, 52, 250n23
Hogarth, William, 102–3, 106, 109, 132, 250n32
Holy Club, 10, 18–20, 38, 221, 233n1
Hopkey, Sophy (Sophia), 30–32, 141, 172, 236n57, 256n38
Hosier, Harry, 212
Hume, David, 101
Hunt, Leigh, 46, 96, 110–11, 114, 117–18, 239–40n8

Ingham, Benjamin,
itinerancy. *See* circuits (of preachers); preachers

Jarratt, Devereux, 106
Jesus: example of, 53; invoked in ecstatic language, 92, 118–19, 184; as object of love, 117–19, 121, 133, 150
Johnson, Samuel, 102, 197, 250n29
Jones, Sarah, 118–19
journal writing, 32, 50–52, 67–69, 125–26, 160, 207, 220, 243n58
Juster, Susan, 6–7, 9, 14

Kingswood school, 80–81, 104, 159
Kobler, John, 123

Lambert, Frank, 11, 245n13
Lavington, George, 99
Lawrence, Sarah, 150, 181
Lee, Jarena, 86–87, 214
Lee, Jesse, 201, 204, 258n84
Livingston, Catherine (Garrettson): conversion of, 64, 66; childhood of, 64–66; and madness, 67; joining Methodist culture, 67, 69, 244n83; and marriage, 152–53, 163, 170; as Methodist leader, 54, 80; separating from family, 66, 68–69, 71
Locke, John, 101, 191, 266n6, 266–67n17
London, 20, 22, 36, 57–58, 80, 103, 142, 146
love feasts, 98, 103–5, 107, 124, 195, 211, 251n41
loyalism, 99, 189, 196–98, 205, 210, 249n14
Lyerly, Cynthia Lynn, 9, 42, 117, 188, 240n16, 241n31

MacDonald, Michael, 73, 240n10
Mack, Phyllis, 109, 148, 270n1
Maddern, Mary, 45
Manchester, 60, 94, 134
Mann, Thomas, 135
marriage: arguments against, 133–57; arguments for, 158–59, 161, 163, 171–76, 180–86; companionate, 191–92, Methodist, 15, 158–86, 218, 220; Methodist threat to, 90, 115–16, 129–30, 140–41; Moravian, 29–30; parental control of, 2, 149, 157–58, 161–62, 167–70, 173, 186; providence in, 161–62, 164–70; Puritan, 254n.3; regulation of, 236n57, 257n56; romantic 2, 72, 162, 228n8, 261n14, 261n17; spousal choice in, 2, 164, 170, 186, 220
Martin, Ann, 84
masculinity. *See* gender
Mathews, Donald, 41, 217, 251n47, 254n108
Matthias, John, 122, 177
Meacham, James, 105–6
Mead, Stith, 45, 48–50, 70–71, 78, 92–93, 97, 123–24, 130
mental illness, 45–48, 58, 62, 67, 71, 89, 130, 233n8, 242–43n48
Methodist Episcopal Church, 86, 203, 214, 217, 222, 269n78
Methodist men: conversion of, 44, 48–49, 52; and ecstatic language, 121–24; fraternity of, 81–82, 93–94; as itinerants, 6, 44, 77, 81–82, 86, 93–94, 151–52, 206, 222; as local preachers, 151–52, 177–79; as rakes, 108, 115–16. *See also* brother; father; gender; preachers
Methodist spiritual family: compared to Muslims, 117; as the connection (or connexion), 5, 72–73, 76, 79, 152, 158, 221, 229n17; friendships in, 72–73, 75, 120, 122–23, 137; as kinship, 5, 7, 72–74, 79–80; as network, 2, 7–9, 19–20, 74, 79–80, 180, 187, 221; supposed promiscuity of, 97–100, 104–5, 109–16
Methodist women: English and American, 85–87, 117–19, 156; leadership of, 9, 85–88, 146, 150–51, 206, 212, 230–31n30–31, 247n47; and susceptibility to seduction, 109–16. *See also* exhorters; gender; mother; preachers, female; sister
Methodist missions, 4–5, 17, 23–33, 37–39, 42–43, 208, 221, 235n30.
Minter, Jeremiah, 154

Methodists, an Humorous Burlesque Poem, The (1739), 111, 114
Miss D——ple; The Pious Preacher (1775), 111, 113
mobs, 21, 37, 59, 99, 129, 198
Moll Flanders (1722), 149, 258n70
Moravians, 3, 22–24, 99–100, 124, 134, 229n16, 232n39; contrasted with Methodists, 29–30, 36–37; family organization of, 5; influencing Methodism, 18, 26–30, 38, 75, 104
Methodist Itinerant System (ca. 1810), 75–76
mother: authority of, 6–7, 85–88, 156; in blood families, 48, 53–54, 56–64, 66–68, 74, 167–69; ideal of, 110; spiritual, 59, 78–79, 85–91, 120, 129, 133, 156; Susanna Wesley as model, 19–20, 28
Mother in Israel. *See* mother, spiritual
Murphy, Terrence, 73
Murray, Grace, 141–44, 172, 256n38

Native Americans, 23–26, 235n30, 235n31
new birth, 66, 69–70, 82–83, 114, 221, 246n31. *See also* conversion
New York: Catherine Livingston in, 64, 68–69, 80; Methodist organization in, 21, 33, 40–41, 54, 85, 193, 195, 214; preachers in, 141, 177, 207
Nightingale, Joseph, 97–98
Norman, Jeremiah, 78, 105, 126–28, 254n108
North Carolina, 80, 85, 105, 126–28, 135, 179, 200, 205
novels, 2, 101, 116, 147–49, 257n67–68, 258n70

O'Brien, Susan, 11
Oglethorpe, James, 31–32, 234n29
Ohio, 80, 177–78, 213, 217
O'Kelly, James, 205–6, 269n78
Ormond, William, 126
orphanages, Methodist, 59, 80–81, 88, 159, 165–66, 261n25
orphanhood, 44, 58–59, 70, 80, 94–95
Oxford University, 10, 18–20, 233n1

paternalism, 188, 213, 216.
patriarchy: in families, 3, 117, 190–92, 213, 241–42n31, in family religion, 28, 159–60, 259n1; in Methodism, 10, 91, 97, 221; and societal order, 107, 110, 141, 190–92
Perrin, Sarah, 119–21, 130, 145, 252n78, 253n83–84

Pilmore, Joseph, 193
preachers, 17, 37, 68, 75–78, 80–84, 91–94, 125–30, 192; in America, 12, 41–42, 44, 106, 122–24, 160, 188–206, 209–12, 216; criticism of, 3, 8, 21, 49, 96, 98, 111, 114 ; and families, 159–61, 260n3; female, 9, 85–88, 146, 150–51, 212, 230–31n30–31, 247n47; as fraternity, 6, 77, 81–82, 93–94, 151–52, 206, 248n83; local, 151–52, 177–79; meetings of, 14, 75, 94, 151–53, 200–205, 240n17; in Great Britain, 119, 125, 128–30, 188, 263n68, 263–64n72; and marriage, 161, 163–66, 170–80, 185, 264n78–79; ordination of, 27, 189; relating to female followers, 144–45; as supposed seducers, 110–14, 119–20, 129; and sexuality, 135–39, 150–57. *See also* brother, preacher as; celibacy, among itinerants; circuits (of preachers)
polygamy, 146–49, 257n56
print culture, 11, 17, 22–23, 36, 50–54, 75–77
Propagation of the Gospel in the East (1709–10), 28
providence, 13–16, 87, 122, 166–67, 170–74, 181, 186, 220–21
Puritanism: in America 11, 21, 229n10, 249n18; commonalities with Methodism, 50, 96–97, 99, 241n25, 241n27, 248n2; in England, 47; and family, 81, 134, 138, 162, 190–91, 218, 254–55n3, 259–60n2. *See also* Calvinism

Quakers, 2, 6, 22, 87, 99, 229n.10
Quinn, James, 77

Rack, Henry, 31, 143, 171, 231n35, 233n1, 235n31, 236n54, 262n52
radicalism of Methodists, 13, 156–57, 206, 209–12, 217, 220, 223
Rankin, Thomas, 140–41, 195–99, 202, 207, 209, 267n27, 267n29, 268n44
religious toleration, 20–21
republican: citizenship, 110, 192; familial ideas, 191–92; politics and Methodism, 13, 189, 192, 203–6
Republican Methodist Church, 205–6, 269n78
Revolutionary War: anti-Methodism during, 99, 197–99; differences between American and English Methodists during, 12, 18, 187–90, 193–206; and disestablishment, 14; Methodist growth during, 10, 41; Method-

Revolutionary War (*continued*)
ists' views of, 99, 189, 196–98, 205; preacher recall during, 12, 196–99; and views of family order, 191–92; women's status during, 110, 149
Richardson, Samuel, 148–50
Richey, Russell, 81
Robin John, Ancona and Ephraim, 208, 269n86
Rodda, Martin, 198
Rogers, Hester. *See* Roe, Hester
Roe, Hester: childhood, 60–62; compared to Catherine Livingston, 64–67; marriage, 124, 166–68; rejecting customs and status, 49, 62–63, 70–71, 97; relationship to mother, 48, 53, 62–64, 69, 71, 243n64; as transatlantic model, 54, 86. 243n58
Rogers, James, 167–68
Rowson, Susanna, 149, 257n68
Ryan, Sarah: death of, 59, 88–89, 184–85; narrative of, 145–50, 257n56, 257n64

Sacramental Controversy, 16, 189, 200–203, 221
same-sex attachments, 59, 88–89, 121–24, 184–85
sanctification, 35, 37, 63, 84, 90–92, 120, 184
Second Great Awakening, 107–9, 221
sensibility, 101, 114, 131–32, 162, 208
sensual language, 116–24
sexual activity, 20, 125–30, 144–45
sexual attraction, 124–26, 154–55; between preacher and convert, 110–14
Shakers, 134, 136
Shine, Daniel, 212
Short History of the People Called Methodists, A (1781), 27
Simpson, David, Rev., 62
sister, Methodist, 5–6, 78, 81–82, 87, 91–95, 188, 221, 248n83
slavery. *See* African American Methodists; antislavery
Smith, Daniel Scott, 162, 228n8, 261n14
Smith, Henry, 123
Sneath, Richard, 178
Society for the Propagation of Christian Knowledge (SPCK), 22
Society for the Propagation of the Gospel in Foreign Parts (SPG), 22–23, 35, 42
Song of Solomon, 111, 118

Spangenberg, August, 24
Spencer, William, 78, 85
Stone, Lawrence, 97, 162, 228n8, 261n14–15, 261n17
Story of the Methodist-Lady, or The Injur'd Husband's Revenge, The (1770), 114–16, 124
Strawbridge, Robert, 42, 200
Sunday schools, 160, 223

Tadmor, Naomi, 73, 79, 229n17, 230n25, 245n4
Tennent, Gilbert, 33
Thomas, Mary, 119
Thompson, E. P., 13, 97, 131, 231n32, 232n43, 248–49n6
Thoughts on Marriage and a Single Life (1743), 135, 137, 141, 154, 255n10
Thoughts Upon Slavery (1774), 208
Toft, Mary, 109, 251n50
toleration of dissent. *See* dissent
Toryism. *See* loyalism
transatlantic: network, 68–69, 80, 119–20; politics and leadership, 12–13, 85–86, 187–99, 206; scope of Methodism, 1–5, 10–12; sources of evangelicalism, 17–43, 231n34, 231n36, 232n39;
Tripp, Ann, 81, 94
Tyerman, Luke, 155, 263–64n72

Udall, John, 190–91

Valenze, Deborah, 222
Valton, John: accusations of adultery, 89, 129–30, 248n73; attachments to fellow Methodists, 89–91; marriage, 130, 136–37, 175–76, 180; sexual feelings, 125–26, 154–55
violence. *See* mobs
Virginia, 205, 211, 240n16, 270n112; antislavery in, 203, 151, 160; Fluvanna Conference in, 200–201; Methodist growth in, 22, 200, 210; Methodist preaching in, 78, 118, 154, 179–80, 205, 210, 212

Wales, 19, 28, 128, 172
watch-night services, 104–7
Webb, Captain Thomas, 40–41
Webb, Joan, 140
Welch, Anne, 31
Wesley, Charles: on the American Revolution, 196; and children, 159–60, 174–75, 182;

and conversion narratives, 51, 53, 72, 82–84, 118–19, 125, 140, 241n28; in early Methodism, 36, 42, 221, 262n46; as father to Methodists, 82–85, 171, 175, 263n69; hymns and poetry of, 104, 131, 159–60, 172, 265n99; and John Hutchinson, 122–23; compared to John Wesley, 32, 83, 171–72, 174–75; on marriage, 32, 171–72, 174; and marriage to Sarah Gwynne, 171–75, 186, 263n58, 263n68, 263–64n72; as missionary, 18, 23, 31–32; and Grace Murray affair, 143, 256n45; at Oxford, 18–20; and Sarah Perrin, 121, 253n83; on slavery, 208

Wesley, John: antislavery views of, 208–9; and celibacy, 135–39, 154; compared to Charles Wesley, 32, 83, 171–72, 174–75; conversion of, 18, 23–24; death of, 69, 88, 188, 193, 209, 214–16, 219, 222; and enthusiasm, 102–4; as father to American preachers, 188–90, 192–95, 202–6, 216; as father to Methodists, 12, 66, 69, 166–68, 171, 221–22; founding Methodism, 18–19, 35–39; and Sophy Hopkey, 30–32; alleged infidelity of, 111, 144–45; on marriage, 30, 32, 134–39, 141–44, 164, 166–67, 169, 255n7, 256n38; marriage to Mary Vazeille, 111, 125, 141, 143–45, 171–72; mission in America, 23–32, 236n63, 237n72; political views of, 99, 189, 196–97, 205; publishing the *Arminian*, 118, 120–21; relationship to Church of England, 48; sexual power of, 119–20; support of female leadership, 9, 27–29, 88–89

Wesley, Mary Vazeille, 111, 125, 143–45, 156, 172, 256n38, 257n49, 262n52

Wesley, Samuel, Sr., 28

Wesley, Susanna, 19, 28, 119, 233n2, 235n43

Wesley family, 256n.22

Wesleyan theology. *See* Arminianism

Whatcoat, Richard, 204

Whitefield, George: and African Americans, 33–35, 209; conversion of, 18; criticism and satire of, 8, 34, 102, 111, 115; in early Methodism, 10, 18, 39; orphanage of, 80; as transatlantic itinerant, 11, 19, 33–35, 84, 93, 140

Wigger, John, 153, 156–57, 258n81, 260n12

Winscom, Jasper, 205

Winthrop, John, 190

women. *See* families; gender; Methodist women; mother; preachers, female

Wright, Richard, 193

Yewdall, Zachariah, 128–29, 135, 139

Zizendorf, Count Nikolaus Ludwig von, 29, 36

Acknowledgments

There are many people to thank for their intellectual insights, encouragement, and material sustenance over the course of this project. I want to give special thanks to the editors of the American studies series at the University of Pennsylvania Press, Kathy Brown and Dan Richter. Kathy saw both the big picture and the relevant details of the project, helping immensely in my revisions of the manuscript. Bob Lockhart has also provided the clarity necessary to take this book through the final stages of publication.

The assistance I received at a number of archives has made this project not just possible but also enjoyable. I have immense gratitude for the help I received at the British Library, the Methodist Archives and Research Centre at the John Rylands University Library of Manchester, the Duke University Rare Book, Manuscript, and Special Collections Library, and the Southern Historical Collection at the University of North Carolina. The Rylands's rich and seemingly endless archives could have kept me there for years, and the added benefit of its knowledgeable staff was instrumental to my work there. In particular, Dr. Peter Nockles and Dr. Gareth Lloyd were central in the assistance they provided. Dr. Lloyd has been helpful in continually sending nuggets my way, above and beyond the call of duty. I also want to thank Elizabeth Dunn of the Duke University Perkins Library Special Collections for her kind help. Special thanks are also due to Mark Shenise at the General Commission on Archives and History for the United Methodist Church for his help in securing many of the illustrations. As well, I am indebted to the professionalism of the staff at the Lewis Walpole Library of Yale University and the British Museum for their assistance with artwork.

Portions of Chapters 4 and 5 were published in a different version as an article appearing in the *John Rylands University Library Bulletin*. These portions appear courtesy of the Librarian and Director of the John Rylands University Library at the University of Manchester. In addition, some segments of Chapter 7 appeared in *The American Revolution: People and Per-*

spectives, edited by Andrew Frank, Social Perspectives in U.S. History (New York: ABC Clio Books, 2007). These portions are reproduced with permission of ABC-Clio, LLC.

Numerous grants and fellowships made this project feasible at various points in the research and writing of this book. The Andrew W. Mellon Foundation fellowships were essential for completing the beginning stages of this project. The University of Michigan's Department of History and Rackham School of Graduate Studies also provided generous grants. The Mary Lily Research Grant funded my research at Duke University's Special Collections, and the Archie K. Davis Fellowship supported my time at the University of North Carolina's Southern Historical Center. I also received support from the University of Michigan's Institute for Research on Women and Gender's Community of Scholars Program. Recent grants from the Dorothy L. Schmidt College of Arts and Letters at Florida Atlantic University have been instrumental in the completion of the book's research.

Over the years, I have benefited from the generous advice of several friends and colleagues. Most especially, I am tremendously thankful for Susan Juster's insights. She read earlier drafts of this project and was always intelligent, attentive, responsive, professional, and supportive. I hope that her excellent wisdom and guidance show through these pages. In addition, Julie Ellison, Carol Karlsen, and Michael MacDonald gave tremendously sharp feedback on the content and style of early drafts of this book. I also want to especially thank Alice Ritscherle, Ruth Hartman, Phyllis Mack, Erik Seeman, Andrew Frank, Kenneth G. C. Newport, Janet Moore Lindman, Cynthia Lynn Lyerly, Dee Andrews, and Ann Braude. They read chapter drafts and conference papers; they all gave insightful feedback and generally prodded me to go further with this project. As well, the endgame of this book would not have been nearly as enjoyable without the support of my delightful colleagues in the Department of History at Florida Atlantic University. They have been unstinting with their personal and intellectual support.

Throughout the entire process of research and writing about the Methodist family, my own family has been the constant. My parents have assisted me over the years in ways that could never be enumerated or remunerated. In reading earlier drafts of the manuscript, they pushed me in all the right ways. My husband, Daniel, has been central to my completion of this book, in every mundane, unpaid, and absolutely crucial task from chief babysitter to writing critic. Emma and Jonah have been lovely and worthwhile distractions from the book at hand.